Contents

Scenic Driving

the OZARKS

including the Ouachita Mountains

Don Kurz

FALCON™

HELENA, MONTANA

A FALCON GUIDE

Falcon Press is continually expanding its list of recreational guidebooks. All books include detailed descriptions, accurate maps, and all the information necessary for enjoyable trips. You can order extra copies of this book and get information and prices for other Falcon guidebooks by writing Falcon Press, P.O. Box 1718, Helena, MT 59624 or calling toll-free 1-800-582-2665. Also, please ask for a free copy of our current catalog. Our e-mail address is: falconbk @ ix.netcom.com

© 1996 by Falcon Press Publishing Co., Inc., Helena and Billings, Montana.
Printed in the United States of America.
Reprinted 1997
10 9 8 7 6 5 4 3 2

All rights reserved, including the right to reproduce this book or parts thereof in any form, except for inclusion of brief quotations in a review.

Cover photo: Talimena Scenic Drive, by Don Kurz
Back cover photo: Yellow Coneflowers, by Don Kurz
All black and white photos by the author.
All photos in color section by the author.

Library of Congress Cataloging-in-Publication Data

Kurz, Don
    Scenic driving the Ozarks including the Ouachita Mountains / Don Kurz.
        p. cm.
    Includes bibliographical references.
    ISBN 1-56044-485-1 (pbk.
    1. Ozark Mountains--Tours. 2. Ouachita Mountains (Ark. and Okla.)..Tours. 3. Automobile travel--Ozark Mountains--Guidebooks.
    4. Automobile travel--Ouachita Mountains (Ark. and Okla.)--Guidebooks. I. Title.
    F417.O9K87 1996
    917.67' 10453--dc20   96-8581
                                                               CIP

Text pages printed on recycled paper.

CAUTION

Outdoor recreational activities are by their very nature potentially hazardous. All participants in such activities must assume the responsibility for their own actions and safety. The information contained in this guidebook cannot replace sound judgment and good decision–making skills, which help reduce risk exposure, nor does the scope of this book allow for disclosure of all the potential hazards and risks involved in such activities.

Learn as much as possible about the outdoor recreational activities you participate in, prepare for the unexpected, and be cautious. The reward will be a safer and more enjoyable experience.

This book is dedicated to Paula and Molly for their patience and understanding of my need to travel and see new landscapes; and to my parents, Ken and Milly, who taught me to live up to my commitments and to do the best job I can.

Acknowledgments

My sincere appreciation goes to several people from the public and private sector whom I met along this journey. Their information and advice helped me produce a better book. My thanks goes to Tom Foti, who shared with me his favorite Arkansas drives, and to Frank Oberle for his encouragement and suggestions.

My special thanks goes to Chris Cauble, publishing director of Falcon Press, who suggested this project, and to Megan Hiller for seeing this book through the editorial and production processes.

Locator Map

Map Legend

Scenic Drive (paved)

Scenic Drive (gravel)

Interstate

Other Roads

Hiking Trail

Campground

Point of interest

Interstate

U. S. Highway

State and
County Roads

Forest Road

Pass or Saddle

Mountain

River or Creek

Lake

Scenic Drive
Location

National or State
Forest or
Reservation
Boundary

State Boundary

Map Orientation

Scale
of Miles

0   5   10   15   20

Miles

Introduction

The Ozark region is one of the most identifiable in the United States. One does not need to have actually visited the area to be able to conjure up thoughts of rugged, wooded landscapes, clear-flowing streams, and abundant wildlife. However, it is a region of geographic contrasts. The Ozarks encompass unbroken woodlands and crop fields and pastures; broad, slow-moving rivers and swift mountain streams; nearly level plateaus and river valleys and dramatically rugged terrain; and sloughs and swamps and some of the driest forests in eastern North America.

The Ozark region extends across five states but lies mainly within Missouri, Arkansas, and Oklahoma. Its northwestern boundary just nicks southeastern Kansas. In the geologic past, the Mississippi River carved through the eastern Ozarks, isolating a portion of the highlands in what is now Illinois. The total geographic extent of the Ozarks is approximately 50,000 square miles, an area the size of Florida.

This book also includes the Ouachita Mountains. This region, which covers 22,500 square miles, stretches across part of the midsections of Arkansas and Oklahoma. Although it was formed by the same process that created the Ozarks, its east-west trending mountains, with their craggy ridges, steep slopes, and narrow valleys have always been considered separate from the Ozarks.

These regions were historically inhabited by the Osage, Illinois, Caddo, and Quapaw Indian nations. The Osages occupied most of the interior and western Ozarks, the Illinois lived along the Mississippi River border, the Caddos covered the southern half of the Ozarks and the Ouachitas, and the Quapaws hunted in the southeastern hills of the Ozarks and Ouachitas. European settlement of the region began as a result of the French mining for lead and iron ore in the area between Ste. Genevieve and Potosi, Missouri. Later, settlers of Scotch-Irish descent from Tennessee, Kentucky, and nearby parts of the southern Appalachians moved into the Ozarks and Ouachitas. The rugged terrain made education, socializing, and travel difficult, and modernization came slowly. In spite of these obstacles—or perhaps because of them—the hill people, or "hillbillies," became known as honest, kind, skilled craftsmen perservering to wrest a living from the rugged hills. The term *hillbilly* was first used during the Great Depression to describe the individuals living in poverty in these mountain districts deep in the heart of the Ozarks. Since then, training, education, and employment have made this image a thing of the past—except for the occasional caricature displayed on roadside advertisements.

The formation of the Ozarks and the Ouachitas goes back about 300 million years; to when the continents of South America and Africa drifted

Impressive limestone bluffs overlook vast wetlands at Pine-Hills-LaRue Swamp.

up from the south and collided with the North American plate. This process, which lasted more than 200 million years, uplifted a high, flat plateau called the Ozarks. Just to the south, where the impact of the collision was stronger, the rock wrinkled like an accordion and sometimes folded over, forming the long ridges of the Ouachita Mountains. These east-west trending mountains are unique in the United States. The Sierras, Rockies, and Appalachians are all north-south trending mountains formed by previous collisions of continental plates from the east and west.

The mountains of the Ozarks and Ouachitas offer far-reaching views unparalled in the midcontinent region. The most dramatic relief in the Ozarks occurs in the Boston Mountains with their elevations of up to 2,500 feet; however, the highest point in the Midwest is Mount Magazine in the Oachitas, at 2,753 feet. This mountain stands as a sentinel above the Arkansas River valley and is considered part of the Ouachitas. The oldest rock in the midcontinent region is found in the St. Francois Mountains in the eastern Ozarks. Here, exposed igneous rocks of volcanic origin date back two to three billion years.

The Ozarks and Ouachitas are divided into geographic regions based on geology, soils, topography, and plant and animal communities. Although specialists divide the Ozarks and Ouachitas into finer detail, for the pur-

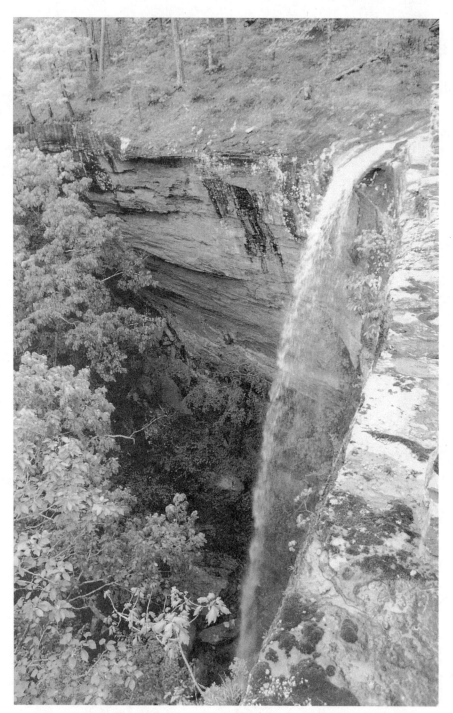

The falls at Kings Bluff plunges 100 feet down a sheer sandstone cliff.

poses of this book, the Ozarks are composed of the Springfield and Salem plateaus, the St. Francois and Boston mountains, and the Ozark Border. The Ouachitas consist of the Arkansas River valley and the Ouachita Mountains. These geographic regions are discussed and their interesting features described as they are encountered along the drives.

The geology of the Ozarks and the Ouachitas is complex and fascinating. Travelers may encounter a variety of rocks including igneous, dolomite, limestone, chert, shale, and sandstone. Because different bedrocks erode at varying rates, their weathering produces different shapes. The Ozarks and Ouachitas display a diverse array of interesting features including mountains, hills, knobs, mounds, shut-ins, waterfalls, rapids, bluffs, narrows, cutoffs, lost hills, faults, sinkholes, caves, springs, arches, bridges, tunnels, and isolated rock prominences.

The varied topography and numerous bedrock and soil types give rise to a great variety of terrestrial and aquatic natural communities. The scenic drives in this book lead to forests, savannas, prairies, glades, cliffs, caves, fens, swamps, marshes, springs, creeks, and rivers. There are numerous opportunities to observe and enjoy a diversity of plant and animal life when visiting these habitats. The Ozarks and Ouachitas are renowned for providing displays of roadside wildflowers and fall colors along with occasional glimpses of interesting and unique wildlife. Although it is common to see deer, turkeys, foxes, coyotes, beavers, vultures, herons, songbirds, snakes, and lizards, rare occasions might also include sightings of bald eagles, ospreys, prairie chickens, bears, and river otters. There are also elk and bison that have been introduced into specific areas, as well as some rare sightings of mountains lions in the more rugged regions.

Before You Begin

Scenic Driving the Ozarks contains thirty-one drives that provide the traveler with the opportunity to experience the wonders of this unique region. The drives cover more than 1,500 miles of highways and backroads. Varying from five to ninety-five miles in length, the routes were chosen for the quality of their scenery, natural features, recreational activities, and historic significance. Points of interest along the way are highlighted in **bold** in the text.

The highways and gravel roads are passable by all types of vehicles unless otherwise noted. A few sections of road are steep and winding and demand extra caution from the motorist. Avoid low water crossings that appear flooded and fast moving. Some scenic views offer no safe pulloffs, so it is best to keep moving to the next designated stop. Distances in this guide

A view of Hot Springs National Park from Hot Springs Mountain Tower.

were measured using a vehicle odometer and may vary slightly from distances given by highway signs or other odometers. Be aware of highway signs, junctions, and other vehicles while traveling the sometimes busy roads. Be alert for wildlife on the road. Snakes and turtles are especially vulnerable during the day, while armadillos, opossums, raccoons, skunks, and deer are more active at night.

The weather in this region is very changeable throughout the year and is especially fickle in the winter. The Ozarks average up to 15 inches of snow per year, but it usually lasts only a few days. Freezing rain, although uncommon, can create very hazardous road conditions for up to a day or two. The most popular times to travel are during the spring, summer, and fall. Spring rain brings waterfalls and wildflowers. Summer offers opportunites for families to share in outdoor activities. Autumn brings lower temperatures and lower humidity, plus a spectacular palette of fall colors. Some of the higher elevations, especially in the Ouachita Mountains, experience fog on occasion, but it usually burns off by midday.

Unlike the situation in many western states, there is usually enough activity on most of the roads in the Ozarks and Ouachitas to minimize the chances of being stranded for long periods of time. Having a vehicle in good condition and with plenty of gas helps to avoid possible problems on the road. Travelers should carry water, especially in the summer. Unfortunately, vandalism is always a possiblity wherever you travel, so be sure to conceal all valuables out of sight when parking your vehicle for any length of time. The drives in this book pass through public and private lands. Respect private property by not trespassing, and never litter. Allow others to enjoy the beauty of clean, uncluttered settings.

These drives offer plenty of opportunities to see the best of what the Ozarks and the Ouachitas have to offer. The routes were chosen for leisurely travels; to really benefit from the experience, consider involving at least one overnight camping or lodging stop. These drives take on different appearances in different traveling seasons. A scenic drive in springtime can be totally different when revisited in the fall. These drives may also be traveled in reverse adding another new perspective.

The amount of time it takes to explore each special feature is up to you. The Ozarks and the Ouachitas offer unique and memorable experiences that will draw you back time and time again, for regardless of when they are traveled, every stop is a reward in itself.

Drive 1: River and Hill Country
Cape Girardeau to Grand Tower, Missouri/Illinois

SITES

1. Cape Girardeau Conservation Service Center
2. Cape Rock
3. Union County Conservation Area
4. Pine Hills Campground
5. Winters Pond
6. Tower Rock
7. Devil's Backbone Park
8. Trail of Tears State Park

To Chester

Grand Tower

Big Muddy River

CLEAR SPRINGS/BALD KNOB WILDERNESS AREA

LARUE-PINE HILLS ECOLOGICAL AREA

Grand Tower Island

Mississippi

Winters Pond

Wolf Lake

ILLINOIS

To Trail of Tears State Forest

To I-55

River

MISSOURI

Ware

To Jonesboro

N

Reynoldsville

Cape Rock Drive

To St. Louis

To Jackson

Country Club Drive

Broadway

Cape Girardeau

Devils Island

McClure

To Grapevine Trail Campground

East Cape Girardeau

To Sikeston

To Cairo

0 1 2 3 4 5
Miles

1

River and Hill Country

Cape Girardeau to Grand Tower

Missouri/Illinois

General description: A 70-mile drive starting in Cape Girardeau and following the eastern Ozark border on both sides of the Mississippi River.
Special attractions: Cape Girardeau, Mississippi River, Trail of Tears State Park, Port Cape Girardeau, Cape River Heritage Museum, Glenn House, Union County Conservation Area, LaRue—Pine Hills Ecological Area, Clear Springs/Bald Knob Wilderness Area, and Grand Tower; scenic views, hiking, camping, fall colors, spring wildflowers, hunting, and fishing.
Location: Eastern Ozarks. The drive begins on the northwest side of Cape Girardeau at the junction of U.S. Interstate 55 and U.S. Highway 61.
Drive route numbers: U.S. Interstate 55, U.S. Highway 61, Missouri Highway 177, Illinois Highways 146 and 3, and Forest Roads 236 and 345.
Camping: Trail of Tears State Park has 35 basic campsites in wooded riverside hills, 12 campsites with electrical hookups, and 8 campsites with electricity and sewer hookups located near the river. Campgrounds include modern restrooms, laundry facilities, hot showers, and a dumping station. Two primitive camping areas bordering the Peewah Trail are available for use by backpackers. Pine Hills Campground has 12 Forest Service campsites with water and pit toilets. Grapevine Trail Campground has 5 basic campsites with water and pit toilets. Trail of Tears State Forest in Illinois has 4 basic camping areas with pit toilets. Grand Tower has a campground at Devil's Backbone Park with restrooms, showers, electricity, and water.
Services: All services at Cape Girardeau. Gas and food at East Cape Girardeau, McClure, Ware, and Grand Tower.
Nearby attractions: Bollinger Mill State Historic Site, Grand Tower Natural Area, Steam Train Ride, and Jackson (in Missouri); Trail of Tears State Forest, Ozark Hills Nature Preserve, and Cache River State Natural Area (in Illinois).

The drive:

Located on the easternmost edge of the Ozarks, this drive follows the rugged river hills and floodplain of the Mississippi River. The Ozarks extend about 10 miles into Illinois. This section of the Ozarks was once part of a much larger Ozarks millions of years ago until a new, southward-flowing river system formed and cut deep into the landscape. The geology, plants, and animals are basically the same on both sides of the Mississippi River, but the Illinois side is forever isolated. The river is still a dominating force on the landscape, and this drive provides opportunities to see it in action.

Begin the drive just north of **Cape Girardeau** at the junction of I-55 and US 61 and head south on US 61 for about a mile. Turn left at the first lane crossover and enter Cape Girardeau County Park. The first stop is the **Cape Girardeau Conservation Service Center** operated by the Missouri Department of Conservation. Open from 8 a.m. to 5 p.m., Monday through Friday, the center offers publications and brochures on activities in the area, plus interesting exhibits. Interpretive displays show why this border region of the Ozarks is unique and diverse. A large aquarium displays fish that can typically be found in nearby streams. About two hundred yards north of the building, a 0.5-mile paved trail winds through woods and over a creek, affording close-up views of plants and animals characteristic of the region.

Return to US 61, which also bears the city street name of Kingshighway, and follow it into town. Just before the first traffic light, which is at the junction of Mt. Auburn Road, you will find the Cape Girardeau Convention

One of the oldest buildings west of the Mississippi River,
Port Cape Girardeau dates back to before 1836.

and Visitors Bureau on the right. The people there can supply you with brochures and maps to guide you through interesting areas of the city. After about 3 miles, turn left onto Broadway Street at the traffic light. Follow Broadway, passing Southeast Missouri State University, and in about 2 miles take MO 177 north through a residential part of town. Follow MO 177, and in 1.5 miles, turn right onto Country Club Drive. Notice the monument with the inscription "To Cape Rock Drive." In about two city blocks a road to the right begins Cape Rock Drive. Follow it past the city water plant to a promontory overlooking the Mississippi River.

The view from **Cape Rock** is the best in the city. You can look up, down, and across the mighty Mississippi; observe the Illinois floodplain with its cottonwood and willow trees; and view the distant hills of the Illinois Ozarks. This view was also appealing to Jean Baptiste Giradot, a French soldier stationed at Kaskaskia, Illinois, who in 1720 stood on this point and envisioned a trading post. He noticed the current of the river striking the base of this prominent outcrop and making a cove or "cape" just downstream that could provide shelter for boats. The site was the perfect spot for trappers and river travelers to stop. The area soon became known by voyagers traveling the Mississippi as *Cape Girardot*, which later was modified to "Girardeau." But Girardot was a trader, not a settler, and it is not known just how long he remained at the trading post. In the late 1800s, much of this promontory was removed to create riverfront space for the Frisco Railroad tracks.

The man credited with settling the area around the rock promontory is Louis Lorimier. In 1792, he was commissioned by the Spanish Governor General to establish a trading center in the area for himself and the Indians. Over time, **Cape Girardeau** became one of the most populated and important districts west of the Mississippi River, not excepting St. Louis. The town prospered between the arrival of the steamboat in 1835 and the Civil War. During the war, Cape Girardeau was occupied by Union soldiers who erected four forts to protect the city and river. One minor conflict occurred west of town, with both sides claiming victory, but Cape Girardeau was spared the devastation of total war. The city is rich in history. As the site of Southeast Missouri State University, Cape Girardeau has been the educational and commercial center of southeast Missouri for more than a hundred years.

At this point of the drive you have a decision to make. You can continue on Cape Rock Drive, which wraps around the "Cape" affording a closer view of the river and barge traffic, and proceed to MO 177 which leads 10 miles to **Trail of Tears State Park** as a side trip. Alternatively, you can return to Country Club Drive and then MO 177 south to continue the main drive. Trail of Tears State Park is an exceptional state park with beautiful forested hills that are spectacular in the spring, when dogwoods bloom, and in the fall, when there is a myriad of beautifully colored foliage. The state park

A sheer limestone cliff towers over a levee road and nearby LaRue Swamp.

contains a nature center with exhibits and on-duty naturalists. There are several trails that wind through oak, tulip, poplar, and beech-maple forests and a scenic overlook that rivals Cape Rock. The park is named for the 13,000 Cherokee Indians who were forced to march from their homeland in the southeastern United States to a reservation in Oklahoma during the winter of 1838—1839. One of the groups that crossed the Mississippi River did so here, where the park now stands. The nature center has exhibits telling the story of this sad chapter in America's history.

Returning to downtown Cape Girardeau by way of MO 177, turn left at Broadway and park two blocks downhill along Water Street. Walk through one of the gates along the flood wall and stroll along the river walk. Evenings are particularly relaxing times to watch the river's never-ending journey down to the Gulf of Mexico.

Just about a block south on Water Street, **Port Cape Girardeau** stands much the way it did when it was occupied by Ulysses S. Grant during the Civil War. The construction of the building dates back to before 1836, a fact that establishes this as one of the oldest buildings west of the Mississippi. Although you can't buy three-cent Coca-Colas now, as an old sign on the building advertises, the restaurant inside offers a delicious barbecue menu that is hard to beat.

There are numerous historic buildings in the downtown area of Cape Girardeau. For more information, visit the **Cape River Heritage Museum** located at the corner of Independence and Frederick streets. This two-story brick building is open March through December, from Wednesday to Saturday, 11 a.m. to 4 p.m. It is open at other times by appointment.

Follow MO 177 south, and after a few city blocks notice the historic **Glenn House** on the right. The two-story Victorian home, built in 1883, is open for tours Tuesday through Saturday from 1 to 4 p.m. Turn left at the next intersection and drive over the Mississippi River Bridge. Completed in 1928, it was a toll bridge until the 1950s. Proceed on IL 146, through the town of **East Cape Girardeau** for three miles. Notice the depressions in the nearby fields, some of which hold water. These are remnants of the Great Flood of 1993, when the rain-swollen Mississippi River broke through a levee upstream from here and sought out a new high-water course. Parts of the highway were destroyed by the force of the river, and many Illinois residents who depended on work in Cape Girardeau were subsequently unable to drive to their jobs. It was several months before the highway could be repaired.

Turn left at the junction of IL 3 and proceed to **McClure**. This town was established in 1896 and at one time supported a canning factory, five general stores, three churches, a hotel, and a restaurant. A sign for the **Grapevine Trail** is posted at an unnamed road heading east out of town. A Forest Service campground is located 4 miles down that road.

Continue on IL 3 for 3 miles and enter the small community of **Reynoldsville**, which once maintained a ferry across the Mississippi River just west of town.

After another couple of miles on IL 3, turn right at the entrance to **Union County Conservation Area**. In late fall and throughout the winter months this refuge drive offers excellent opportunities for viewing Canada geese and bald eagles. The eagles come to feed on the geese that are sick and injured. About 85,000 geese use the refuge, making it one of the few places in Illinois where so many geese can be closely observed and photographed.

Follow the refuge drive to IL 146 and turn left, returning to IL 3. (If you turn right on IL 146 and go 8 miles east to Jonesboro, you will find signs leading to the Forest Service's Jonesboro Ranger Station. Maps and brochures are available at the office, which is open during business hours.) Proceed north on IL 3; pass through the community of **Ware** and continue 5 miles to **Wolf Lake**. A fairly prosperous community, Wolf Lake's main employer is the Trojan Powder Company, a gunpowder manufacturer. The town is named for a lake at the base of Pine Hills. Take the road leading east from town. Follow the directional signs to Pine Hills (0.5 mile) and Trail of Tears State Forest and State Nursery (4 miles).

Trail of Tears State Forest is operated by the Illinois Department of

Natural Resources. The site superintendent's office provides several maps and brochures on recreational activities in the area. Although 120 acres of the state forest is devoted to growing nursery trees, the remaining 5,000 acres provides picnicking, trails, camping, and hunting. A drive through the 222-acre Ozark Hills Nature Preserve provides opportunities to see such unusual plants as red buckeye, wild azalea, and cucumber magnolia. The narrow road, however, is not recommended for motorhomes or vehicles pulling trailers.

Return to the entrance to the **Pine Hills**, which is 0.5 mile east of Wolf Lake. A gravel road, FR 236, passes towering stands of American beech, tulip poplar, and white oak that are of old growth dimensions. At 0.6 mile, Pine Hills Campground is visible on the right. Between its two camping sections, White Pine Trail heads northeast for a moderate 3-mile, one-way hike that ends just south of a picnic area called Allen's Flat. You can return by way of the trail or walk 2.5 miles back to the campground along FR 236.

Continue on FR 236 and in about 2 miles the road begins to climb to the top of the Pine Hills. Along the way, a sign marks the boundary of the **LaRue—Pine Hills Ecological Area**. This designation was the first of its kind in the national forest system. It is said that there are more plant and animal species in this 3,000 acres than in any other area of similar size in the nation. This specially designated area contains more than 1,150 species of plants, which is more species than occur in all of the Great Smokey Mountains National Park. There are also 41 mammal, 24 amphibian, 35 reptile, and 173 bird species that inhabit the area. The diversity of the plant and animal life correlates with the diversity of habitats or natural communities found here, ranging from high, wooded ridges, steep, moist-to-dry slopes, and 350-foot bluffs to a vast floodplain of swamp and bottomland forest. There are more habitats here than in any other place in the Ozarks. To celebrate this outstanding landscape, a LaRue—Pine Hills Appreciation Day is held biannually with field trips and nature talks by botany, zoology, and geology interpreters. Check with the Jonesboro Ranger District for more information.

In less than 0.5 mile, **Allen's Flat** provides picnic tables and pit toilets. No scenic views are available here. Just beyond Allen's Flat, **McGee Hill** provides one of the finest views of the Mississippi River valley. LaRue Swamp is below, and, in the distance, you can see the Missouri Ozarks. **Crooked Tree Trail** is 1.3 miles north of McGee Hill on FR 236. From the signed pullout, there is a short (0.2-mile) trail leading to a bench overlooking the valley. **Saddle Hill** vista is next, only 0.5 mile from Crooked Tree Trail. Unfortunately, the view is being closed in by tree growth. **Pine Grove** is 0.7 mile beyond Saddle Hill. A short trail leads to a valley overlook and a stand of shortleaf pine, the namesake of the ecological area. Shortleaf pine is endangered in Illinois and exists in only two areas in the Illinois Ozarks. It is much more common in the Ozarks of Missouri, Arkansas, and Oklahoma.

In another 0.2 mile on FR 236, **Government Rock** provides a 0.1-mile hiking trail to an old fireplace and view of the lowlands. Beyond Government Rock 0.2 mile, **Old Trail Point** offers views east to Bald Knob and the Bald Knob Cross and west to the Mississippi River valley. Proceed on FR 236 for 0.4 mile to the head of the Godwin Trail and the **Clear Springs/Bald Knob Wilderness Area**. The trail extends 6 miles east to Bald Knob blacktop road, which is 3 miles southwest of Alto Pass. There are some confusing turns along the way, and it is best to use a topographic map or consult the Jonesboro Ranger Station for trail conditions.

Follow the road to **Inspiration Point**, which is 0.3 mile north of the wilderness trailhead. An easy 0.25-mile walk leads to great views of the Mississippi River valley, including LaRue Swamp and the Big Muddy River bottoms. It is best to stay on the trail because the steep, cherty slopes are unstable, especially along the bluff. The trail continues another 0.5 mile through a north-facing cool valley with large beech trees to **McCann Springs Picnic Area**.

If you continue on FR 236, the road will immediately descend out of the Pine Hills, past McCann Springs Picnic Area, to the intersection of FR 345. Turn left and enter **LaRue Swamp**. After 0.3 mile, turn right and take a side trip on the levee road. Go a few hundred yards and turn around. Be

Tower Rock stands sentinel against the swift waters of the Mississippi River.

prepared for a spectacular view of the Bailey limestone bluffs rising 350 feet above the valley floor. At the top is Inspiration Point. Return to FR 345 and turn into the entrance of **Winters Pond**. This 0.3-acre depression was created when fill material was taken to help build the levee. Picnic tables and a boat launch are provided here. You can view interesting swamp vegetation from the water's edge, or you can launch a canoe or boat to explore the extensive swampland. Winters Pond is a good place to park and walk along the level, 3-mile road. This road is closed to all but foot traffic during the last three weeks of April and the last three weeks of October. Limiting traffic this way helps protect the amphibians and reptiles as they migrate between their winter retreats at the base of the bluffs and their summer homes in the swamp. The swamp is dominated by pumpkin ash around the margins (look for swollen buttresses at the base), buttonbush, swamp loosestrife (with its arching stems), American lotus, yellow pond lily, and, of course, a carpet of duckweed.

The road affords excellent views of LaRue Swamp, a spring at the base of the bluff, dense bottomland hardwood forest, massive limestone bluffs supporting small grassy openings on top, and beautiful displays of wildflowers in the spring.

Continue on the gravel road as it turns and heads west; use caution as you approach the double railroad crossing. At IL 3, turn right and head north to **Grand Tower**, and cross the Big Muddy River. The land west of the road is Grand Tower Island, which is part of Missouri. Late in the 1800s, the main channel of the Mississippi River took a westward course, thereby isolating this part of Missouri. After another couple of miles, turn left onto Grand Tower Road and proceed 0.5 mile west to Front Street. The town was surveyed and platted in 1867 and named for the prominent rock outcrop on the far side of the river. The rock outcrop of Bailey limestone, now called Tower Rock, is a designated Missouri State Natural Area. It was first recorded and described in 1673, when the French explorers Joliet and Father Marquette penetrated the region. Around 1680, La Salle noted the stately grandeur of the "Grand Tower," which has for thousands of years withstood the continual torrents of the mighty Mississippi.

On the north side of Grand Tower, **Devil's Backbone Park** offers camping, hiking along Devil's Backbone, and strolls along the sandy beach. Walk north of Devil's Backbone to the natural gas pipeline that extends across the river. Devil's Bake Oven, a prominent rock formation with a shallow, south-facing cave, rises at the base of the pipeline. A trail winds its way to the top for a great view of the Mississippi River.

2

Great River Settlements

Ste. Genevieve to Fults Hill Prairie
Missouri/Illinois

General description: A 28-mile drive through historic French settlements along the Mississippi River with a side trip to picturesque sandstone outcrops and canyons.

Special attractions: Ste. Genevieve, Great River Road Interpretive Center, Felix Valle House State Historic Site, Pickle Springs Natural Area, Hawn State Park, Mississippi River (may be closed to ferry traffic during high waters, especially in spring), Modoc Rock Shelter, Fort de Chartres, Prairie du Rocher, Fults Hill Prairie Nature Preserve, and Maeystown; scenic views, hiking, camping, fall colors, hill prairies, and weathered sandstone features.

Location: Northeastern Ozarks. The drive begins at the junction of U.S. Interstate 55 and Missouri Highway 32.

Drive route numbers: Missouri Highways 32, 144, and AA; and Illinois Highway 155.

Camping: Hawn State Park has 50 campsites, including 17 with electrical hookups. The camping area includes modern restrooms, hot showers, laundry facilities, a dumping station, and playground equipment.

Services: All services at Ste. Genevieve and Maeystown. Gas and food at Prairie du Rocher.

Nearby attractions: Amidon Memorial and Magnolia Hollow conservation areas, and Ball Mill Resurgence Natural Area (in Missouri); Fort Kaskaskia State Park (in Illinois).

 The drive

Before entering the town of Ste. Genevieve, a side trip to **Pickle Springs Natural Area** is highly recommended. It is truly one of the most interesting areas in the Ozarks; a well-designed 2-mile trail system takes you to outstanding features of sandstone outcrops.

To get to Pickle Springs Natural Area, take MO 32 at the junction of I-55 and drive west. Proceed through the small communities of New Offenburg

Drive 2: Great River Settlements
Ste. Genevieve to Fults Hill Prairie
Missouri/Illinois

To Maeystown

6.

To Ruma

Fults

5.

155

7.

155

Prairie du Rocher

Mississippi River

Bluff Road

4.

Modoc

To Roots

SITES

1. Great River Road Interpretive Center
2. Felix Valle House State Historic Site
3. Ste. Genevieve-Modoc Ferry
4. Modoc Rock Shelter
5. Fort de Chartres
6. Fults Hill Prairie Nature Preserve
7. Creole House

To Bloomsdale

To St. Louis

3.

61

1.

32

2.

Gabouri Creek

55

Ste. Genevieve

61

32

To Perryville

O

New Offenburg

C

Weingarten

Jonca Creek

N. Fork

144

S. Fork

Pickle Creek

32

N

To Farmington

AA

Pickle Springs Natural Area

0 1 2 3 4 5

Miles

and Weingarten. After about 11 miles you will meet MO 144, which leads to **Hawn State Park**. The 3,271-acre state park offers two trails that explore oak-pine forests, savannas, rock outcrops, and Pickle Creek. Hawn State Park is downstream from Pickle Springs Natural Area, and there are plans for a trail connecting the two areas. Information on recreational activities at the park can be obtained at the superintendent's office.

Continue on MO 32 another 4.8 miles and turn left on MO AA. Proceed another 1.5 miles, turn left on Dorlac Road, follow it about 0.2 mile, and pull into the parking lot of Pickle Springs Natural Area. The sandstone bedrock here has been sculptured by the forces of wind, rain, and ice. The resulting narrow fissures, rock pillars ("hoodoos"), gigantic boulders, arches, and box canyons were formed over more than 500 million years of geologic time. This is the oldest sedimentary rock in the Ozark region. Imagine a time when land animals and plants had not yet appeared: Vast seas covered most of what is now the United States and marine invertebrate animals and primitive fish ruled the waters. Active and inactive volcanoes protruded above the ocean, and rain and waves continually pounded them, breaking their igneous rock down into fine sediments. This sand was eventually covered by additional sediment, cementing it all together to form sandstone. Today, this sandstone, the LaMotte, crops out in just a small portion of the St. Francois Mountains region of the Ozarks.

A trail leads from the parking lot along a gentle to moderately difficult hike through special places like The Slot, Cauliflower Rocks, Double Arch, Spirit Canyon, and Headwall Falls, to name a few. Be sure to obtain a trail booklet at the trailhead for complete descriptions. The natural area, named after William Pickles who owned the land in the mid-1800s, exhibits a wide array of plant life. Mosses and lichens form colorful patterns on the rocks while ferns thrive in moist nooks and crannies. Wild azaleas are a special treat, blooming in early May, and box canyons display waterfalls during spring runoff and after heavy rains. Listen for pine warblers in spring and watch for wild turkeys any time of year.

Return to MO 32 and head for **Ste. Genevieve**, the first permanent European settlement west of the Mississippi River. Upon entering town, follow the signs to the historic downtown area, which is reached by bearing right on MO 32 and crossing over US 61. The road now becomes Center Drive and shortly changes into Fourth Street. Cross over the railroad tracks and turn right onto Market Street at the first stop sign. Proceed three blocks to the **Great River Road Interpretive Center**. Parking is available behind the building. This is a good place to explore exhibits depicting historic events and obtain tourist information including maps and brochures.

Ste. Genevieve was founded around 1735 by French Canadians who moved into the Mississippi Valley to avoid British rule in Canada. They settled first on the east side of the river at Kaskaskia, then moved across the

*Ste. Genevieve's Bolduc House, originally constructed in 1770 by Louis Bolduc,
was moved and rebuilt after a major flood in 1875.*

river when prospectors discovered lead at Mine La Motte in Madison County, 30 miles to the west. After St. Louis became established upstream, the two settlements competed for river trade. St. Louis finally emerged predominant, because it had a better geographical location for commanding trade on the Missouri, the upper Mississippi, and the Illinois rivers. Ste. Genevieve declined as St. Louis grew.

Today, Ste. Genevieve is an architectural treasure trove. Houses and buildings from the 1700s, 1800s, and early 1900s make a tour of Ste. Genevieve a fascinating walk through history. Many of the original log cabins of the early settlers still stand. As you walk or drive through the town, you will notice that many private homes have plaques bearing their construction date. There are presently 89 historic properties listed in Ste. Genevieve's preservation ordinance record. Because there are so many wood, brick, and stone buildings to see, you may want to ask the staff at the interpretive center for advice based on your interests.

A "must" visit is the **Felix Valle State Historic Site** on Merchant and Second streets. Built in 1818, the home is decorated with furnishings of the period; tours are provided by guides in period costume. The building was also used by a trading firm, and today's visitors can enjoy the Menard and Valle Store, stocked with the trade goods and furs that would have filled its shelves in 1830.

While in the area, consider strolling to 10 South Main Street, where an art studio houses works by the nationally known artist Al Agnew. A local resident, he has been widely acclaimed for his renditions of fur-bearing animals such as mountain lions, wolves, bears, and otters, as well as fish and birds of prey. His excellent depictions of wild animals in their natural habitats are well worth the visit. Signed and numbered artworks are available for purchase.

Along the streets closer to the **Mississippi River** floodplain, you will notice remnant sandbags and rebuilt levees, all reminders of the Great Flood of 1993. Ste. Genevieve received international attention when the floods of that year threatened the town and, in some cases, engulfed buildings along the bottoms. During the "Summer of the Sandbag," more than 1,500 volunteers from across the country came to fill and stack more than 98,000 sandbags on water-soaked levees. There has been a long-standing feud between the "Mother of the West," as Ste. Genevieve is known, and the "Father of Waters"—in 1993, the historic community held its own. That summer, the river crested at 49.67 feet during what the U.S. Army Corps of Engineers described as a "500-year flood" (meaning a flood of this intensity occurs, on an average, only once every 500 years). Extraordinary efforts to save the historic buildings paid off: only four of the eighteenth- and nineteenth- century buildings were inundated by the flood.

Floods have grown more destructive and have reached higher water levels mostly as the result of man's efforts to contain the river. The massive levee system along most of its length confines the Mississippi River for the sake of flood control, commercial navigation, agriculture, and hydropower generation. When the river swells, as it did in 1993, there are no safety valves to relieve the pressure. Before the levees were built, marshes, sloughs, lakes, and backwater areas were the overflow points where the river released some of its energy. These critical areas have now been cut off by the levees, drained, and filled for agriculture, a process that also eliminated important habitat for many kinds of wildlife. The Corps of Engineers and other government and state agencies are beginning to rethink and study some of these issues. Much work is still needed, however, to properly address this problem.

The rest of the drive is on the Illinois side of the Ozarks, which can be reached by taking a ferry across the Mississippi River. Follow the ferry crossings signs on Fourth or Main streets, to the river, about 2 miles away. If you have not been on a ferry before, it is a pleasant experience. The **Ste. Genevieve-Modoc Ferry** is in operation from 6 a.m. to 6 p.m. except on Sundays and holidays, when it is open from 9 a.m. to 6 p.m. The fee is $6.00. On the rare occasions when the river rises above 28.5 feet, the entrance ramps are closed due to high water. The ferry holds up to nine vehicles, and motorhomes are allowed.

On the other side, the road leads to Modoc, a distance of 3.4 miles.

Follow the river road through Modoc and head north on Bluff Road. After another 1.5 miles, pull off on the right side of the road at the base of a bluff. This is the **Modoc Rock Shelter**, a national prehistoric site. The bluff is Aux Vases sandstone, parts of which are stained by iron oxides. *Aux Vases* is French for "of slime/mire/ooze"; a possible referrence to the staining of the rock or the fact that this formation is a petroleum reservoir at some locations. At the base of the cliff is a rock shelter of archeological significance. Excavations have uncovered many Indian artifacts whose age makes this the earliest known human habitation east of the Mississippi River. Skeletons from here were found to have been buried between about 6,219 and 2,765 B.C. and artifacts have been dated to 8,000 B.C. An interpretive sign describes the historical uses of the rock shelter.

Continue on Bluff Road another 1.6 miles to **Prairie du Rocher**, which means "Prairie on the Rock." Notice the prairie grasses dominating the openings above the limestone cliffs. Later in the drive, you will have a chance to visit a hill prairie that has been designated a state nature preserve. Prairie du Rocher was founded by French settlers in 1722 and is Illinois's oldest town. A Creole house dating back to 1800 is featured in the town, along Bluff Road.

Proceed another 2.3 miles and turn left on IL 155 for 4 miles to **Fort de Chartres**. The fort is named in honor of Louis duc de Chartres, son of the regent of France. An earlier fort, which was closer to the Mississippi River, was completed in 1720. It consisted of a fence of squared logs surrounded by a dry moat. The fort, subject to frequent flooding from the river, deteriorated rapidly. A second fort, more inland from the river, was built in 1725 and served until 1742. Since the 1730s, French leaders had discussed building a stone fort to protect their interests on the Mississippi River. After much disagreement and delay, construction finally began on a new fort only a short distance from its predecessor. Stone was quarried and hauled from the bluffs north of Prairie du Rocher.

The stone Fort de Chartres served as France's Illinois Country headquarters for only ten years. In 1763, France surrendered Illinois and most of its North American possessions to Great Britain in the Treaty of Paris, which ended the Seven Years' War. British troops took possession of the fort in 1765. They showed little interest in maintaining the fort, and by 1772, the south wall and bastions had collapsed into the Mississippi River. The fort continued to deteriorate. By 1900, none of the wall existed above ground level, since much of it had either been silted in or carted off for other building use. In 1913, the Illinois legislature authorized purchase of the stone fort site and by the 1930s the Works Progress Administration (WPA) had reconstructed the gateway and two stone buildings.

Fort de Chartres was also inundated by the flood of '93 when water levels reached thirteen feet. Damaged areas have been repaired and visitors can investigate the various buildings, a museum, and a gift shop, that carries an impressive array of books, crafts, and items of the period. Check the special events schedule for festivals and reenactments held during the year.

Return on IL 155 to Bluff Road and turn left, heading north. For the next few miles, look for large limestone mines tunneled into the cliff face. Called St. Louis limestone, this rock is high in calcium and makes excellent road rock. About 5 miles from IL 155, an entrance and sign on the right indicate that you are at **Fults Hill Prairie Nature Preserve**. Dedicated in October 1970 as the thirtieth Illinois Nature Preserve, the 532-acre tract is owned and managed by the Illinois Department of Natural Resources. Fults Hill Prairie lies within the rugged topography of the northern section of the Illinois Ozarks.

The site contains the largest assemblage of the highest quality loess hill prairies along the Mississippi River. *Loess* is a German term for the wind-deposited silt that is usually derived from glacial activity. Although no glacier has ever touched this area, 200,000 years ago the Illinoisan glacier came within 3 miles of overtopping the bluff on its southward path. Glacial meltwaters from the Illinoisan and from the more recent (10,000 to 40,000 years ago) Wisconsinan glacial period had a remarkable influence on this land. The tremendous meltwaters from the glaciers helped to scour the Missis-

Double Arch is one of the many unique sandstone features found at Pickle Springs Natural Area.

sippi River valley, ever-enlarging the cliff face. In the winters, when the glaciers stopped melting and the waters receded, winds from the northwest would whip across the dry 4-mile riverbed, creating clouds of fine silt. As the winds lifted over the cliff face, heavier particles of silt dropped out, depositing hundreds of feet of loess. Over time some of the silt wore away, but prairie plants, which are adapted to steep slopes and hot, dry, westerly exposures, colonized the soil and slowed erosion.

Hill prairies are rare worldwide. They occur along the eastern side of the Mississippi River valley from Wisconsin to southern Illinois; along the eastern side of the Missouri River from Council Bluffs, Iowa, to just north of Kansas City, Missouri; along the Rhine River in Germany; and along the Yellow River in China.

Two paths lead from the parking lot: one north, the other south. The northern path is the most rewarding. The first 200 feet are just like climbing steps—take it slow and easy. The trail passes through stands of walnut, sugar maple, honey locust, flowering and gray dogwood, white oak, red oak, slippery elm, box elder, and hickory. Watch out for poison ivy. The first opening is a limestone glade. The southern exposure is ideal for glade-loving Ozark animals like the plains scorpion, coachwhip snake, and narrow-mouthed toad. This is a natural area; please leave the rocks in place and wildflowers to bloom for others to enjoy. The dominant grasses are little bluestem, side-oats grama, Indian grass, and big bluestem. Wildflowers, particularly many diverse members of the sunflower and legume families, are abundant throughout the season.

Continue up the path through a wooded area where the trail soon opens onto a hill prairie. It differs from the rocky limestone glade by having a deep layer of loess. Follow the path west along the ridge for a spectacular view of the Mississippi River valley. Many visitors are content to sit here and enjoy the view from this point. If you decide to go farther, the route does lead down to the cliff's edge, so exercise great caution, because it is a long drop to the bottom.

If you choose, you can continue your drive by stepping back in time and exploring the nineteenth century German village of **Maeystown**. From the nature preserve, continue north on Bluff Road, passing what is left of the community of Fults after the Great Flood of 1993. After 5 miles, cross over Chalfin Bridge and turn right, following the signs to Maeystown. Founded by Jacob Maeys in 1852, the village was settled by German immigrants predominantly from the former Bavarian Rheinpfalz. Sixty historically significant buildings still exist, including Maeys's log house; the original 1865 stone church; Zeitinger's Mill; and various outbuildings, barns, and smokehouses made of limestone, brick, and wood. Gift and bakery shops, a general store, a restaurant, and bed-and-breakfast are also featured. Maeystown was listed on the National Register of Historic Places in 1978.

3

Mineral Mines

Bonne Terre to Millstream Gardens
Missouri

General description: A 33-mile drive that begins at Bonne Terre and travels through the historic mining region to the scenic granite shut-ins of Millstream Gardens Conservation Area 9 miles west of Fredericktown.

Special attractions: Bonne Terre Mine, Mineral Mines State Historic Site, Silver Mines Recreation Area, and Millstream Gardens Conservation Area; scenic views, hiking, camping, fishing, canoeing, kayaking, off-road-vehicle (ORV) trails, and geology.

Location: Northeastern Ozarks. The drive begins at the junction of U.S. Highway 67 and Missouri Highway 47 at the Bonne Terre exit.

Drive route numbers: U.S. Highway 67 and Missouri Highways 72, 47, 32, and D.

Camping: St. Francois State Park is 4 miles north of Bonne Terre on US 67. The park offers 47 basic campsites and 63 improved sites with modern facilities. St. Joe State Park, along the south edge of Park Hills, provides 35 basic campsites, plus 15 modern ones that are primarily for ORV users. A daily fee is charged for camping at both state parks on a first-come, first-served basis. Mark Twain National Forest's Silver Mines Recreation Area, located south of MO 72 along Missouri Route D, offers 91 campsites.

Services: All services at Bonne Terre, Deslodge, Leadington, Park Hills, Farmington, and Fredericktown.

Nearby attractions: Washington, Elephant Rocks, Hawn, and Taum Sauk Mountain state parks; Hughes Mountain and Pickle Springs natural areas and Amidon Memorial Conservation Area (Missouri Department of Conservation); the Ozark Trail; and Marble Creek Recreation Area and Rock Pile Mountain Wilderness Area (in Mark Twain National Forest).

 The drive

This drive begins in the Ozark border's rolling, wooded hills and their broad, open valleys and clear streams. This area is part of the largest lead-producing region in the world. The hills become more pronounced and rugged as you head south. Here, US 67 edges along the eastern flank of the

Drive 3: Mineral Mines

Bonne Terre to Millstream Gardens, Missouri

St. Francois Mountains, a landform that contains the oldest exposed rock (2 to 3 billion years old) in the midcontinental region. Most of the rock is covered by dense forests of oak and pine, but grassy openings called glades and boulder-strewn streams known as "shut-ins" provide interesting places to explore the geologic past.

Start the drive at the intersection of US 67 (a four-lane route) and MO 47. Take the exit ramp west onto MO 47 and proceed into the town of **Bonne Terre**. The French called this area *La Bonne Terre*, "the good earth," in reference to its mineral wealth. Bonne Terre is the oldest of a series of closely spaced lead-mining towns. In 1864, 946 acres were purchased by the newly incorporated St. Joseph Lead Company of New York. The next year a company store was established to supply the miners and their families with necessities. A post office was built the following year. Mining was confined to digging from four to eight feet below the surface to extract horizontal sheets of lead. It was not until the introduction of the diamond drill in 1869 that larger amounts of lead ore could be extracted from deep below the surface. For more than a hundred years, lead mining and smelting dominated the communities in the area in what is today known as the Old Lead Belt. There are nearly 1,000 miles of multi-level mine tunnels in this region, testifying to the many operations in this area. In 1976, after the mines played out, the renamed St. Joseph Mineral Corporation moved its offices to Viburnum, in what is known as the New Lead Belt.

Signs of past mining activities can still be seen in Bonne Terre. One-half mile west on MO 47, a large, bare hill of "chat," or mine tailings, can easily be seen to the north. Go another 0.5 mile and enter the parking lot of the **Bonne Terre Mine**. This replica of a 1864 mining town sits atop the first underground lead mine in Missouri. Commercially guided tours lead you into underground rooms, some as high as 200 feet and in some places filled with water as deep as 400 feet. Bonne Terre Mine is on the National Register of Historic Places.

Around the corner, on Main Street, you will find the Bonne Terre Memorial Library. Established in 1867 and moved to its present location in 1904, the library, built of Bedford limestone, is one of the oldest in Missouri. A clock, handmade in England in the late 1700s, decorates the entrance. The adjacent Shepard House was built by Cornish miners in about 1865. Tours are provided, and a museum is located on the second floor. While at the Shepard House, which also serves as the Visitor Center/Chamber of Commerce, ask about other places to visit in the area. To continue the drive, return to US 67 and proceed south. Notice the roadcut at the highway intersection; it is Bonne Terre dolomite, the rock from which layers of lead were once mined. This dolomite, which was formed about 500 million years ago, is composed primarily of magnesium carbonate. This tan dolomite differs from limestone in that limestone is made of calcium carbonate and is whitish.

After 6 miles on US 67 south, take the MO 32 exit ramp. Turn right on MO 32 and follow the signs to the **Missouri Mines State Historic Site**, approximately 1 mile west. You are now in the south part of the city of Park Hills which, prior to January 1994, was composed of the towns of Flat River, Esther, Elvins, and Rivermines. The citizens of these four financially strapped communities voted to pool together their duplicate resources and emerge with increased services, a stronger tax base, and a projection of future growth and development.

Plan to spend a couple of hours at the Mineral Mines State Historic Site. A guided tour will take you through old Federal Mill Number 3. Closed in 1972, this complex consisted of twenty-five buildings whose operations were aimed at crushing, grinding, and concentrating lead ore. Prior to its closure, the Federal Mill became the largest operation of its kind in the world. In 1976, 8,244 acres of land, including the mill complex, were donated to the state of Missouri and became St. Joe State Park. The mill complex became a state historic site soon after in 1980. Within the old mill there are exhibits on geology, mineral resources, and an outstanding array of mineral specimens; this museum has been rated one of the best in the Midwest. Selected pieces of restored underground mining equipment are also on display. Ask to see the videotape that explains mining history and

Bonne Terre Memorial Library, built in 1904 of Bedford limestone, continues to operate on funds donated by the local community.

*The St. Francis River cascades over granite boulders
at Millstream Gardens Conservation Area.*

technology.

Return to US 67 and proceed south. In about 4 miles there is an exit ramp to **Farmington**. If you decide to visit this town note that there is no access back onto US 67 south. You must take US 67 north to the first cross-over and carefully pull onto the southbound lane. Why there isn't a south-bound ramp from Farmington is a mystery!

Five miles beyond the Farmington exit, you cross over the St. Francis River for the second time. Notice the roadcut to the right of the highway. The pink rock is granite overlain by the yellow sandstone. The granite is your first contact with the St. Francois Mountains.

Proceed another 5 miles and then turn onto a small road on the right. It is easy to miss, so be prepared to turn onto the side road after a long climb up a large hill called **Knob Lick Mountain**. The side road immediately branches, so be prepared to turn right. A wooden sign designating Knob Lick Lookout Tower is then visible. Follow the road, which eventually turns to gravel, for 1 mile to the top of the large hill. The last part of the road is rather steep but can be handled by most vehicles. A walk from the parking lot leads to the lookout tower. A sign warns you to climb at your own risk. It is recommended that no more than five people be on the tower at one time. A moderately strenuous climb to the top affords a commanding pan-oramic view of the countryside. The distant hills to the south and west are also part of the St. Francois Mountains. Below the parking lot, the moss-covered ground thins to expose large areas of granite. Here, drought-adapted plants survive in a desert-like environment called a glade. Take the time to walk around and inspect the boulders and open pavement. Post oak and blackjack oak grow immediately upslope, where the soil is a little deeper. These trees are stunted and slow-growing because of the poor conditions. Many are more than 100 years old; however most rarely reach a second century.

Return to US 67 and head south another 7 miles to the Fredericktown exit. Turn right onto MO 72 and go 4 miles to MO Route D. This road leads to **Silver Mines Recreation Area**, a U.S.D.A. Forest Service campground. A self guiding brochure leads you to interesting geologic formations, scenic views, and an abandoned silver mine.

Once back on MO 72, go 4 miles and look for a wooden sign indicating **Millstream Gardens Conservation Area** to the left. Turn on the gravel road, which leads to a parking lot and trailhead. The 0.5-mile, paved Turkey Creek Trail leads to spectacular views of the St. Francis River Natural Area. Here, the river has cut through the igneous St. Francois Mountains forming a gorge, or "shut-ins," that extends over 2 miles downstream into Silver Mines Recreation Area. In the spring, whitewater boating is popular in the shut-ins when the water is high and reaches Class IV in difficulty. The area is not suitable for large boats. There is a 2.5-mile hiking trail along the river from Millstream Gardens to Silver Mines that is especially rewarding in the spring and fall.

4

Ancient Rocks

Potosi to Taum Sauk Mountain, Missouri

General description: A 40-mile drive that begins at Potosi, heads south into the St. Francois Mountains, and ends at Taum Sauk Mountain, the highest point in Missouri.

Special attractions: Big River; Hughes Mountain Natural Area; Arcadia and Belleview valleys; Buford Mountain Conservation Area; Elephant Rocks, Johnson's Shut-Ins, and Taum Sauk Mountain state parks; Fort Davidson State Historic Site; and the Ozark Trail; scenic views, hiking, camping, fishing, hunting, canoeing, and geology.

Location: Northeastern Ozarks. The drive begins at the junction of Missouri Highways 21 and 8 on the east side of Potosi.

Drive route numbers: Missouri Highways 8, 21, U, RA, N, V, and CC.

Camping: Taum Sauk Mountain State Park is a new park with 8 primitive campsites, pit toilets, and water. Johnson's Shut-Ins State Park has 52 campsites, half of which have electrical hookups. Facilities include modern restrooms that are wheelchair accessible, hot showers, a dumping station, and coin-operated laundry. A daily fee is charged for camping at both state parks. Mark Twain National Forest has campgrounds nearby. Check at the Potosi Ranger District office or the forest headquarters in Rolla for more information. Primitive camping is allowed at Buford Mountain and Ketcherside Mountain conservation areas.

Services: All services at Potosi, Pilot Knob, and Ironton.

Nearby attractions: Washington, St. Francois, and St. Joe state parks; Mineral Mines State Historic Site; Royal Gorge Natural Area and Ketcherside Mountain and Bismarck Lake conservation areas (Missouri Department of Conservation); Bell Mountain Wilderness Area and Council Bluff Lake Recreation Area (Mark Twain National Forest); and exhibits at Union Electric Hydroelectric Power Plant.

 The drive

This drive leads through the heart of the St. Francois Mountains to Taum Sauk Mountain, the highest point in Missouri. This region was formed by ancient volcanoes more than 1.5 billion years ago, making it the oldest

Drive 4: Ancient Rocks
Potosi to Taum Sauk Mountain, Missouri

To Steelville

8

21
To Desoto

Potosi

8
To Park Hills

Big River

Bootleg Access
To Irondale

Cedar Creek

Hughes Mountain
Natural Area

To Belgrade

C

Caledonia

32
To Bismarck

21

To Salem

32

Buford Mountain
Conservation Area

Belleview

U

N

0 1 2 3 4 5
Miles

W

RA

Graniteville

Elephant Rocks
State Park

Pilot
Knob

V
To Farmington

N

Pilot Knob
Mountain

To Johnson's Shut-Ins
State Park

Fort Davidson
State Historic Site

Shepherd
Mountain

Ironton

72
To Fredericktown

Russell
Mountain

Arcadia

Taum Sauk Mountain
and State Park

CC

21

72

To Piedmont

landform in the midcontinent.

The drive begins on the eastern side of **Potosi** at the intersection of MO 8 and 21. (For information on maps, hiking, camping, and points of interest in the Mark Twain National Forest go west through Potosi on MO 8 for 1.5 miles to the Potosi Ranger Station.) Potosi, with a population of 2,683, is the seat of Washington County and a former lead-mining and smelting town. It was once an important shipping point for railroad ties, and it had one of the largest sawmills of the era located nearby. The lead deposits were discovered in 1773, and Mine Au Breton (later Potosi) became one of the first settlements in the Ozarks. In 1797, Moses Austin, an experienced metallurgist, opened several mines and built furnaces at Potosi to smelt the ore. He soon became wealthy but went bankrupt in 1818, following the collapse of the Bank of Saint Louis and the worldwide depression caused by the Napoleonic Wars. The following year he went to Texas to form a colony, which he passed on to his son Stephen A. Austin, who later became "the Father of Texas." Moses Austin died in 1821 when his health failed during one of his trips to Texas. Austin is buried in the cemetery one block northwest of the courthouse.

Most of the hills around Potosi are pockmarked with numerous shallow pits dug with only a pickax and a wooden shovel. Early prospecting amounted to digging four-foot-deep test holes with which to judge the quantity of ore each might produce. Ore prospecting continued until the 1850s, when tiff (barite) mining became important. This resulted in more shallow holes being dug. Tiff is a relatively soft, white-to-gray mineral which is used in oil drilling to contain gas pressure. It is also used as a filler in paint, ink, paper, textiles, and asbestos products.

Proceed south on MO 21 for 8 miles to the **Big River**. Just before the bridge, a road to the left takes you to **Bootleg Access**. There is a developed trail in the hills above the river valley. The river, which stretches a permanent distance of 117 miles, is shallow along this section and offers opportunities to explore the gravel bars and view small fish. Although it suffers from agricultural runoff and heavy loads of gravel from erosion in the watershed, it is better off here than farther downstream. Lead mine tailings around Deslodge and Bonne Terre sometimes drain into the Big River. Toxic heavy metals accumulate in aquatic animals, resulting in unsafe levels in the bodies of fish. Nevertheless, the Big River remains a popular float downstream from here, and canoes are available for rent near the deeper water at Washington State Park.

Of geologic interest at this stop is the **Palmer Fault Zone**. Notice the rugged hills to the north and their cherty soil covered with trees. To the south of the Big River, the landscape is open, rolling, and suitable for farming. The contrast in the two areas is the result of a massive, thousand-foot vertical uplift on the south side and its subsequent erosion down to the

At Hughes Mountain Natural Area, unique weathered rocks resembling fence posts comprise the core of an ancient volcano.

present level. The south side's older bedrock of sandstone and dolomite was exposed and weathered, producing a richer soil. This fault zone extends more than 45 miles trending east and west; it is thought to have been formed along the northern boundary of the St. Francois Mountains as they were uplifted.

Return to MO 21 and drive 8 miles south to MO M. Turn left, and after 2 miles notice the prominent mountain to the southeast. That is **Hughes Mountain**, one of the premier natural areas in Missouri. Proceed 3 more miles, cross over Cedar Creek, and turn right onto the first gravel road. Drive to the crest of a small hill, then turn left and park in the lot. Follow the slightly strenuous trail less than 0.5 mile to a large opening. This is an igneous glade ("igneous" describes a rock of molten origin) and is covered with various lichens, mosses, wildflowers, and grasses. Continue to the top and notice that the rocks resemble columns or fenceposts. This formation is called Devils Honeycomb and was formed when molten rock cooled and contracted into vertical polygonal joints. These formations are much like those found at Devils Tower National Monument in Wyoming and Devils Postpile National Monument in California, though on a much smaller scale. Be sure to take the time to enjoy one of the few panoramic views in the Ozarks.

Return to MO 21 and proceed south, passing the Caledonia Methodist

Cemetery established in 1834. Notice the colorful red granite tombstones that were quarried just a few miles south of here. There is also a historical marker worth reading. Travel another 0.5 mile to **Caledonia**, which was founded in 1819 and named for New Caledonia in Scotland. The town has several preCivil War houses located in a seventeen-acre historic district along Main and Central streets. The area is on the National Register of Historic Places.

Continue another 6 miles to **Belleview**. The road just before and a few miles beyond Belleview is quite dangerous, with sharp turns and one-lane bridges. Be sure to yield to oncoming traffic. Historic **Belleview Valley** and **Arcadia Valley** (to the south) are known as one of the most scenic cultural landscapes in the Ozarks. In the 1880s, the area was "discovered" by wealthy families from St. Louis, and it became popular with vacationers after the Civil War. Today, many of the farmhouses have been remodeled to serve as country retirement homes.

As you leave Belleview, notice the prominent landform to the east that extends for miles in either direction. This is **Buford Mountain**, which is perhaps the most scenic mountain in Missouri; but for only 32 feet, it would be the tallest mountain in Missouri. It is accessible by taking MO U, 2 miles south of Belleview. The road leads to a parking lot where a primitive trail winds up and along the top of the mountain. Most of Buford Mountain is owned by the Missouri Department of Conservation.

Proceed on MO 21 to **Graniteville**, which is home to the "World's Finest Red Granite," as the quarry company sign proclaims. The attractive red granite, adorning several of the buildings in the small community, has been quarried here since 1869. The stone was also used for the piers on historic Eads Bridge and many other structures in early St. Louis, as well as for cobbles in that city's streets.

From Graniteville, take MO RA to **Elephant Rocks State Park**. At the north end of the large parking lot, a trail weaves through large, rounded granite boulders that resemble elephants. These extraordinary rocks were formed more than a billion years ago when subterranean molten rock (magma) pushed upwards to just below Earth's surface and slowly cooled to form granite. As it cooled, nearly vertical cracks (joints) developed and these were strained further by the uplift that formed the Ozarks. Over time, natural weathering (freezing and thawing) has widened the cracks and rounded off the corners to produce elephant-shaped boulders. Although there are other locations in the St. Francois Mountains where ancient granite has been exposed, Elephant Rocks is the only place where the huge, oblong granite boulders can be found. It was designated in 1978 as a state natural area.

Return to MO 21, and drive south for 0.5 mile towards Ironton, turn right onto MO N. This road leads to **Johnson's Shut-Ins State Park**, which is

A combination of special fracturing and weathering has sculpted these huge granite boulders at Elephant Rocks State Park.

well worth the visit. Here, the swift waters of the East Fork Black River flow through a canyonlike gorge called a "shut-in", which can be seen by taking a 0.4 mile walkway to an observation deck overlooking the shut-ins. The park also has several scenic hiking trails, one of which is the Ozark Trail that goes to the top of Taum Sauk Mountain.

Back on MO 21, the next stop is Arcadia Valley. Here, the towns of Pilot Knob, Ironton, and Arcadia flank the historic railroad line that once transported hematite, a type of iron ore, out of the mining towns. In Pilot Knob, turn left on MO V and proceed 0.5 mile to **Fort Davidson State Historic Site**. The prominent mountain to the east of the visitors center is Pilot Knob Mountain, for which the town is named. In the mid-1800s, iron ore mining began on the north part of the mountain and continued until the 1930s. Then, from the 1950s to 1980, shafts were driven into the base of the mountain to extract more iron ore, but low ore prices eventually caused the mine to shut down. A chain-link fence now surrounds the mountain to keep the public from entering the extremely dangerous mine openings. Over a century of weathering has caused numerous breakdowns, which are sometimes triggered by would-be explorers. A major rescue effort in the mid-1980s to free a trapped young man convinced the mining company to give up its claim on the mountain. It was then donated to the U.S. Fish and Wildlife Service to manage for the thousands of federally endangered Indiana bats that live in the numerous passageways. A census conducted in 1978 estimated that 139,000 Indiana bats—or one-third of the world's popu-

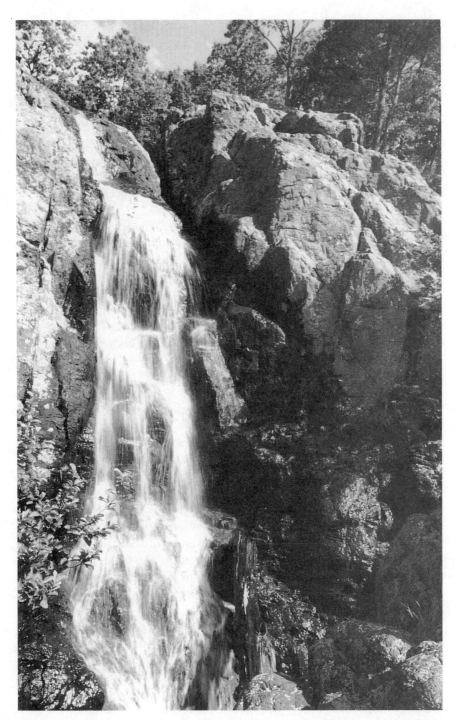

Mina Sauk Falls plunges 132 feet over several cascades at Taum Sauk Mountain State Park.

lation of this species—call Pilot Knob Mountain their home.

The new visitors center at Fort Davidson State Historic Site contains exhibits that interpret the Civil War battle that was fought here. Plan to spend some time visiting the displays and walking over the grounds which still resemble a small earthen fort.

Return to MO 21 and proceed through Ironton. As you leave town, the road begins climbing up the flanks of **Taum Sauk Mountain**. In a couple of miles, turn right onto MO CC and begin the 3-mile climb to the top. Halfway up, you will notice a pullout and a sign on the left. This is the entrance to the Russell Mountain Trail, a section of the **Ozark Trail**. The trail leaves Russell Mountain, heads south through a part of Ketcherside Mountain Conservation Area, and ends at a parking lot off MO 21 near Royal Gorge. This 2-mile trail is maintained by the Missouri Department of Conservation.

As MO CC nears the top of the mountain, there is a choice of stops. To the left, you can enjoy a 360-degree view of the surrounding countryside from the Taum Sauk Mountain Lookout Tower; to the right, you can enter **Taum Sauk Mountain State Park**. Both stops are recommended. The newly designated state park has camping facilities and a short trail that takes you to the highest point in Missouri, which is 1,772 feet above sea level. Another trail goes to Mina Sauk Falls, which is the highest waterfall in Missouri. It falls a total of 132 feet in cascades, with the main cascade falling a distance of nearly 105 feet. The waterfall does not flow the year around and is best seen in the spring or after a good thunderstorm. The trail is 3 miles round-trip.

One mile beyond Mina Sauk Falls, the trail passes through Devil's Toll Gate. This is an 8-foot-wide gap in a 50-foot-long, 30-foot-high ridge of orange and red igneous rock. The gap probably began as a vertical rock fracture that was enlarged by weathering. The trail passing through this gate is a historic military road leading to the Southwest Territory and, according to some, is also a portion of the infamous Trail of Tears endured by the Cherokee Indians during their forced relocation of 1838-1839. The Devil's Toll Gate was aptly named because it was as if the Devil was collecting his toll by forcing the unloading of long wagon trains, unhitching the horses, and swinging the wagons around a sharp turn by hand in order to penetrate the narrow passage.

The trail through the Devil's Toll Gate is now a part of the Taum Sauk section of the Ozark Trail. The Ozark Trail, although not yet complete, will someday extend from St. Louis through western Arkansas, a distance of more than 500 miles. This section of the trail extends to Johnson's Shut-Ins State Park, a hiking distance of 12.8 miles. The state park office can provide you with more information on the various sections of the Ozark Trail that are available to hikers.

5

Meramec Hills

St. James to Onondaga Cave, Missouri

General description: A 44-mile drive that begins at St. James and winds through the scenic wooded hills of the Meramec River valley to Onondaga Cave State Park.

Special attractions: St. James, Maramec Spring Park, Onondaga Cave State Park, and Vilander Bluff and Spring's End natural areas; wineries, canoeing, hiking, auto tour, camping, trout fishing, and hunting.

Location: Northeastern Ozarks. The drive begins at the junction of U.S. Interstate 44 and Missouri Highway 8 at the St. James exit.

Drive route numbers: U.S. Interstate 44 and Missouri Highways 8, 19, and H.

Camping: Private and public land is available for camping along the drive. Maramec Spring Park offers 58 campsites between March 1 and October 31. Each campsite in the campground is furnished with a picnic table, grill, fire-ring and lantern stand. Water is available at the modern shower house. Recreational vehicles are welcome but generators are not allowed. Reservations can be made by calling the privately owned park anytime between March 1 and October 31. Onondaga Cave State Park has 72 campsites, 17 of which have electrical hookups. The campground area includes modern restrooms with hot showers and a dumping station. Nearby Huzzah Conservation Area offers primitive camping at designated sites.

Services: All services at St. James, Steelville, and Cuba.

Nearby attractions: Meramec State Park, Dillard Mill State Historic Site; Meramec and Indian Trail conservation areas; Meramec Caverns (commercial); and Berryman Trail and Red Bluff recreation areas (Mark Twain National Forest).

 The drive

This drive begins on the eastern edge of the narrow plateau that separates the Gasconade River drainage (15 miles to the west) from the Meramec River hills (just to the east). Small patches of prairie once grew on this more level, open plateau but the grasses quickly gave way to forest on the steep hills leading down to the Meramec River, a drop of about 300 feet in elevation. Very little erosion occurs in these densely wooded hills, resulting in

Drive 5: Meramec Hills

St. James to Onondaga Cave, Missouri

clear-flowing streams and springs.

Begin the drive at the intersection of I-44 and MO 8 at **St. James**. On the northwest side of the intersection, the St. James Tourist Information Center is a good place to obtain brochures and learn about area attractions and services. There are several local wineries that offer tours, wine tasting, and a variety of German foods.

Proceed on the overpass above the interstate (formerly Route 66) to St. James. The town was settled in the early 1800s as a trading post on Big Prairie. Indians of the Shawnee and Osage tribes bartered their pelts at the post and the pioneers replenished their supplies there. Legend has it that a local band of Shawnee Indians once traveled to Washington, D.C., to visit the "great white father," President John Quincy Adams. One day in 1825, these journeyers camped on the grounds of Thomas James, a banker and merchant from Chillicothe, Ohio. He noticed their decorative red paint, which he recognized as hematite, an agent of iron ore. His interest was piqued when they told of the red earth beside a huge spring in the West. Upon their return trip, James's business partner accompanied the Shawnee group to inspect the enormous spring and red earth. A favorable report led to construction of the Maramec Iron Works in 1826. Six miles north of the works, a town was founded on Big Prairie to serve as a source for grain and cattle to be used at the works. The James family proposed the town to be "Jamestown." When the post office notified them that name was already in use elsewhere, they followed a custom prevalent at the time by prefixing "James" with "Saint."

St. James, known for its trees, is called the "Forest City of the Ozarks." *Time* magazine called St. James "the most handsomely wooded town in the nation" in an article in 1967. The trees were planted as a project started in the late 1950s. Each autumn, residents enjoy the brilliant reds of the planted sweet gum trees, which are actually native to southeastern Missouri and states further south.

A descendant of the early Iron Works family, Lucy Wortham James, inherited the land surrounding the old Iron Works. Upon her death in 1938, she willed her estate as part of a trust that was later known as The James Foundation. The foundation has provided many gifts to the city of St. James including the city hall, the fire station, the library, and a city park. Most noteworthy of all was its establishment of Maramec Spring Park, where the old Iron Works had been.

Proceed 6 miles east on MO 8 to **Maramec Spring Park**. As you leave St. James, notice the transition from level terrain to the rugged, forested hills leading to the Meramec River valley. At the bottom of a steep hill, turn left and enter the park. A nominal fee is charged. Before entering the park, note the building to the right, which is an office of the Missouri Department of Conservation. Here, information is available on public lands in the region.

In 1971, Maramec Spring Park was designated as the first Registered Natural Landmark in the State of Missouri by the National Park Service. The 1,856-acre park contains a small restaurant, picnic and camping facilities, comfort stations, sports fields, an auto trail and observation tower, a historical museum, an agriculture museum, a nature center, the ruins of the Maramec Iron Works, trout rearing pools, and trout fishing. The best place to start is the **Maramec Museum**, where exhibits recreate the days from 1826 to 1876 when the Maramec Iron Works produced iron. The museum contains exhibits, dioramas, and working models that trace the origin of the works, the iron manufacturing process, the life of the miners and their families, and life of the Shawnee Indians.

Leaving the Maramec Museum, you can walk through Maramec Village as it was in the 1870s. The trail passes through what was a company town that once supported a community of 500 residents. Interpretive signs illustrate where buildings once stood. Remnants of the cold blast furnace and the five refinery forges have been preserved and restored in their original locations. Also, be sure to tour the nature center and agriculture museum.

A visit to **Maramec Spring**, the seventh largest spring in Missouri, is a must. A rustic path leads around the spring opening, which issues an aver-

*Five iron refinery forges are among the historical structures
that can be viewed at Maramec Spring Park.*

age of 96 million gallons of water a day. The water rises almost vertically from a depth of 190 feet into a pool, which was formed when the original channel was dammed during construction of the Iron Works. The water source is from a drainage basin approximately 15 to 20 miles south and southwest of the park. The water courses through porous dolomite rock and joins into one main artery that feeds the spring. Below the spring pool, notice the trout-rearing raceways. More than 180,000 trout are released annually into the spring branch after they attain a length of 10 inches. The Missouri Department of Conservation stocks 2.25 trout for each fisherman they anticipate will be fishing the next day. Trout fishing season occurs between March 1 and October 31; a daily trout tag can be purchased at the park office along with a state fishing license.

An **auto tour road** within the park leads to the Maramec Iron Works Cemetery, the Maramec Iron Works Mine, and the old Stringtown Road. This road once connected the industrial area of the ironworks with the mine; it was the first road in this area between Ste. Genevieve and Springfield, Missouri. The area was called "Stringtown" because of the string of homes that bordered the winding, busy mine road. In 1982, four large murals depicting different types of homes were erected along the road. These murals also give some insight into the lives of these early pioneers.

There are more than 4.5 miles of hiking trails throughout the park. A map is available at the office. A short distance off of trail #5, which follows along the Maramec Spring Branch, is **Spring's End Natural Area**. This state-designated natural area is part of the Woodson K. Woods Conservation Area and features a 14-acre old growth bottomland forest. Here, large towering trees more than 150 years old dominate the canopy. Species include bur oak, bitternut hickory, white oak, sycamore, butternut, and northern red oak, and an understory of spicebush, elderberry, and a variety of wildflowers. To reach the natural area, follow the Spring Branch Trail to the suspension bridge over Spring Branch. There is a fisherman's trail at the base of a hill. Follow it, going downstream, past the point where Spring Branch joins the Meramec River. Continue along the trail about 100 yards to a gravel road, which leads through the natural area. A short walk brings you to one of the best examples of an old growth bottomland forest in the Ozarks.

Leave the main part of Maramec Spring Park and continue east on MO 8 toward Steelville. After a mile, the road crosses the **Meramec River**; an access road to the left leads to a popular public canoe-launching site. A good view of the river is available just beyond the parking lot. There are several canoe and raft rental operators in the area who can provide all the equipment you need (even a put-in and take-out service) for single-day or overnight floats down the Meramec River. Ask for information about local canoe outfitters at the St. James Tourist Information Center.

The Meramec River, which empties into the Mississippi River just below St. Louis, is classified as an easy floating stream with a permanent flow distance of more than 201 miles. It is also one of the most popular recreational streams in Missouri. Numerous caves, scenic bluffs, and a diversity of wildlife can be seen along the river. Just past the river access road to the left stands the Brinker House, a historic site, which is part of Maramec Spring Park.

Continue on MO 8 to Steelville, which has a population of 1,465. A welcome sign proclaims Steelville as the "population center of the U.S.A." and the "floating capital of Missouri." Steelville was founded in 1835 when James Steel sold 40 acres of land to the Crawford County Court for fifty dollars. The court named the little settlement in honor of Mr. Steel. A tourist information center is located on the east side of town along MO 8.

Leave Steelville on MO 19 and head north to Cuba, a distance of 8 miles. About halfway there you will cross over the Meramec River again as it flows northeast. **Cuba** advertises itself as the "Gateway to the Ozarks," a common claim made by several towns along the border of the Ozarks. Access I-44 north on the other side of Cuba, travel 3 miles to Exit 214, and leave the interstate. Turn right and proceed on MO Highway H for 2 miles to Leasburg and continue another 5 miles to **Onondaga Cave State Park**. Follow the signs to the new visitors center; plan to spend some time exploring its interesting exhibits and be sure to take the Onondaga Cave tour.

Missouri, which has more than 5,000 caves, is known as the "Cave State"; however, a detailed inventory of Tennessee has revealed more than 6,000 caves there! Arkansas is third, with more than 2,000 caves. Of course, these numbers are subject to change as new caves are discovered each year.

Onondaga Cave was discovered in 1866 by two young explorers who entered the cave by navigating their johnboat into a spring outlet. Onondaga Cave became the official name in 1904 following a name-the-cave contest. Onondaga means "Spirit of the Mountains" and is the name of a northeastern Iroquois tribe. The tribe, and therefore the name, have little to do with local history. The cave was one of the feature attractions during the 1904 St. Louis World's Fair. As a commercial enterprise, Onondaga Cave gained national recognition in the 1950s and 1960s when it was owned by Lester B. Dill, who was often called "America's Number One Caveman."

Onondaga Cave and the surrounding region were threatened in 1967, when the U.S. Congress authorized the U.S. Army Corps of Engineers to construct a dam across the Meramec River for flood control and recreation. In 1973, when Mr. Dill learned that the proposed lake would flood up to eighty percent of Onondaga Cave, he joined the farmers, environmentalists, and conservationists opposing the dam. Because of their letters, petitions, hearings, and other efforts, a non-binding vote of sixty-four percent against the dam convinced political leaders to deauthorize the dam in 1981. Prior to his death in 1979, Mr. Dill approached the Missouri Department of Natu-

Massive flowstone provides a backdrop for unusual rimstone features in Onondaga Cave.

ral Resources with the idea of making Onondaga Cave a state park. With the help of The Nature Conservancy, this became a reality in 1982. The cave is also a National Natural Landmark. The 75-minute tours are almost a mile long and visitors can experience the cave from lighted concrete walkways with handrails. The temperature of the cave is 57 degrees Fahrenheit year-round. Visitors see spectacular cave formations including soda straws, stalactites, stalagmites, and columns; flowing water has created rimstone dams and massive flowstones.

While in the area, ask at the park office about access to **Vilander Bluff Natural Area** which is 10 miles from the park. While no trail is currently available, the hike up to one of the highest and most spectacular bluffs along the Meramec River is well worth the effort. Eastern red cedars up to 500 years old cling to a ledge on a sheer, 200-foot cliff. An excellent view of the bluff is also available when floating the river.

Another recommended stop is **Meramec State Park**, which is located north of Onondaga Cave State Park and east of Sullivan on MO 185. The park offers many interesting sites, including a new visitors center with excellent exhibits, tours of Fisher Cave, scenic views, and access to the Meramec River.

6

Missouri Rhineland

Busch Conservation Area to Hermann, Missouri

General description: A 50-mile drive beginning at Busch Conservation Area and traveling through the German-settled Missouri River valley and hills to historic Hermann.

Special attractions: August A. Busch Memorial, Grand Bluffs and Weldon Spring conservation areas, Katy Trail State Park, Missouri River, Daniel Boone Home and Monument, Augusta, Marthasville, and Hermann; German festivals, wineries, scenic views, hiking, biking, fall colors, fishing, hunting, and wildlife viewing.

Location: Northeastern Ozarks. The drive begins at the junction of U.S. Highway 40 and Missouri Highway 94.

Drive route numbers: Missouri Highways 94, 19, D, and F.

Camping: Primitive camping is permitted only in designated areas at Daniel Boone and Little Lost Creek conservation areas. No facilities are provided.

Services: All services at Hermann, Washington, and nearby St. Charles and St. Peters. Gas and food at Marthasville. A bed and breakfast, food and gas at Augusta.

Nearby attractions: Babler State Park; Shaw Arboretum; Rockwoods Reservation and Howell Island conservation areas; and Powder Valley Conservation Nature Center.

The drive

The northern edge of the Ozarks extends just across the Missouri River into hills that barely escaped Missouri's last glacier more than 500,000 years ago. The Missouri River has been a major influence in this region of the Ozarks. Beginning as a coldwater trout stream in Montana, it flows 2,522 miles before joining the Mississippi River. The Missouri River, also known as the "Big Muddy," was a marvel to early explorers because of its natural resources. They reported fish large enough to capsize canoes and described extensive wetlands arranged along the river margins like pearls on a necklace.

The Missouri River was not always the single channel it is today. Called

Drive 6: Missouri Rhineland

Missouri Rhineland Busch Conservation Area to Hermann, Missouri

SITES

1. Lost Valley Hiking/Biking Trail
2. Weldon Spring Hiking Trail
3. Daniel Boone Home
4. Daniel Boone Monument

A tour guide stands ready to greet visitors at the home of the legendary Daniel Boone.

Pekitanoui by the Osage Indians, the river was a braided stream with many chutes, sloughs, islands, and channels. Drastic channel modification began in the early 1900s, and by 1972 about fifty percent of the original surface of the river had been lost. Backwater habitat was eliminated and the main channel was deepened and narrowed for navigation. Most of the natural vegetation has now been replaced by agriculture. The Great Flood of 1993 awoke many to the consequences of river confinement when record high waters broke through levees, flooding towns, farmland, and highways over a three-month period. A near repeat of this event occurred again in the spring of 1995. To help prevent major catastrophes like this in the future, federal and state agencies are working together to try to partially restore natural floodways. This involves acquiring floodplains in critical areas and setting back levees to allow more room for the river to expand at high water levels. These changes will also create more wetlands and bottomland forests in which fish and wildlife can thrive.

The drive begins at the junction of MO 94 and US 40. Proceed 1 mile west on MO 94 and turn onto MO D. Follow it for 1.5 miles and turn into the entrance of the **August A. Busch Memorial Conservation Area**. This 6,987-acre area was acquired by the Missouri Department of Conservation in 1947 from the federal government. A donation of $70,000 toward the purchase of the area was made by Mrs. August A. Busch as a memorial to her late husband, owner of Anheuser-Busch Brewing Company of St. Louis. Maps and information are available at a small visitors center. You may also wish to pick up a map to Weldon Spring Conservation Area, which is the next stop on this drive. Plans are underway to construct a modern visitor center with exhibits.

The Busch conservation area provides opportunities for wildlife viewing, hiking, fishing at its thirty-two lakes and ponds, and hunting during special seasons. At the headquarters, you can pick up a brochure outlining an 8.7-mile auto tour of the area that begins and ends at the main parking lot. There are seven hiking trails varying from 0.2 to 3.0 miles in length at selected stops along the tour route. If you decide not to take the auto tour, at least visit the waterfowl refuge at the beginning of the route. Follow road "C" to the first parking lot on the right. A boardwalk and viewing platform provide opportunities to see giant Canada geese and other wildlife, including fish.

The return of the giant Canada goose is a wildlife success story. Giant Canada geese look much like common Canada geese, except that they are up to one and one-half times larger than the latter and they do not migrate. Giant Canada geese originally nested over much of the Midwest. As settlement increased, these birds were practically eliminated. By the early 1900s there were no known nesting populations of giant Canadas in the entire country. It was later discovered that a few isolated populations were nesting along small ledges and depressions in cliffs above the Missouri River near here. The first efforts to restore nesting Canada geese were made at Busch in the late 1940s and early 1950s. As the population grew, the geese were moved to other areas to start new flocks. Giant Canada geese are now doing fine, and in some city parks and in yards around lake-edge homes they have actually become pests. They are remarkable birds, however, and these resident giant geese would be sorely missed if they had been allowed to go extinct.

As you continue on MO 94, the road enters **Weldon Spring Conservation Area**. This 7,356-acre area was purchased in 1978 from the University of Missouri, which had received it in 1948 from the federal government for use as an agricultural experiment station. Weldon Spring is named for the nearby town founded by John Weldon. He came to this area in 1796 with a Spanish land grant for 425 acres including the spring. The conservation area has diverse natural features. In addition to the Missouri River, with its rugged limestone cliffs, the area contains seven ponds, Femme Osage Slough, and Prairie Lake. A unique 385-acre natural area contains examples of upland and bottomland forests, and limestone cliffs that extend for a mile along the Missouri River.

About 1.5 miles west from MO D, the Weldon Spring Hiking Trail begins on the left at a parking area. Two trails, the 8.2-mile Lewis Trail and the 5.3-mile Clark Trail begin and return here. A Weldon Spring Conservation Area map showing these trails and other features is available at the Busch Conservation Area headquarters. The trails enter the natural area and offer scenic views on bluffs overlooking the Missouri River.

After another 2.7 miles on MO 94, a road on the left leads to **Katy Trail State Park**. Formerly, the old Missouri-Kansas-Texas (M K T) Railroad, which ceased operation in 1986, the right-of-way of was purchased by the late Edward D. "Ted" Jones Jr. and donated to the State of Missouri for a state park. After its development as a hiking-biking trail, the MKT (nicknamed the "Katy" Trail) became the longest continuous trail in the United States, at 235 miles in length. Just after most of the trail was completed, it suffered a major setback during the Great Flood of 1993 and again in the spring of 1995. Major restoration efforts by the state of Missouri have it back in operation. This drive will encounter the trail at several crossings.

After another 0.7 mile on MO 94, the Lost Valley Hiking-Biking Trail begins beyond a parking area on the right. The 8-mile trail is more rigorous than the Katy Trail, following valleys and climbing up and over hills that provide challenges for mountain bikers.

In another 0.4 mile, a side trip on MO F on the right leads about 5 miles to the **Daniel Boone Home**. A fee is charged to help maintain the historic buildings and grounds. In 1766, the legendary Daniel Boone helped explore Kentucky and other areas west of the Appalachians. He was a trailblazer, Indian fighter, scout, trapper, surveyor, Virginia state legislator and judge. In 1799, at the age of 66, Boone left Kentucky and came to Missouri when the region west of the Mississippi River was still ruled by Spain. While hunting along Femme Osage Creek, he came upon a spring flowing from a hillside near an enormous elm tree. It was here, in 1803, more than a day's ride from the nearest settlement, that he and his son Nathan began building the house their families would share. The Boones built a magnificent house entirely from materials found in the valley around them. Walls were constructed of quarried limestone. Floor timbers, beams, doorways, and fireplace mantels were made of black walnut. Even the primitive, wrinkled glass in the windows was made using valley limestone. When it was finished, the home was considered the finest house west of the Mississippi River. Daniel Boone lived out his final years in his rock mansion and died there in 1820, a year before Missouri became a state. His son Nathan continued to live in the house until 1837, when he sold it and moved his family to Ash Grove in southwest Missouri. Today the home is filled with furnishings of the era and interpreters in period costume describe life in the early 1800s.

Return to MO 94, and after 1.5 miles enter the small community of **Defiance**, which earned its name in 1894 by building a depot that lured the railroad away from Augusta. From here to Hermann, you are in wine country, and there are several vineyards along the route. Their exploration will be left to you.

Continue on MO 94, pass **Matson**, and after 8 miles enter **Augusta**, which is on a side road heading south. The town is situated on the hills and bluffs overlooking the Missouri River valley. It was founded in 1836 by Leonard Harold, one of the settlers who followed Daniel Boone to this region. The town grew predominantly with German families who brought their wine-growing and agricultural expertise with them.

In the 1870s, flooding caused the Missouri River to cut a new channel away from the town, depriving the town of its boat landing but providing several hundred new acres of fertile bottomland. Today, Augusta is officially recognized as America's First Wine District. Much of the recent tourism interest in these old German towns has been spurred by the revival of the vineyards in the 1960s. In Augusta, you will find specialty shops, wineries, bakeries, bed and breakfasts, restaurants, and access to the Katy Trail.

Return to MO 94 and proceed 7.7 miles to **Dutzow**, where Missouri's German heritage first took root. In the 1820s, Gottfried Duden established a farm and sent enthusiastic accounts of his experiences back to Germany by way of a book he authored. The book was widely circulated and gave a glowing description of the climate and agricultural potential of the region. Because it described the region's similarity to Germany, Duden's book attracted thousands of Germans to this area. The settlement grew and was eventually established as a town by Baron Von Bock in 1832.

Continue on MO 94 to the junction of MO 47. A side trip south for 4 miles takes you to **Washington**. Founded in 1839, this town also drew German families that would shape the area's economy, arts, architecture, and culture. The city has two registered historic districts, along Main Street and Front Street.

After another 3 miles on MO 94, the town of **Marthasville** provides a popular access point for the Katy Trail and a variety of services. Founded in 1766, the town was originally a French village called La Charrette. Located at the mouth of Charrette Creek, it was a convenient place for hunting, trapping, and trading with the Indians. The village was the westernmost settlement of white men when the Lewis and Clark Expedition went up the Missouri River in 1804 and when it returned in 1806. After the purchase of the Louisiana Territory in 1803, the French villagers of Charrette began selling their land claims to Americans. The French settlement had become an American one when Dr. John Young refounded the town, named it for his wife, Martha, and advertised its founding in the *Missouri Gazette* of St. Louis on June 21, 1817.

Daniel Boone was familiar with the Marthasville area and selected a site on a tree-covered knoll overlooking Toque Creek to be his final resting place. The monument to Daniel and his wife, Rebecca, still stands as a tribute to the old fighting Quaker. To visit the **Daniel Boone Monument**, head east on MO 94 from the entrance to Marthasville about 1.8 miles and turn left on a side road that may or may not be marked as the Boone Monument Road. After 0.5 mile, turn left at the junction and proceed another 0.5 mile to a parking area along the left side of the road. Steps lead up a small knob to the monument. In 1845, a group of developers persuaded the surviving Boone relatives to move the remains of Daniel and his wife back to Kentucky, where they were reburied in a Frankfort cemetery. There is some skepticism that the remains are actually that of Daniel Boone; however, exhuming the graves for possible identification has been ruled out for now.

Continue on MO 94 another 10.5 miles to a parking area on the left. This stop is the only roadside view of the Missouri River other than that in the town of Hermann. With its confined, single channel, the river is traveling faster now than in the days of Lewis and Clark. In the cold of winter, when the temperature remains below freezing for several days, ice floes form on the river. Although too small to support anything but a bird, their circular shapes are interesting to watch as they go floating by.

Travel another 15 miles on MO 94 to the junction with MO 19. A 7-mile side trip west on MO 94 for 7 miles leads to the most dramatic stretch

Hermann's Octoberfest is a popular attraction complete with parades, pageants, foods and music celebrating the town's German ancestry.

of bluffs along the Missouri River. Towering dolomite cliffs rise over the Missouri River valley and parallel the highway for 3 miles. The Missouri Department of Conservation has purchased a section of this impressive feature, now called **Grand Bluffs Conservation Area**. Access to the area is reached by following the entrance sign at the west end of the bluff and turning north on a side road to a parking lot. A trail has not been developed yet and you must find your own way to the top of the bluff. Access will improve when more land is acquired. October is a particularly rewarding time, when the sugar maples turn crimson red against the white cliffs. Returning to MO 19, you pass through the town of Rhineland, which after the devastation of the 1993 flood, is in the process of moving into the hills.

At the junction of MO 94 and 19, turn south and proceed to **Hermann**. As you cross the Missouri River valley, notice the deep scours and sand deposits across the landscape. During the Great Flood of 1993, the river broke through a levee upstream and for a period of several weeks reclaimed some of its historic course, taking out the highway in the process.

In 1837, a group of German immigrants landed on the rugged south shore of the Missouri River to establish Hermann. The town was named to honor a Germanic hero (called Arminius by the Romans, but Hermann in modern German) who in 9 A.D. gathered a force of Germans and crushed an army of 15,000 to 18,000 veteran Roman soldiers. The victory saved the Germans from being enslaved by the Romans.

Soon after their arrival on the south shore, the immigrants cleared the steep wooded hills of the northern Ozark settlement and established vineyards. By 1870, Hermann had become the second largest wine-producing region in the United States. The community endeavored to preserve its ancestry and culture by building homes, churches, schools, and wineries in traditional German-style architecture; many of these structures still stand today.

Each spring and fall the streets are crowded with visitors during Maifest and Octoberfest, when many of the old houses are opened for tours. There are also pageants and parades with German bands and folk dancing. The historic wineries of Hermannhof, Stone Hill, Bias, and Adam Puchta display their products and serve them with traditional German foods. In addition to the popular festivals in May and October, various gift shops, restaurants, and historic sites are open year-round, which offers an alternative for those that would rather visit Hermann when it is less crowded.

7

Boonslick Country

Columbia to Arrow Rock, Missouri

General description: A 55-mile drive beginning in Columbia and heading west across the northern edge of the Ozarks through historic towns and trails.

Special attractions: Rock Bridge State Park, Eagle Bluffs Conservation Area, Columbia, Rocheport, Katy Trail State Park, Old Franklin State Historic Site, New Franklin, Boone's Lick State Historic Site, Missouri River, Santa Fe Trail, Boonville, and Arrow Rock; scenic views, hiking, camping, boating, fishing, hunting, fall colors, and wildlife viewing.

Location: Northern Ozarks. The drive begins on Missouri Highway 163 at the junction of U.S. Highway 63 south of Columbia.

Drive route numbers: U.S. Interstate 70; U.S. Highways 63 and 40; and Missouri Highways 5, 87, 41, 163, 187, 240, Z, and BB.

Camping: Finger Lakes State Park has 35 campsites with modern showering facilities and water. Water is shut off from November 1 through March 31. Arrow Rock State Historic Site has 22 basic and 23 improved sites with a dump station and modern restrooms. Pine Ridge Recreation Area has basic campsites and a pit toilet.

Services: All services at Columbia and Boonville. Food and bed and breakfasts at Rocheport and Arrow Rock.

Nearby attractions: Finger Lakes State Park; Rocky Fork Lakes and Three Creeks conservation areas; and State Capitol and Runge Conservation Nature Center (in Jefferson City).

 The drive

This drive skirts along the northern edge of the Ozarks over a landscape that was once buried under a massive glacier. This is the only part of the Ozarks that was glaciated, and that occurred more than 950,000 years ago. Traditionally, this has been called the Kansan glacial period, the second in a series of four major ice advances over the three-million-year period called the Ice Age. Each period was named after the present-day states where these glacial fronts pretty much ended. The first was the Nebraskan, then the Kansan, next the Illinoisan, and last the Wisconsinan glaciation, which melted away about 10,000 years ago. However, recent studies cast doubt on

Drive 7: Boonslick Country
Columbia to Arrow Rock, Missouri (east)

SITES

1. Rock Bridge State Park
2. Eagle Bluffs Conservation Area
3. Katy Trail State Park

Drive 7: Boonslick Country
Columbia to Arrow Rock, Missouri (west)

SITES
4. Davisdale Conservation Area
5. Franklin Island Conservation Area
6. Boone's Lick State Historic Site
7. Arrow Rock State Historic Site

the idea that there were only four major glaciations; currently, textbooks refer to early glaciers as "pre-Illinoisan."

Imagine a wall of ice up to a mile thick leveling everything in its path. As the massive ice flowed along, it carried silt, clay, sand, gravel, and a few boulders, (collectively called glacial till), leaving them behind as the climate warmed and the glacier receded. Some rocks found in this area can be traced back to what is now Minnesota and Canada. Some car-sized boulders were ground smooth by the tremendous pressure and friction of transport.

Ahead of these glacial advances, the landscape was much different than it is today. Immediately south of the glacier was tundra, dominated by ground-hugging lichens and mosses; farther south were spruce and fir forests that graded into birch and pine. The gradations continued further south to oak and hickory forests that were found in what is now Louisiana and Mississippi.

Animals that lived in this colder climate included twenty-foot ground sloths; giant beavers that were four feet high at the shoulder; mastodons and mammoths; huge versions of bison and musk ox; horses and camels; and giant American lions and saber-toothed cats, to name a few. These unusual animals became extinct with the changes in climate and habitat and early man's hunting pressure.

Today, it may seem that there is little evidence of past glacial events; but search along eroded soil banks, plowed fields, and gravel-bottomed streambeds and you may just find one of those smooth, rounded rocks of pink or grey granite that was transported here by a glacier more than 950,000 years ago.

The drive begins southeast of Columbia at the junction of US 63 and MO 163. Head west on MO 163 about 5 miles and turn left at the entrance of **Rock Bridge State Park**. Follow the short drive to a parking area that accesses the rock bridge and Devil's Icebox. Follow the trail a short distance to the rock bridge. Actually more like a tunnel, the rock bridge has a 15-foot ceiling, is 150 feet long, and is from 50 to 75 feet wide. This natural bridge is the remnant of a limestone cave that collapsed, leaving only a section of the ceiling still standing. The trail continues to Devil's Icebox, a sinkhole that empties into an underground cave system. Devil's Icebox has so far been explored for a total passage length of 6 miles. Only experienced spelunkers who obtain permission from the park superintendent are allowed to explore the cave's interior. The western part of this state park also contains three trails covering a total of 4.5 miles.

Return to MO 163 and continue west to MO K. A side trip of about 7 miles leads to **Eagle Bluffs Conservation Area**. This is a relatively new acquisition by the Missouri Department of Conservation. Once developed, it will be the largest wetland area in the United States that uses treated municipal wastewater (from Columbia) to supplement its water needs. The area was nearly completed and operational when it was devastated by the Great Flood of 1993. Sections of newly built levees, designed to hold water in pools for waterfowl use, were overtopped and washed away. As of this writing, the 4,156-acre complex is almost totally repaired and ready for operation. In addition to providing feeding and resting areas for migrating ducks and geese, the area will eventually have hiking trails and viewing blinds along the levees and in a marsh, allowing visitors to observe wildlife firsthand. The area will also be used for outdoor classroom studies by nearby schools. After acquiring the prominent cliff and upland overlooking the vast wetland development, the Missouri Department of Conservation plans to develop a loop hiking trail with observation decks that will provide sweeping views of the Missouri River valley.

Before entering Eagle Bluffs, the road crosses over **Katy Trail State Park**. Beginning in St. Charles, this state park is 235 miles long and 60 feet wide—making it the longest, narrowest state park in the United States. This reconditioned bed of the old Missouri-Kansas-Texas Railroad (MKT) was purchased by the late Edward D. "Ted" Jones Jr. and donated to the State of Missouri for a state park. The MKT, nicknamed "Katy" Trail, is now a popular hiking-biking trail extending from St. Charles to Boonville and southwest to Sedalia. An abandoned railroad spur from Columbia to the Katy Trail is being developed by the city as a hiking-biking route to the main trail.

Return to MO 163 and proceed northwards into **Columbia**. Settlers began to arrive here as far back as 1819, but it was not until 1836 that the settlement really began to grow. New arrivals came largely from Kentucky, attracted to the area's similarity in soils and landscape to their Madison County, Kentucky homeland. Columbia is the seat of Boone County, which was formed in 1820. This was almost nine months before Missouri's official entrance into the union on August 10, 1821, making the county older than the state. At the time Boone County was formed, members of the legislature were wearing black arm bands to mourn the death of Daniel Boone on September 26, 1820; naming the county in his honor seemed a fitting tribute.

It is said that Columbia was probably named after the county seat of Adair County, Kentucky, in the hope that it, too, would be a county seat. One of the most popular names in the United States, "Columbia" has been used in some thirty-two of the fifty states. By the 1840s, Columbia was steadily growing into a prosperous town, serving as a retail center for a wide area. It was also in the 1840s that the most influential event in all of Columbia's history came about—the acquisition and organization of the University of Missouri. This established Columbia as a center of education. Today, the university's Columbia campus enrolls more than 22,000 students and specializes in teaching, research, and extension services. Two other colleges, Stephens College and Columbia College, help to make Columbia

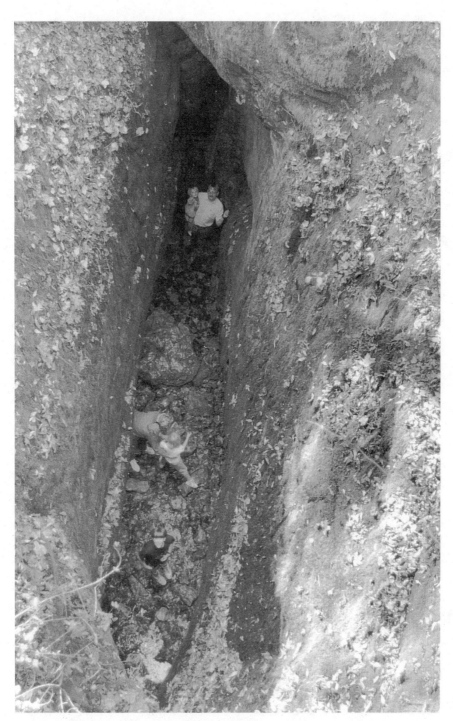

A family explores Devil's Ice Box, a sinkhole whose roof has collapsed.

Arrow Rock's historic Lyceum Theatre provides summer plays performed by nationally known professional actors.

worthy of its nickname, "College Town, U.S.A." To obtain information about events and points of interest in Columbia, visit the City of Columbia Convention and Visitor Bureau (see Appendix for address and phone number).

The next stop is **Rocheport**. Continue on MO 163 to I-70 and travel west on the interstate for about 2 miles until it intersects US 40 at Exit 121. (An alternative is to continue on the interstate to Exit 115 and follow MO BB into Rocheport.) US 40 was America's first highway west and begins at the docks in Baltimore, Maryland. Travel west on US 40 for 8 miles to MO 240 and proceed south for a mile to Rocheport. Founded in 1825, the settlement was first intended to be called "Rockport," but the name was changed to "Rocheport" at the insistence of a French missionary who happened to be in the area. The name refers to a large rock outcrop just west of the town. The Missouri River once flowed against this rocky point, creating a safe harbor just below it. Moniteau Creek, or "Creek of the Great Spirit," still flows by this rocky point today.

During their expedition up the Missouri River, Lewis and Clark landed here in June 1804 and explored the surrounding countryside. They noted the "painted rocks" in their journal as being "very remarkable. They are covered with strange and uncouth hieroglyphics and representations. We were prevented from making a careful inspection by reason of the presence of so many ferocious rattlesnakes, which are very venomous at this season of the year, and which were crawling among the rocks in great numbers."

After settlement, the town grew along with the steamboat transportation on the river. Nothing remains of the large tobacco and lumber warehouses that once occupied the busy dock area. During the Civil War, Rocheport was raided by both Confederate and Union troops. The town was also the site of important Underground Railroad efforts to aid runaway slaves in their escape northward. The popular harbor is now gone because the Missouri River, having shifted about 0.25 mile south, no longer flows against the rocky point.

Today, Rocheport is an attractive historic site with restored nineteenth-century homes and buildings. Restaurants and shops are found about town, and a winery is perched nearby on the high bluffs overlooking the river valley. The popular Katy Trail State Park occupies the old Missouri-Kansas-Texas Railroad bed along the south side of town. Bike rentals, refreshments, a restroom, and parking are found along the trail. Be sure to take the short walk west to see Moniteau Creek and the only tunnel along the Katy Trail.

Return to US 40 and continue west, passing the 2,521-acre **Davisdale Conservation Area**, which features an 8-mile hiking trail and opportunities for hunting and fishing. In another 4 miles, the 1,517-acre Franklin Island Conservation Area lies to the south. The Missouri River once cut a channel on the area's north boundary and the land was surrounded by water. In 1952, the remnant chute was permanently closed by a flood-control levee. The conservation department purchased the land in 1978. The area offers fishing along streams and the Missouri River, plus deer and turkey hunting.

A side trip on MO 5 north to **New Franklin** provides an opportunity to visit numerous pre-Civil War homes. A self-guided tour brochure is available at the information center. The town was established in 1828 in the hills above the Missouri River valley after the original Franklin was destroyed by floodwaters. The **Old Franklin State Historic Site** west of New Franklin has markers that describe the original town that as it was laid out in 1816.

As you continue on US 40/MO 5, a side trip on MO 87 goes to **Boone's Lick State Historic Site**. Follow MO 87 across the Missouri River valley 8.5 miles to Boonesboro. Notice the sand deposits and scour holes that resulted from the Great Flood of 1993. The **Santa Fe Trail** auto tour signs along the road mark the 900-mile route to Santa Fe, New Mexico. Its first travelers left Franklin in 1821. Pass the town of Boonesboro, and after 1.2 miles, turn left on MO 187 and follow it for 2.5 miles to Boone's Lick State Historic Site. An interpretive center and short trail are provided. The site contains a natural saltwater spring—a salt lick—that was named for Nathan and Daniel M. Boone, sons of famed pioneer Daniel Boone. In the early 1800s, the brothers processed salt here for other early settlements along the Missouri River. As a measure of the salt lick's importance, communities in, and indeed, the region itself were named for the family's and the lick's legendary status. Boone's Lick Road became an important thoroughfare for westward expansion in the Missouri Territory.

Return to US 40 /MO 5 and enter **Boonville** by way of the Boonville Bridge. A walkway on the bridge connects the Katy Trail as it heads south to Sedalia. Boonville was established in 1817 as a river port and its merchants, along with fur trappers and traders, explorers, soldiers, and educators, contributed to the opening of western lands for settlement. An important battle in the western campaign of the Civil War was fought just 4 miles downstream on June 7, 1861. Confederate soldiers were defeated by Union forces at the battle of Boonville, and Missouri was preserved for the Union. A well-known Boonville landmark, the Kemper Military School and College, is located at Center Avenue and Third Street. Founded in 1844 by Federick Kemper, it is the oldest boys' school and military academy west of the Mississippi River. It is now co-ed.

Continue on US 40 /MO 5 through Boonville to I-70 and follow the interstate west for 5 miles to Exit 98 and MO 41. Once on MO 41, follow the signs 13 miles to **Arrow Rock. Arrow Rock State Historic Site** is located on the right just before you enter the town. A new visitor center interprets Booneslick country in the early nineteenth century. The nearby Arrow Rock bluff was a significant landmark and a crossing place on the Missouri River for Indians, explorers, and early westward travelers. The town's name first appeared in 1732 on a French map drawn by D'Anville, who called it *Pierre a Fleche*, or "Rock of Arrows." Lewis and Clark passed through this area on June 9, 1804. Clark recorded in his journal, "We set out early, and reached a cliff called Arrow Rock, near to which is a prairie called the Prairie of Arrows and Arrow Creek . . . " In 1819, the explorer Stephen Long reported that the bluff was so named because the Indians gathered flint from the bluff for arrowheads.

Located above the Missouri River and across from Boone's Lick, Arrow Rock became an important trading center for area farmers and, as an outfitting town, provided supplies for westward expeditions on the Santa Fe Trail. By the mid-1800s, Arrow Rock's population had grown to more than 1,000. By the late nineteenth century, more modern means of transportation had replaced river travel, and Arrow Rock declined in importance. Fires devastated the business district in 1873 and again in 1901, hastening the decline. Today, Arrow Rock is a quiet village where visitors to the site often outnumber the town's population of 70.

Many of the buildings have been restored in Arrow Rock, and walking tours are offered from Memorial Day through Labor Day, as well as by special arrangement during the rest of the year. Special events and historical reenactments are held at different times throughout the year. Of particular note is the Baptist Church, which was built in 1872 and has since been converted into a summer theater. Now called the Lyceum Theatre, it houses Broadway-caliber shows featuring professional actors from around the country.

8

Lake of the Ozarks
Bagnell Dam to Ha Ha Tonka, Missouri

General description: A 22-mile drive starting at Bagnell Dam and the Lake of the Ozarks. Attractive features along the way include picturesque hills, bluffs, glades, caves, and springs.

Special attractions: Osage River, Bagnell Dam, Lake of the Ozarks, Ha Ha Tonka and Lake of the Ozarks state parks, Castle Ruins, Ozark Caverns, and Grand Glaize Recreation Area; Dogwood Festival; wildlife viewing, camping, hiking, wildflower displays, fall colors, scenic views, fishing, hunting, boating, horseback riding, and swimming.

Location: Northern Ozarks. The drive begins at the junction of U.S. Highway 54 and Missouri Highway W.

Drive route numbers: U.S. Highway 54 and Missouri Highways 42, 134, A, D, and W.

Camping: Lake of the Ozarks State Park has 230 tent and trailer campsites, both basic and improved. Facilities include a dumping station, modern restrooms, a laundry, and a store. Four group camps are available for use by nonprofit organizations. Reservations must be made in advance with the park superintendent. Each group camp accommodates from forty to two hundred campers and includes sleeping cabins, restrooms with showers, a dining lodge with kitchen, a playing field, and swimming facilities. Ha Ha Tonka State Park offers picnicking only.

Services: All services at Osage Beach and Camdenton.

Nearby attractions: Bennett Spring State Park, Fiery Forks Conservation Area, Bridal Cave (commercial), and State Capitol and Runge Conservation Nature Center (in Jefferson City).

 The drive

The Lake of the Ozarks is a resort-based destination for water recreation, restaurants, roadside gift shops, shopping malls, family rides, and country music halls. The lake also draws people looking for second homes and retirement homes. Amidst all of this development remain special areas where one can experience and enjoy what the rugged Osage River Hills have to offer.

Drive 8: Lake of the Ozarks

Bagnell Dam to Ha Ha Tonka, Missouri

SITES

1. Bagnell Dam
2. Bagnell Dam Access
3. Lake of the Ozarks State Park
4. Grand Glaize Recreation Area
5. Ozark Caverns
6. Ha Ha Tonka State Park
7. Castle Ruins
8. HaHa Tonka Spring

The Osage Indians were the first inhabitants of this region. East of here, a village site remained as late as 1822. The first white man to record his visits to this area was Zebulon M. Pike, who with a group of Osageans, traveled up the **Osage River** in 1806. Like the other large rivers in the Ozarks, the Osage served as a highway for settlers into the roadless interior. Special steamboats that required only about a foot of water in which to float were built for the Ozark rivers in the mid-1800s. The boats were also built shorter than their big river counterparts in order to navigate the many sharp bends. These paddlewheelers traveled as far upriver on the Osage as Warsaw, Missouri. The Osage River remained important for river traffic well into the twentieth century.

The main industry in the early years was cutting timber and making railroad ties. The ties were made along the Osage and adjacent rivers and then floated down to the city of Bagnell, the site of the closest railroad spur, for shipment.

In 1923, a study was conducted on damming the Osage, Niangua, and Glaize rivers. Six years later, Union Electric Company began to build Bagnell Dam across the Osage River. Four months into construction, the stock market crashed, initiating the Great Depression. Because this was just about the only major construction project going on in the country, it drew some 4,600 workers to the area. Many earned only a dollar a day working on the dam, which took only two years to complete. When the dam was finished in 1931, the water backed up and formed a channel 92 miles long, ranging from 0.5 to 2 miles wide, and creating over 1,370 miles of shoreline, more than the state of California. The lake covered 58,500 acres, forming the shape of a ragged-looking dragon, a symbol promoted by businesses in the area.

The drive begins at the junction of US 54 and MO W at Lakeland. Turn onto MO W and proceed only 0.3 miles. The turn to **Bagnell Dam** is on the left. For a scenic view of the Lake of the Ozarks, bypass the turn and continue on U.S. 54 to a pullout on the right side of the road. Continuing down the hill, the highway crosses over Bagnell Dam and into the town of **Lake Ozark**, the "Miracle Mile" of amusement, antique, and bric-a-brac, the oldest commercial development in the area to accommodate tourists.

Return to the side road that is highlighted by the sign "Union Electric Dam Tours" and follow it to the dam. In 0.6 mile, a picnic area overlooking the lake is provided by Union Electric. After another 0.5 mile the road descends, with some sharp turns, to the bottom of the hill at the Osage River floodplain. Turn right and proceed to **Bagnell Dam**. There are overlooks near the dam, and tours show the inner workings of the hydroelectric power plant. When the spillway gates are open, there is sometimes a frenzy of avian activity as gulls, terns, and great blue herons dive at injured or stunned fish that have been swept through the rushing waters.

Below the dam, snagging for paddlefish is a popular event in the spring. Since paddlefish feed only on microscopic plankton, they will not take baited hooks. Fisherman, using special hooks, snag the fish bodies which can weigh more than a hundred pounds and can be up to seven feet long. The paddlefish has declined drastically from its former nationwide range due to destruction of its habitat and over fishing. The impoundments of the Osage River at the Lake of the Ozarks and upstream at Truman Lake eliminated many of the paddlefish's spawning areas, which were the gravel bars along the river and its bordering streams. Fortunately, the Missouri Department of Conservation has been successful in its efforts to spawn and raise paddlefish for release into their historic waters.

In the winter, another type of "angler" can be seen patrolling the waters below the dam—the bald eagle. Eagles fly all around the lake, but when the surface water freezes, they concentrate below the dam where the water remains open. Eagles perch in trees along the river and occasionally swoop down to snatch a stunned fish that has gone through one of the power plant's turbines. A majority of these eagles only winter here, and spend their summers in Minnesota, Wisconsin, and Canada. Eagles had not nested in Missouri or most of the other lower 48 states since the 1950s, due to habitat destruction and the widespread use of DDT. DDT, a long-lived insecticide, was washed by rainfall from cropland into lakes and streams, where it entered the food chain and grew increasingly concentrated as it passed from plankton to aquatic insects to fish to eagles. DDT in birds was discovered to reduce the amount of calcium in egg shells, allowing the eggs to be crushed by the birds' own weight during incubation. After the banning of DDT use in the U.S., meat-eating birds started making a comeback. Now, with an annual winter count of over two thousand eagles, Missouri ranks second only to the state of Washington with the most eagles in the lower 48. And, thanks to a ten-year release program of young eagles into Missouri by the conservation department, by 1995 there were twenty-three active bald eagle nests and their number promises to grow. The bald eagle has returned to nest in the Ozarks.

Continue down the river road to **Bagnell Dam Access**, where boats may be launched into the Osage River. The access also provides an opportunity to see wildlife feeding along the river. After 0.5 mile the road meets US 54; turn right onto the highway and cross the Osage River Bridge. After climbing a long, steep hill, the highway follows a ridge bordered with an 8-mile-long development of tourist attractions.

In a mile, a sidetrip on MO 42 leads to **Lake of the Ozarks State Park**. In 3.3 miles MO 134, on the right, enters the 17,087-acre state park, the largest in Missouri. The park was originally established by the National Park Service in the mid-1930s, following the damming of the Osage River and the creation of the lake. The recreational area was turned over to the state in

1946. Lake of the Ozarks State Park has ten hiking trails that lead through dense oak-hickory forests and lush ravines, across open glades with showy wildflowers, and along towering bluffs overlooking the lake. There are also two equestrian trails and trail rides are available at the park stables for a nominal fee. A rental service provides boats for fishing, skiing, and taking a self-guided aquatic trail, marked by buoys, which has been developed on the Grand Glaize arm of the lake. Ask for brochures at the park office upon entering the park.

Return to US 54 and continue west through **Osage Beach**. This 8-mile-long community has become the shopping destination for tourists from as far away as Chicago and Indianapolis. Cross the Grand Glaize Bridge and continue about 3 miles to the **Grand Glaize Recreation Area** on the left provides swimming, picnicking, restrooms, and the Rocky Top Trail with

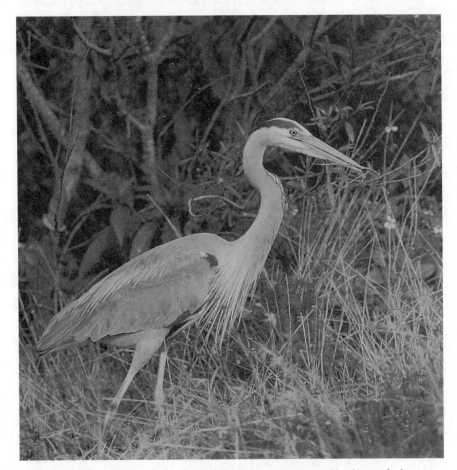

Commonly seen along the shore below Bagnell Dam, great blue herons feed and search for nesting materials.

Visitors stand at the doorway to the ruins of a European-style castle at Ha Ha Tonka State Park.

two 1.5-mile loops.

The south end of Lake of the Ozarks State Park is reached from MO A. Continue on US 54 to the junction of MO A. A side trip leads to **Ozark Caverns**, which is part of the park. You can reach it by traveling 6.5 miles to MO A-33 and following the signs another 2 miles to the caverns. A small parking lot is next to the visitor center. A naturalist is on duty to lead daily cave tours throughout the summer months and at varying times the rest of the year. This cave tour is unique in that visitors are given their own lights to carry. You feel like an explorer entering the cave for the first time.

The Coakley Hollow Self-guiding Trail interprets a variety of habitats including a rare Ozark fen. Fens are open areas that resemble meadows but are fed year-round by seep water percolating down through the hills and emerging at their base. Special plants grow in these fens and nowhere else. If you do not have time to walk the mile-long trail, be sure to at least see the fen. Walk behind the visitor center and follow the path to a boardwalk overlooking the fen.

Return to US 54 and continue west. You will pass through what is left of **Linn Creek**. Once the seat of Camden County, the townsite that once supported five hundred residents was inundated when the water rose to form the Lake of the Ozarks. The residents of Linn Creek fought the lake project in court, but lost. The town was moved up the hill 3 miles west to the newly formed town of Camdenton, which became the new county seat. Thirty-two cemeteries and seventy-four scattered graves were also relocated. **Camdenton**, often called the hub city of the lake area, is home to the Dogwood Festival. This event, which is timed to coincide with the blooming of the flowering dogwood, had its forty-fifth anniversary in 1995. Around the third weekend in April, the white-bracted flowers of the dogwood are at their peak. They are particularly visible in the understory of the tall oaks and hickories because the hardwoods are then only just beginning to leaf out. Of course, nature does not always cooperate, and an early spring sometimes causes the festival's main attraction to look a bit faded. This does not dampen spirits, however, as there are plenty of activities for all ages.

MO 5 heads north from the center of Camdenton and in about 2 miles passes the Camdenton Office of the Missouri Department of Conservation, located off Lake Road 5-88 on the left. Maps and information about recreational opportunities on public lands are provided. The lake road continues to Bridal Cave, a commercial cave that offers tours and is also a popular location for wedding ceremonies.

Proceed west out of Camdenton on US 54 for 2 miles to MO D and follow the signs to **Ha Ha Tonka State Park**. The name is said to be an Osage Indian phrase, meaning "Laughing Water." This probably referred to the sound made by Ha Ha Tonka Spring as it once cascaded over rocks on its course to the Niangua River. With the establishment of the lake, the spring now forms a pool, and the rocks are silent. The spring issues an average of 48 million gallons of water a day, making it the twelfth largest spring in Missouri. The Spring Trail has a barrier-free section that goes to a viewing platform overlooking the spring branch. A boardwalk extends beyond this point to the spring.

Ha Ha Tonka is considered to be one of the most outstanding combinations of geologic and human history in the Ozarks, with both in an area of less than one square mile. Geologically, the Ha Ha Tonka area is a classic example of collapsed structures in a karst landscape. "Karst" is a term taken from an area in the former Yugoslavia that is known for its solution features of sinks, caves, underground streams, and large springs. The Missouri Ozarks, because of its large areas of dolomite and limestone, are also known for its numerous karst features. They include: Counterfeiters', Robbers', and River Caves; Dry Hollow; Natural Bridge; Devil's Promenade; Devil's Kitchen; and Red and Black sinks. Pick up a trail map at the park office or at the Castle parking lot for directions to these fascinating features.

Ha Ha Tonka Spring was one of the first features to lure humans to the area. The Osage Indians used the large sinkhole southwest of the natural bridge for tribal powwows. Indians from Minnesota prairies and the Teton Indians were known to winter here by the "Great Spring." Daniel Boone and his son Nathan visited the area in 1801 when they followed the Niangua drainage to the spring. Reportedly, their first winter's catch of pelts was confiscated by the Osages; the Boones returned the following year and kept their pelts by hiding them in nearby caves.

Counterfeiters' and Robbers' caves were named for a local group of counterfeiters and robbers operating here in the 1830s. In 1903, Robert M. Snyder, a wealthy Kansas City businessman, visited the area on a fishing expedition and conceived of a private retreat having as its centerpiece a magnificent European-style mansion or castle. In 1905, stonemasons from Scotland began construction with stone quarried from about 0.25 mile away. Snyder did not live to see the completion of the castle, for on October 27 of that year he was killed in an automobile accident near his Kansas City home. The castle stood unfinished until his son completed it in 1922. In 1942, however, sparks from a fireplace caught the roof's wooden shingles on fire and the building was gutted. Then, after many years of semi-commercialization and general neglect, the property was acquired by The Nature Conservancy and sold to the state to become Ha Ha Tonka State Park. The impressive karst features of the park have been designated a state natural area.

With a self-guided tour brochure in hand, be sure to hike the 0.75 mile Turkey Pen Hollow Trail off MO D in the park. The trail passes through a savanna, which is a scattering of open-grown trees with a grassy understory, and crosses interesting glades with weather-worn rocks. The glades are rich in showy wildflowers from April through October. In the spring, look for Indian paintbrush, yellow star grass, downy phlox, and wild indigo. Early summer is ablaze with large stands of yellow coneflower, butterfly weed, and Missouri primrose.

9

Two Rivers

Salem to Blue Spring, Missouri

General description: A 64-mile drive that starts at Salem and travels south into the scenic river hills of the Current and Jacks Fork rivers.

Special attractions: Alley and Round Springs, Current and Jacks Fork rivers, Devils Well, Akers Ferry, Blue Spring Natural Area, Rocky Falls, Ozark Trail, and Virgin Pine Forest; scenic views, fall and spring colors, hiking, canoeing, swimming, camping, fishing, hunting, and large springs. (Exceptional drive for fall colors in October and white-flowering dogwoods in April.)

Location: Central Ozarks. The drive begins at the junction of Missouri Highways 19, 32, and 72 on the south side of Salem.

Drive route numbers: Missouri Highways 19, 106, KK, H, Y, and NN.

Camping: Akers (81 campsites), Round Spring (60 campsites), Alley Spring (187 campsites), Pultite (55 campsites), Two Rivers (10 campsites), and Powder Mill (10 campsites) all have restrooms and water and are maintained by the National Park Service. Other possibilities include Little Scotia Pond Campground and Picnic Area (14 campsites) and Loggers Lake Recreation Area (41 campsites) in the Mark Twain National Forest. Primitive camping is allowed in the Missouri Department of Conservation's Sunklands, Angeline, Rocky Creek, and Current River conservation areas.

Services: All services at Salem and Eminence.

Nearby attractions: Montauk State Park (trout fishing). Peck Ranch Conservation Area (includes five natural areas); Sunklands, Burr Oak Basin, Mill Mountain, and Cardareva Bluff natural areas, (Missouri Department of Conservation). Jam Up Cave and Prairie Hollow Gorge natural areas and Klepzig Mill (National Park Service).

 The drive

The highway travels across a broad, gently rolling upland plains, that is part of the Salem Plateau. As you head south, the plateau is deeply dissected by rugged hills whose steep slopes drain into spring-fed streams. Some of the largest springs in the United States—even in the world—are within this region.

Drive 9: Two Rivers
Salem to Blue Spring, Missouri

Begin the drive on the south side of **Salem** at the intersection of MO 19, 72, and 32. To the south, just beyond the intersection on the right is the Salem Ranger Station of the Mark Twain National Forest. It has information on nearby recreational opportunities in the national forest. Salem, with a population of about 5,000, is the northern gateway to the scenic riverways and the big springs country. Founded in 1851, Salem has had a long and steady growth as a mining and shopping center. The Tower Inn, a ten-story motel and shopping center, is a dominating landmark that can be seen for several miles.

About 7 miles south of Salem, as the road begins to curve along narrow ridges, notice the broad upland plains giving way to hill country. Short-leaf pine trees become more prominent, favoring the thin, cherty soils on south and west slopes. After 9 miles the road descends to Gladden Creek. Notice the prominent rock outcrop in the creek to the right of the bridge. Called Standing Rock, it is composed of sandstone that is so thoroughly cemented it is quartzlike, making it resistent to erosion. Gladden Creek is typical of many modern Ozark streams; it is gravel-choked and has a less-than-permanent flow. Long-time residents can recall that these smaller streams once contained deep pools for fishing and swimming; however, extensive logging and open-range grazing earlier in this century caused considerable erosion of the hillsides. Heavy rains carried loads of chert gravel down the slopes and into the streams. Today there is less erosion, but it will take centuries for some of these streams to reclaim some semblance of their original character.

After another 9 miles, MO KK appears on the right. A side trip to see Devils Well and Akers Ferry is recommended. Just 2 miles down MO KK is a sign and entrance road on the left. The gravel road goes two miles to **Devils Well**, which is on the Ozarks Riverways. You can see the well by peering through a two-foot-wide sinkhole opening to the underground lake a hundred feet below. The lake is more than four hundred feet wide and one hundred feet deep, and emerges a mile south at Cave Spring on the Current River. An estimated 22 million gallons of water per day flows through the sinkhole.

Return to MO KK and proceed almost 4 miles to **Akers Ferry**. The National Park Service provides a campground and access to the Current River. Akers Ferry, a commercial outfitter, rents canoes and sells supplies for float trips. Akers Ferry also operates a ferry crossing over the Current River for those traveling on MO K. The ferry has been in operation since the mid-1800s.

The **Current River** flows through the heart of the Missouri Ozarks for 133 miles to its confluence with the Black River in Arkansas. The Current River is fed by more springs than any other river in the Ozarks; this is evident in its water quality. The Current, along with its tributary, the Jacks

Fork, was protected by the establishment of the Ozark National Scenic Riverways Act on August 27, 1964, and is managed by the National Park Service. The Current River is rated the most popular river for recreational value in Missouri. Unfortunately, the summer months are crowded with canoes, kayaks, float tubes, and, farther down river, jet skis and johnboats. Increased regulations may be implemented to maintain a quality experience for all who enjoy the river. Because springs maintain the river's flow year-round, fall, winter, and spring can provide more solitude on the river. This particular stretch of the Current River is the most popular; a one-day float trip (lasting six to seven hours) from Baptist Camp near Montauk State Park to Akers Ferry can be arranged through several commercial operators in the area. Shorter or longer floats are also possible.

Back on MO 19, proceed another 11 miles to where the highway crosses the Current River. A bridge for pedestrians parallels the highway bridge; you can get to it by turning onto a campground road on the left, parking, and walking over to the bridge. The **Round Spring** entrance is just down the highway. Besides providing camping and a river access, a short trail with interpretive signs leads to the fourteenth largest spring in Missouri. A daily flow of 26 million gallons emerges through a collapsed cave roof. Part of the roof remains intact as a natural bridge, beneath which the waters of the spring flow toward the nearby Current River. Round Spring Cave is located on the west site of the highway; guided tours are offered during the summer for a small fee.

The road climbs a steep hill after leaving Round Spring. A pullout on the right offers a dramatic view of the rugged wooded hills and narrow valleys of the Current River country. After 2 miles, you enter an area of old growth shortleaf pine trees known as **Virgin Pine Forest**. This native stand of towering pines, many more than 200 years old, extends for a mile along the highway and for 200 feet on either side of the center line. It was donated to the State Highway Department by Leo A. Drey, owner of Pioneer Forest and the largest private landowner in the state. Pine forests were once common in this part of the Ozarks, but extensive logging and fire suppression have eliminated most of them. Several public agencies are now working to manage some areas for native pine as a natural component of the Ozark forest.

After 8 miles, watch for a scenic overlook and parking lot on the left. On the eastern horizon, a fire tower marks the summit of Coot Mountain. This prominent hill and the ones surrounding it are volcanic in origin and are considered an outlier of the St. Francois Mountains, which are more than 50 miles to the northeast. One mile beyond this overlook, the Missouri Department of Conservation's Eminence Forest District office is located. It offers information describing recreational opportunities on M.D.C. lands in the area.

The ever-flowing Alley Springs discharges through a gate adjoining Alley Mill.

Continue down the steep highway to the **Jacks Fork River** crossing, just north of Eminence. The Jacks Fork was named for John Jacks, a Shawnee Indian who settled near the headwaters of the river. The Jacks Fork has a permanent flow of 39 river miles, with much of it through dramatic steep-walled canyons. Beginning at the MO Y access, the river is most floatable during the higher water levels in spring. Just upstream from here, however, it can easily be floated from Alley Spring to where it joins the Current River, about 11 river miles below Eminence. Like the Current, the Jacks Fork is a river that is being loved to death, but by picking the right time of year, you can be rewarded with some very memorable experiences.

Eminence has a population of 582. Organized in 1841, it is the seat of Shannon County. The county was named after George "Pegleg" Shannon, who at age 17 was the youngest member of the Lewis and Clark Expedition. He reportedly later lost a leg to an infection following a skirmish with Indians. Pioneers from Kentucky and Tennessee first settled this area in the 1820s. Missouri's first copper mine was opened near here by Joseph Slater in 1837. Eminence was first located farther north, along the Current River. The town was burned in the Civil War by guerrilla bands. After the war, Eminence was rebuilt at its present location by the Jacks Fork.

Proceed west on MO 106 through West Eminence, which was established by a lumber company in 1906. After 5 miles, the highway crosses the Jacks Fork and the **Alley Spring** section of the Ozark Riverways. An entrance on the right leads to a parking lot, picnic area, and path to Alley Spring and Mill. A turnoff just beyond this entrance allows easy access to the mill for elderly and disabled visitors. Alley Spring is the seventh largest spring in Missouri, with an average of 81 million gallons passing through the mill race each day. In 1894, a three-story mill was completed with a steel turbine to drive the roller mill rather than the commonly seen waterwheel. The mill originally provided finely ground wheat flour for local farmers. Later, its services expanded to include corn grinding, a sawmill, and an electrical generator for the community. A small museum in the millhouse is open to visitors during the summer. There are two hiking trails (1.5 and 0.3 miles) located near Alley Spring. Camping and access to the river is available on the other side of the highway.

Return to Eminence and continue on MO 106 east for 5 miles. A 3-mile side trip on MO V goes to **Two Rivers**, an Ozark Riverways campground and access to the Current River. While traveling to Two Rivers, watch for a large hill with a fire tower on top. This is Coot Mountain, which could be seen from the scenic overlook above Eminence. The fire tower is closed to visitors.

The highway ends at the base of a steep hill. It is here that the Jacks Fork flows into the Current River. An excellent view of this convergence is from the deck of the Two Rivers Store.

Back on MO 106, proceed east another 2 miles and turn right onto MO H, and travel almost 4 miles to MO NN. Turn left and go another 2 miles, then turn right onto the gravel road for 0.3 mile to the entrance to the **Rocky Falls** parking lot. Follow the short trail down to the falls. Although best seen in the spring and after heavy rains, Rocky Falls Shut-Ins is impressive year-round. Here, the waters of Rocky Creek tumble in a forty-foot cascade down a steep slope of pink to purple igneous rock. The large plunge pool at the base of the falls is a popular swimming hole during the hot summer months. A path along the right side of the falls leads to the top . Autumn is also an excellent time to visit, because the site supports a variety of colorful vegetation.

Returning to MO 106, turn right and head east for 5 miles. The road enters the Current River valley and provides scenic views of the broad valley, hills, and cliffs that continue to be reshaped by the carving action of the river. The trailhead for the Current River section of the **Ozark Trail** begins in this valley and heads south. Contact the Mark Twain National Forest for a map and access information. Just after the bridge, a road to the right leads to **Powder Mill**. Although the visitor center is presently closed, picnicking, camping, and access to the Current River are possible. At the end of the campground road, a 1-mile trail leads to Blue Spring.

You can also reach **Blue Spring** by returning to MO 106 and driving east for about 2 miles, then turning right onto a gravel road. The first part of the 2.5-mile road is steep and not recommended for vehicles pulling trailers. The well-maintained road is accessible by two-wheel drive vehicles and ends at a parking lot. From here, a 0.5-mile walk affords glimpses of the Current River and eventually skirts along a roaring spring branch leading to Blue Spring. The Indians called it "the Spring of the Summer Sky." Of all the springs in the Ozarks, this is certainly the bluest. Ranked sixth in Missouri, with a daily flow of 90 million gallons per day, it is also the deepest known spring in the Ozark region, with an explored depth of 256 feet. The intense blue color is caused by the extreme depth and angle of the emerging water and the scattering of blue light by minute particles of mineral or organic matter suspended in the water.

Blue Spring is a state natural conservation area and is owned by the Missouri Department of Conservation. A deck along one edge of the spring pool affords a view into the depths of the spring orifice. A short path to the left leads to an observation deck overlooking the intensely blue waters below. Blue Spring has been a popular attraction for generations. However, heavy usage caused the banks to be worn bare and the vegetation trampled. The conservation department decided to "harden" the site by establishing walkways and viewing platforms a few years ago. Although some feel that this took away from the pristine look of Blue Spring, the vegetation has come back and the banks have healed, giving the area a more natural look.

10

Big Spring

Van Buren to Big Spring, Missouri

General description: A 7-mile drive beginning in Van Buren, crossing the Current River following the Forest Service's Skyline Drive, and ending at Big Spring.

Special attractions: Van Buren, Ozark National Scenic Riverways, Skyline Drive, Big Spring, Big Spring Pines Natural Area, and Mark Twain National Forest; floating, swimming, fishing, camping, hiking, boating, hunting, fall colors, and spring wildflowers.

Location: East-central Ozarks. The drive begins in Van Buren on U.S. Highway 60 and ends at Big Spring.

Drive route numbers: U.S. Highway 60, Missouri Highways 103 and Z, and Forest Road 3280.

Camping: Big Spring Recreation Area has more than 100 campsites with restrooms, showers, playgrounds, water, barrier-free campsites, and boat access. Rental cabins are available by calling the Big Spring Lodge. In Van Buren, Watercress Spring Recreation Site has 17 campsites, restrooms, picnicking, and boat access. Primitive camping is allowed in the national forest.

Services: All services at Van Buren.

Nearby attractions: Peck Ranch and Current River conservation areas; Spring and Two Rivers scenic drives; the Ozark Trail, and Irish Wilderness Area (Forest Service).

 The drive

Van Buren is the headquarters for the National Park Service's Ozark National Scenic Riverways. The riverways system includes both the Current and the Jacks Fork, a total of 134 miles of managed river. To help protect the river systems, 80,788 acres of land (61,374 of them federally owned) border the rivers. The riverways celebrated its twenty-fifth anniversary in 1989.

Controversy over what to do with the Current River country began early in the 1900s. Some wanted to protect it in its "natural state," while others wanted to dam the rivers for hydroelectric power. The region began to draw more visitors in the 1920s and 1930s when the state of Missouri

Drive 10: Big Spring
Van Buren to Big Spring, Missouri

To ②①
D
To
Poplar Bluff
Watercress Spring Recreation Site
60
Van Buren
Pike Creek
M
Current River
60
To
Winona
103
Chicopee
Ozark National Scenic Riverways
Reeves Roadside Park
Drive 3280
M A R K   T W A I N
Skyline
N. F.
Sweezie Hollow
103
3281
3280
103
Big Spring
Spring Valley
Big Spring Lodge
Recreation Area
N
Chub Hollow
Z
Big Spring Pines Natural Area
Z
0   0.5   1
Miles
Big Spring Lookout Tower

developed state parks at Montauk Springs, Round Spring, Alley Spring, and Big Spring. Love and passion for the river rose to a new level in the mid-1930s when the United States Corps of Engineers proposed damming the Current River. Editorials in the *St. Louis Post Dispatch* and *Kansas City Star* opposed the dam. The Missouri Conservation Commission and the Missouri Department of Conservation also opposed the dam and then-governor Forrest Smith announced there would be no dam built on the Current River as long as he was in office.

Finally, on August 27, 1964, President Lyndon Johnson signed the act establishing the Ozark National Scenic Riverways. By mid-1966, the first tract was acquired. There was much bitterness and resentment among the local landowners who were against a national park. Missouri signed over the state parks at Round, Alley, and Big springs in 1969, but kept Montauk. The national park was formally dedicated on June 10, 1972, when Tricia Nixon Cox "christened" the Ozark National Scenic Riverways by tossing a bouquet of flowers into the waters of Big Spring.

The drive begins in **Van Buren**, a small town that serves as an outfitter for canoes, kayaks, float tubes, jet skis, and johnboats. Summer months often find the town and the river overcrowded with recreational users. Permanent springs maintain the river's flow year-round, so it is possible to enjoy the river in fall, spring, and winter when there is more solitude and space.

Probably the most historic building in Van Buren is the Carter County Courthouse, located on the square. The original building, built in 1837, was a two-story, wood-frame, four-room building held together with wooden pins. This early courthouse was located on the west bank of the Current River, 0.5 mile west and across the river from the present county seat. It was used when Carter County was part of Ripley County, before the counties separated in 1859. A commission voted to retain Van Buren as the county seat. In 1871, court officials authorized a new courthouse to be built on the square. It was built with hand-planed pine lumber on a rock foundation.

Several proposals to build a new courthouse were defeated early in the twentieth century. Instead, the 1871 building was remodeled, expanded, and covered with native cobblestones. It is the only courthouse in Missouri known to have been built with cobblestones. The building was last remodeled and expanded in 1936. Behind the courthouse is a log cabin that dates back to 1851. It was moved there in 1959 to commemorate the county's first one hundred years.

In 1994, a new bridge and a bypass around Van Buren were completed. The old bridge is now closed to vehicular traffic and pedestrians can walk leisurely across the old roadbed. Great views of the Current River, both up- and downstream, are now possible. The disabled accessible bridge can be reached by parking at either end. The Current River was once used to float railroad ties and logs from a huge sawmill in West Eminence. The log rafts were collected just downstream from Van Buren at a place called Chicopee. From there, the wood was transported to the west. Much of this wood was used in the railroads that crossed the Great Plains. The log drives were not popular with local residents because logjams often blocked the river for days, causing property to be flooded and barring passage across the river. The government imposed regulations in 1915 restricting the use of the Current River for floating ties and logs. The last recorded log drive on the Current was in 1935.

The Information Center at the National Park Service headquarters is located north of the square along Main Street. Open from 8:00 am to 4:30 pm, Monday to Friday, the headquarters offers information on local natural, historic, and recreational sites along with a selection of books, tapes, and other items.

To continue on the drive, take US 60 south across the Current River and immediately turn left onto MO 103. The first mile is a steep climb up an unnamed Ozark mountain. On the right, Reeves Roadside Park, maintained by the Missouri Highway and Transportation Commission, provides a picnic area and a place to rest. Take FR 3280 on the right, and begin the **Skyline Drive**. This 4-mile loop provides fifteen scenic vistas of the surrounding Ozark hills. Also along the drive, the privately owned Skyline Lodge

The unique Carter County Courthouse is built with cobblestones
gathered from the surrounding area.

*Canoeing and tube floating the Current River are popular activities
during the hot summer months.*

and Supper Club offers a bed-and-breakfast and evening dining with a commanding view of the river, farmstead lights, and distant mountains. About
midway along the drive, FR 3281 heads southwest and in just over a mile,
crosses the Ozark Trail. Just before joining MO 103, the last two vistas reveal Big Spring Lookout Tower on the horizon, 1.5 miles to the south.

At MO 103, turn right and follow the signs to **Big Spring**. There is
ample parking with a short trail that leads to the mouth of the spring. The
water roars from the base of a huge dolomite cliff. The rock is named Eminence dolomite after the town some 25 miles northwest of here. (After geologists discover and describe new bedrock, they name the rock after the
nearest town.) This rock was deposited as sediment during the Cambrian
Period, over 600 million years ago. The land was covered by a shallow sea in
which primitive marine life such as trilobites and brachiopods thrived. Today, the compressed sediment that now forms this rock has a weathered face
with nooks and crannies that harbor ferns, columbines, mosses, and other
interesting plants.

Big Spring is appropriately named, for it is ranked as the largest spring
in the United States and one of the largest in the world. The spring has an
average daily flow of 276 million gallons. Water boils upward and out of the
mouth of a cave, instantly forming a river that courses 1,000 feet down-

stream to enter the Current River. Dye tracings have shown the water to come from an area to the west of Big Spring, as far away as Willow Springs—an airline distance of over 50 miles. Some of the water is even "pirated" from the watershed of the Eleven Point River to the southwest. It is thought that the area drained by Big Spring (the Big Spring Recharge Area) covers 967 square miles. It is estimated that Big Spring removes in solution each day about 175 tons of calcium and magnesium carbonate, the chemical component of limestone and dolomite. This means that in a year's time, enough bedrock (640,000 tons) is removed to form a cave passage 30 feet high by 50 feet wide and a mile long. It is interesting to note that the Big Spring system is now larger than it has ever been in the past and that the rate of growth is also greater than ever before. This is because each year, the recharge system grows larger by the removal of rocks by groundwater solution and, each year, more rock is exposed to the dissolving action of the groundwater.

Big Spring was a popular site long before the first European settlers set foot in the area. Today's campgrounds are filled with recreational vehicles and tents but were once also used as camps for prehistoric peoples. From about 10,000 years ago to 4,000 years ago, humans repeatedly camped in this area along the banks of the Current River. They hunted deer, turkey, elk, woods bison, and songbirds; caught fish; and collected plants from the surrounding forest. A recent archaeological excavation in the park has unearthed knives, scrapers, drills, and projectile or spear points that had been

A view from Skyline Drive of Missouri Highway 103 as it winds its way to Big Spring.

buried over time, some six feet deep in the alluvial soil. These are significant finds that will add to our understanding of the early inhabitants of the region.

Returning to the main park road, MO Z passes the **Big Spring Lodge**. There is a display featuring the Civilian Conservation Corps (CCC) at that junction at a pullout. The Big Spring Lodge and cabins were built by the CCC in the late 1930s. President Roosevelt organized the CCC to create jobs and training for the unemployed during the Great Depression. Many structures built by the CCC can still be found throughout the Ozarks. At the lodge, reservations can be made for cabins, and meals are served in a rustic atmosphere.

The **Big Spring Pines Natural Area** is located off MO Z, 1.1 miles from the junction of MO 103 and Z. There is a pulloff on the right and a service road leading to the Big Spring Lookout Tower. It is a comfortable half-hour walk through the natural area to the tower. The trail continues past the tower and ends in the vicinity of the rental cabins. The tower, by the way, is closed to the public. There are other trails at Big Spring, many of which were built by the CCC. A park official has explained that most trails have not been well-maintained, so they are not recommended at this time. The 345-acre natural area contains the largest, highest quality chert forest known in this region of the Ozarks. Old-growth oak and pine trees more than 120 years in age are common throughout this forest. Pine was once more common in this region and was often the dominant forest type. Early accounts by explorers describe this area as open and parklike with abundant grasses and wildflowers in the understory. Because of past logging of the pines and fire suppression, the original forest type has changed dramatically. Plans for managing this natural area include the experimental use of controlled burnings in order to duplicate the open forest conditions that prevailed when Indians traveled the hills.

11

Springs and Rivers

Winona to Mammoth Spring, Missouri/Arkansas

General description: A 57-mile drive traveling from Winona south through rugged hills with large springs and the Eleven Point River to Grand Gulf and Mammoth Spring.

Special attractions: Falling Spring, Turner Mill, McCormack Lake Recreation Area, Greer Spring, Eleven Point River, Grand Gulf and Mammoth Spring state parks, Mammoth Spring National Fish Hatchery, Spring River, Dam 3 Access, Mark Twain National Forest, and the Ozark Trail; canoeing, swimming, hiking, fall colors, spring flowers, fishing, camping, and hunting.

Location: East-central Ozarks. The drive begins at the junction of U.S. Highway 60 and Missouri Highway 19 at Winona.

Drive route numbers: U.S. Highways 60 and 63, Missouri Highways 19, AA, and W, and Forest Roads 3170, 3164, and 3155.

Camping: Greer Crossing Recreation Area provides 19 camping units with drinking water and pit toilets. McCormack Lake Recreation Area has 8 campsites with drinking water and pit toilets. Primitive camping is allowed in the national forest.

Services: All services at Winona, Alton, Thayer, and Mammoth Spring.

Nearby attractions: Irish Wilderness Area, Two Rivers Scenic Drive, and Peck Ranch Conservation Area.

 The drive

When people first laid out MO 19, it seems as though they tried to connect the road "between the dots," which, in this case, are large springs. Beginning in the north and heading south, MO 19 goes by Montauk Spring, Welch Spring, Round Spring, Alley Spring, Blue Spring, Greer Spring, and Mammoth Spring, which are all within 10 miles of the highway. The only spring that did not fit into this scheme is Big Spring, which is near Van Buren, some 20 miles to the east. However, since it is the largest spring in the United States, maybe it should stand alone. These eight springs are among the fourteen highest flowing springs in the Ozarks. The Missouri part of the Ozarks contains one of the nation's greatest concentrations of springs. In an average day, more than a billion gallons of water flow from Missouri's ten largest springs.

Drive 11: Springs and Rivers
Winona to Mammoth Spring, Missouri/Arkansas

SITES

1. Falling Spring Recreation Area
2. McCormack Lake Recreation Area
3. Turner Mill Recreation Area
4. Turner Mill South Recreation Area
5. Greer Crossing River Access
6. Greer Spring
7. Grand Gulf State Park
8. Mammoth Spring State Park
9. Mammoth Spring National Fish Hatchery
10. Dam 3 Access

All these springs are located in a part of the Ozarks called the Salem Plateau. This region, extending from the south-central part of Missouri to just into Arkansas, is composed largely of dolomitic rock. The soluble character of this rock makes possible the extensive cave and spring systems for which the Ozarks are noted. From 1,000 to 2,000 feet of dolomite rock is present in the Ozarks, and this mass has a tremendous volume for storing precipitation. Much rainwater is collected and transported through the connecting systems of conduits we call caves. You can gain a concept of the capacity of the dolomite aquifers by considering the number of caves in the region, many of which sustain large springs. Of a total of 5,000 caves in Missouri, more than 3,500 are in the Missouri Ozarks.

The drive begins at the junction of US 60 and MO 19, just outside of **Winona**. In the 1890s, this town was the home of the Ozark Land and Lumber Company, one of the largest sawmill operations in the region. It processed shortleaf pine and oak for flooring and railroad needs. On July 4, 1895, a disastrous flood destroyed most of Winona. Eleven people drowned, and most of the property on Front Street, along Pike Creek, was destroyed. The town rebuilt on higher ground. Today, sawmill employment continues to be of some importance, but Winona is primarily an agricultural trade and service center. The Eleven Point Ranger Station is located in Winona, on the east side of MO 19. Open during the work week, the station offers information on recreational activities in the district.

Head south on MO 19 across rolling hills that are mostly forested with white oak, post oak, black oak, and shortleaf pine. After 4.3 miles, the character of the road changes. There are stretches of highway from here to the Eleven Point River where the road leaves the ridges and travels across slopes of hills, following the contour of the land. You may find this road is like a roller coaster as you go up and down the drainages. If you can tolerate the effect, the view along the way will set this road apart from many that use cut-and-fill to level out the road. The forest and its wildflowers, flowering shrubs, and towering trees hug the road. It is a special natural corridor that almost makes you forget about the ribbon of black asphalt over which you are traveling.

After just over 9 miles from the start of the drive, take FR 3170 on the left, then after 0.1 mile, turn left again onto FR 3164. Proceed 2.3 miles to **Falling Spring Recreation Area**. Use caution just before the recreation area for the road narrows to a single lane and has two sharp turns. Go slow because it is hard to see oncoming traffic. Falling Spring is unusual because the water shoots out of an opening in the cliff some fifteen feet above ground. The water once provided power for two mills. The present mill was built in the late 1920s. The water power was used to produce electricity, grind corn, and make shingles. This site was settled before the Civil War and the old log cabin, which was the first home built on the site, is more than a hundred years old. A 650-foot trail leads along the edge of the lower pond, which offers fishing. There are no facilities here except for one picnic table and a fire ring.

Return to MO 19. After 3 miles, turn right onto FR 3155 toward **McCormack Lake Recreation Area,** which offers camping, fishing, hiking, and picnicking. Trailhead parking is also provided for access to the Eleven Point River Section of the **Ozark Trail**. This spur trail from McCormack Lake heads south and connects with the main trail. This 30-mile long section was completed in the summer of 1988 and lies completely on land managed by the Forest Service. A trail map is available at the Eleven Point Ranger Station in Winona.

Back on MO 19 and heading south, the road continues on its roller coaster ride. A potential side trip begins in 2 miles: turn left onto FR 3152 and then FR 3190, go 8 miles to **Turner Mill Recreation Area,** the site of an old grist mill. The mill building and wooden flume are gone today, but the wheel and cement flume by the spring outlet still stand. Turner Mill Spring has an average flow of 1.5 million gallons per day. The area has two picnic tables, pit toilets, and access to the Eleven Point River.

After another 1.3 miles on MO 19, the road enters the Eleven Point National Scenic River. On the left, the **Greer Crossing River Access** provides camping, picnicking, and access to the Ozark Trail and the Eleven

Falling Springs issues out of a cliff beside an abandoned mill.

Point River. This is a popular put-in and take-out point on the river. It is said that the Eleven Point was named by a French fur trader for the eleven points, or bends, in a particular stretch of the river. The Eleven Point River was included in the National Wild and Scenic Rivers Act in its initial passage by Congress in 1968. The river is protected from Thomasville to MO 142, a distance of 45 miles. The river is classified as permanent flow for 50 miles of its length. The upper reaches are fed by a number of springs, the largest being Greer Spring, which doubles the volume of the river as it joins the Eleven Point. The Missouri Department of Conservation stocks trout in the Eleven Point below the spring. Floating this river provides a wild, scenic experience with opportunities to see deer, turkey, beaver, belted kingfishers, and other wildlife inhabiting the corridor.

Continuing the drive, MO 19 crosses the Eleven Point Bridge and climbs out of the river hills. In just over a mile, you will see an access to the recently acquired **Greer Spring**. A 1.8-mile round-trip hiking trail leads to the spring. With a flow of 220 million gallons per day, Greer Spring is the second largest in Missouri and the third largest in the Ozarks, when Arkansas's Mammoth Spring is included. Greer Spring has much wild beauty, having escaped dams, mills, and other structures for the past 75 years. Greer Spring flows from two openings, an upper cave outlet and a lower opening in the bed of the spring branch several hundred feet downstream. The Forest Service has developed a brochure explaining the history of Greer Spring. If it is not available at the parking area, stop by the Winona office or write for a copy.

MO 19 continues south passing through the community of **Greer** to the junction of MO AA, which leads 11 miles to **Turner Mill South Recreation Area**, a canoe access to the Eleven Point River. Continue on MO 19 another 2 miles to **Alton**, established in 1859 as a central location for the new Oregon County seat. The original courthouse was burned in 1863 during the Civil War. The present courthouse is made of Missouri red granite from Graniteville, which is on Drive 4. Many old buildings still crowd around the square.

Proceed another 15 miles across a broad, level plateau to **Thayer**. Stay on MO 19, crossing over US 63. This area was once thriving orchard land and the home ground of "Ma" Barker and her boys, notorious criminals of the 1920s and 1930s.

After a mile, turn right onto MO W and follow it for 6 miles to **Grand Gulf State Park**, which is considered one of the most spectacular geologic features in the Ozarks. The major feature of the 159-acre park is the collapsed remains of a major cave system, with a sinkhole, cave, natural bridge, and a gulf, which is often called Missouri's "Little Grand Canyon." The park does not have facilities for camping but does provide picnic tables and interpretive exhibits on how this impressive gulf was formed. Although the do-

The collapsed roof of a huge cavern reveals part of a waterfilled cave system at Grand Gulf State Park.

lomite bedrock here was deposited in seas that covered much of the Ozarks 480 million years ago, the Grand Gulf cave system may be only one or two million years old. The deep valleys are actually the result of a cavern system, the roof of which collapsed several thousand years ago.

Today the gulf is a 0.75-mile-long canyon. A portion of the cave roof that did not collapse remains as a natural bridge. Bussell Branch, which previously flowed above the intact cave system, now flows through the canyon and into a part of the cave that did not collapse; its waters eventually reappear at Mammoth Spring in Arkansas, 7 miles away. The cave used to be accessible up to a length of 500 feet, but in 1921 a tornado filled the gulf with debris, blocking the cave passage. Heavy rains often back up in the gulf, forming a deep lake that slowly drains through the cave into an underground water system. There are four overlooks, one of which is accessible to the disabled. There is also a 0.25 mile loop trail around the chasm with a primitive trail that crosses the natural bridge.

Return on MO W until you reach MO 19, then enter **Thayer**. The town was founded in 1882 by George Nettleton as a division point for the Kansas City, Springfield, and Memphis Railroad. The line from Memphis to Thayer had easy curves and a flat grade, while the Thayer to Springfield line had many sharp curves and a steep grade. Heavy trains from Memphis had to be divided in order to pass through the mountains to Springfield, and Thayer was a halfway point between the two cities. The town was actually called "Division" until George Nettleton proposed Augusta, the name of his second wife. Upon incorporation in 1885, the residents discovered there was already an Augusta, overlooking the Missouri River. In 1886, the name "Thayer" was chosen in honor of Nathaniel Thayer, a director of the railroad. Today, the town is a thriving community with plenty of recreational activities within a short drive.

MO 19 ends at US 63 in Thayer. Follow US 63 south to the Arkansas State Line and **Mammoth Spring**. The spring is located in **Mammoth Spring State Park**, which is on the east side of the road. The state park has an information center that is a good place to find out about activities in the area. It also features exhibits, brochures, restrooms, and souvenirs. On the grounds there are trails (including one to a 1886 depot), playgrounds, historical objects (such as a Frisco caboose), remnants of the mill, and a hydroelectic plant near Spring Lake.

Mammoth Spring is the second largest spring in the Ozarks, with an average flow of 234 million gallons per day. The main source of the spring's water comes from rainfall over the high plains of southern Missouri. The water seeps into the water table and flows along a vast system of interconnected pathways. Water from Grand Gulf, 7 miles away, has been found to emerge at Mammoth Spring.

The spring was shown on early nineteenth century maps as "Great Spring." It was also called "Big Spring" in the 1820s by area settlers who established a village there known as "Head of the River." An early grist mill powered by the spring's water contributed to the town's growth. In 1886, the Frisco Railroad built lines into the area and constructed one of its first train depots in the town, which is now called Mammoth Spring. The town flourished with the railroad and a dam built by the Mammoth Spring Milling Company (a wheat mill) in the 1880s. The Arkansas-Missouri Power Company bought rights to the dam in 1925 and constructed a hydroelectric plant that provided electricity to the area until 1972. In 1957, legislation established Mammoth Spring State Park.

The **Mammoth Spring National Fish Hatchery**, established in 1904, is located in the back of the state park. Operated by the U.S. Fish and Wildlife Service, the hatchery draws from the 58-degree-Fahrenheit water of Mammoth Spring to raise over three million fish a year. In its fifteen ponds and raceways, the hatchery has the unique ability to produce warm-, cool-, and cold-water fish. The hatchery raises trout, smallmouth bass, channel catfish, and striped bass for release in nearby streams. A display aquarium shows native fishes, amphibians, and reptiles. The hatchery is open during the work week.

Speaking of fish, one of the best catfish and hushpuppy dinners in the

Ozarks is found at Fred's Fish House in Mammoth Springs. Expect more than the normal amount of food at a reasonable price.

Mammoth Spring flows into the **Spring River**, which begins as the Warm Fork Spring River north of Thayer. At the point of contact, Mammoth Spring adds tremendously to the volume of the river. The water is ideal for trout and is stocked by the Arkansas Game & Fish Commission from below Mammoth Spring to Many Islands Camp. The Spring River is canoeable from Dam 3 Access to the Black River, a distance of 61 miles. The Spring River has distinctive characteristics not found on other Ozark rivers. Long pools are broken by waterfalls that range from one to five feet in height.

12

Glade Top Trail

Ava to Longrun, Missouri

General description: A 38-mile drive beginning in Ava and proceeding south to a scenic ridge-top gravel road that is designated as a Forest Service Scenic Byway.

Special attractions: Glade Top Trail and Fall Festival, and Mark Twain National Forest; scenic views, colorful glade flowers throughout the season, wildlife, fall colors, hiking, hunting, and horseback riding.

Location: Central Ozarks. The drive begins at Ava on Missouri Highway 5 and ends at Longrun on Missouri Highway 95.

Drive route numbers: Missouri Highways 5, 14, 95, and A and Forest Roads 147 and 149.

Camping: There are no national forest recreation areas along the drive. Primitive camping is available at the Corbit Potter Campground and along the Glade Top Trail except at the picnic areas. Public camping is available at the U.S. Army Corps of Engineers' Theodosia Park, which has 36 sites, 12 of which can be reserved. The sites have water, electricity, fireplaces, tables, parking spaces, and restrooms but no showers are available.

Services: All services provided at Ava and Theodosia. Gas and store in Thornfield.

Nearby attractions: Hercules Glades Wilderness Area, Caney Mountain Conservation Area, Bull Shoals Lake, old grist mills, Assumption Abbey, and Laura Ingalls Wilder home in Mansfield.

 The drive

The most interesting and unique parts of the White River Hills are their glades. Glades evoke thoughts of the desert Southwest with their harsh, dry conditions in the summer and wet, seepy soils and lush vegetation in the spring. These Ozark deserts have cactus plants, scorpions, tarantulas, black widow spiders, pygmy rattlesnakes, lizards, including eastern collared lizards, and roadrunners—similar to the arid lands of the Southwest. Although some of these animals are potentially dangerous, knowledge of their presence should not prevent you from exploring glades. One rarely encounters these animals, and their "horror movie" depictions are greatly exaggerated. Many glade animals escape the fierce summer heat in the cool, moist

Drive 12: Glade Top Trail

Ava to Longrun, Missouri

To Mansfield

To Ozark

76

A

14

Ava

14

To 63

Prairie Creek

To Branson

76

North Spring Cr.

5

To Gainesville

Spring Creek

A

Beaver Creek

South

A

Spring Creek

Bear Branch

N

MARK TWAIN 2. N. F.

1.

3.

4.

5.

Little Northfork River

6.

7.

0 1 2 3 4 5

Miles

To 125

150

8.

Pond Fork

9.

147

To Bradleyville

149

Skyline Drive

10.

To Thornfield

125

95

To 160

Longrun

To 160

SITES

1. Smoke Tree Scene
2. Hayden Bald Natural Area
3. Corbit Potter Campground
4. Arkansas View
5. Watershed Divide
6. Caney Lookout Tower
7. Caney Picnic Area
8. Pinnacle
9. Willie Lee Farm
10. Panorama

environment beneath rock slabs. That is why it is important to avoid "rock-flipping"; it destroys the microhabitat of many of these interesting creatures.

Glades are open areas in the forest that have thin soils with bedrock at or near the surface. They are dominated by plants and animals that can survive the hot, dry conditions of the summer and the moist, sometimes saturated soils of the spring and winter. The Ozarks have an incredible diversity of glade types. There are glades on sandstone, chert, igneous, novaculite, shale, dolomite, and limestone bedrocks. The White River Hills section of the Ozarks contains the largest and best examples of dolomite glades, a sample of which you will see on the Glade Top Trail.

The drive starts at **Ava**. Founded in 1849 upon the establishment of a post office, it was first named "Cow Skin" after a local creek. It was later changed to "Ava" in 1870, for a city in the Old Testament of the Bible. Early settlers to the area came from Kentucky, Tennessee, Indiana, and points south. By 1857, there were enough pioneers to organize into a county. According to local legend, Douglas County (named for statesman Stephen A. Douglas) endured a fierce rivalry for the claim of county seat. Both Ava and Vera Cruz, a community eight miles southeast of Ava, wanted the honor. Ava was successful in its bid when three commissioners, appointed to lay out the town in 1871, successfully stole the county records from Vera Cruz and brought them to Ava. Then the rivalry literally heated up, with each would-be county seat burning the other's courthouse. The feud lasted well into the 1900s. However, Vera Cruz suffered other setbacks in its brief history. On June 1, 1876, Bryant Creek rose 25 feet in 25 minutes and washed away all of the buildings in the town. This flood started the slow demise of Vera Cruz; perhaps the town was destined for problems, for in Spanish, *Vera Cruz* means "edge of sorrow." The community lasted until the late 1950s, when new road improvements allowed cars to travel longer distances, and the need for smaller communities dwindled. Today, there is little left to show the traveler where the town actually existed, just a small cemetery and portions of the Old Vera Cruz Road.

Ava is the world headquarters of the Missouri Fox Trotting Horse Breed Association and its breed registry. The fox trotter is a "hillbilly" horse developed in the Ozarks. Because the hills demanded a sturdy, sure-footed, even-tempered horse, the early settlers bred high-spirited, five-gaited horses with slower, calmer Tennessee Walkers. Later, they used mustang mares to add endurance and decrease size. The fox trotters were bred as a work horse and also to furnish transportation. They are easy to ride because of their rhythmic gait—they walk with their front feet and trot with their hind feet. The name comes from the fox, which, like the horse, leaves only two tracks: its hind foot steps in the track left by the front one. Two annual fox trotting shows are held in Ava, one the second weekend of June, the other during

Labor Day week.

At the intersection of MO 5 and 14, turn east on MO Business Route 5/MO 14 and take a tour through town. The road soon heads south into the center of town and the public square. The Douglas County Museum and the Ava Fine Arts Gallery and Museum, just off the square, provide opportunities to view local history and culture. As you continue south on MO Business Route 5, look for the Forest Service's Ava Ranger District Office located on the east side of the road. Open during weekday business hours, the rangers there can provide information and maps on recreational opportunities in the forest. Be sure to pick up the Glade Top Trail Map.

The road continues and intersects with MO 5; head south. In a mile, the view on the horizon straight ahead is of a formation called the "monadnocks." These mountains are erosional remnants of a broad plateau that has weathered around the edges, leaving only the center high spot to eventually level off. The Glade Top Trail travels along the crest of such a monadnock.

Proceed south 8 miles and turn west onto MO A. After 3.5 miles, turn south on a gravel road and follow the signs for 3 miles to the **Glade Top Trail**. The first stop is a picnic area with an information sign orienting you to the area. Continue on the well-maintained gravel road, which was built by the Civilian Conservation Corps back in the 1930s. After crossing a cattle guard, the next stop is **Smoke Tree Scene**. To viewers looking out over the glades in the spring, this small tree wears what looks like puffs of bluish-grey smoke. The "smoky" parts have been described as feathery blooms but are actually hundreds of fruits and their bracts all arranged in a loose cluster. The small, inconspicuous flowers bloom earlier in the spring. The leaves turn a bright red-orange in October adding to the rusty red color of the glade grasses. Smoke tree is also called "yellowwood" for its inner color, the sap of which was once used to make a yellow dye.

Fire is an important tool used to maintain the openness of the glades. Prior to settlement, natural fires, spread by lightning and assisted by Native Americans, easily maintained these open areas. Today, prescribed fire, not wildfire, can be safely handled during low winds and moderate humidity with fire lines. Without occasional fires, woody plants will eventually outcompete and overshadow glade plants, eliminating habitat for glade species.

Eastern red cedar is the most aggressive of the woody invaders; as you look across the glades you can see that the glades are slowly losing their integrity as the cedars intrude. Because the government has deprioritized this matter and cut funding, the Forest Service has not been able to direct as much attention to this area as it deserves but hopefully this will change. Some of the cedars are so tall that fire would only burn their lower branches. Now, after more than fifty years of fire suppression, the best method of removal is to cut the trees down and burn the debris. Once a fire maintenance schedule of burning every three to five years is initiated, the younger cedars and other small trees can effectively be controlled. (For a glade management success story, visit Caney Mountain Conservation Area north of Gainesville.)

Across from the Smoke Tree Scene, the 40-acre **Hayden Bald Natural Area** is visible. You can reach it by walking 0.25 mile from the road. With dolomite glades on west, north, and east slopes, it is a good representative of the White River Hills section of the Ozarks.

In another 3 miles, the **Arkansas View** provides a scene of the Ozark Mountains near Mountain Home, Arkansas, some 40 miles away. The area around this stop is heavily forested with white oak, post oak, black oak, chinquapin oak, white ash, and various hickories.

After 0.4 mile, the **Corbit Potter Campground** is available for primitive camping. Proceed another 2 miles to the **Watershed Divide**, where the ridge divides two watersheds; water flows east into the Little Northfork River and west into Beaver Creek.

The **Caney Lookout Tower**, although closed to the public, provides a popular resting spot of the local turkey vulture population. The picnic area just beyond the tower is the site for the popular annual Glade Top Trail Festival (also called the Flaming Fall Review), which is usually held during

Missouri coneflowers blanket the grass-covered glades along the Glade Top Trail in July.

the second weekend in October. On Sunday, the town of Ava puts on a barbecued chicken dinner with free entertainment and a craft show. There is music and square dancing on Friday and Saturday, as well as a sausage and pancake breakfast Saturday. During the last half of April, another celebration called the Spring Flowering Tour, is sponsored by Theodosia. It celebrates the dogwood, serviceberry, redbud, and wild plum flowering season. North of the parking lot at the Caney picnic area, a trail leads to a small but interesting cave.

The relatively gentle slope at the picnic area offers a good opportunity to walk through the glade and observe the plants and animals. The grasses here also grow on prairies further west. Big bluestem, little bluestem, Indian grass, switch grass, and sideoats grama are commonly seen. From late March through October, a variety of wildflowers cast a rainbow of colors over the glade. In the spring you will find Indian paintbrush, downy phlox, blue indigo, and yellow star grass. These give way to pale purple coneflower, Missouri primrose, Missouri coneflower, and butterfly weed in early summer. Yellow is the dominant color through summer, as prairie dock, compass plant, and various sunflowers brighten the scene. Fall brings varied hues of asters, goldenrods, and the striking rust-red color of the grasses set against the bright leaves of smoketree, sumac, and flowering dogwood.

Several lizards are found in the glades; they venture forth in early morning or midevening, thus avoiding the relentless midday sun. Since they are cold-blooded, outside temperatures regulate their body temperatures. Lizards cool off by seeking shade under rocks on the glade. The eastern collared lizard, or "mountain boomer" is the largest lizard in the Ozarks. When startled, they can stand up on their hind legs and swiftly run to avoid predators. Their preferred food is other lizards. Look for a gray to green body and head, green legs, a length of up to fourteen inches, and a dark band around the neck. Other lizards found on glades include the northern fence lizard, five-lined skink, ground skink, and six-lined racerunner. Snakes include the red milk snake, speckled kingsnake, great plains rat snake, eastern yellowbelly racer, and the secretive pygmy rattlesnake.

A host of birds use the glades for nesting, feeding, and resting. One bird of particular note is Bachman's sparrow, which is endangered. As habitat diminishes, their numbers are declining dramatically. Past sightings of Bachman's sparrow have been made on Hayden Bald. Other birds include wild turkey, quail, several species of warblers, nighthawk, whippoorwill, yellow-breasted chat, blue-gray gnatcatcher, and northern cardinal, to name a few.

In the forest close to the edge of the glades, look for gray and fox squirrels, chipmunks, whitetail deer, and gray and red fox. Recently a black bear was seen crossing the road and ambling across the glades.

In another mile, the **Pinnacle**, which is a small hill to the left of the road, is the site of an abandoned gold mine. According to legend, a Mrs. Murray from Kansas City had a vision that told her to dig on the Pinnacle, where she would find gold. Mrs. Murray hired help and dug for years, but found no gold. The scars from her activities can still be seen. The Pinnacle, which was once a "bald," or hilltop lacking vegetation, used to serve as a gathering place for local mountain people each first Sunday in May. The religious services often drew a crowd of around five hundred people for the daylong event. There is a trail at the base of the Pinnacle, but it soon loses definition and you are left to explore the hill on your own.

Following FR 147, in a couple of miles the road passes the **Willie Lee Farm**. The homestead, which was abandoned during the depression, served as a schoolhouse for more than forty children during the 1930s. The site is now a picnic area.

The road branches, with FR 149 heading southwest across additional Forest Service land. Called the **Skyline Drive**, the road ends in about 5 miles at MO 125 near Hercules Lookout Tower and Wilderness Area, which you can reach by traveling another 3 miles north on MO 125.

Continuing on FR 147, the next and last stop is **Panorama**, a look-out point which offers a broad eastward view across glades, forest, pasture, and farmsteads.

In another couple of miles, the drive ends at the small community of **Longrun**. Turn left to reach MO 95.

13

Branson Area
Springfield to Branson, Missouri

General description: A 56-mile drive beginning at Springfield and heading south through the scenic and rugged White River Hills to Branson.

Special attractions: Fantastic Caverns, Dickerson Park Zoo, Bass Pro Shop's Outdoor World, Springfield Conservation Nature Center, Busiek State Forest and Wildlife Area, Branson, Ruth and Paul Henning Conservation Area, Shepherd of the Hills Outdoor Theatre, Silver Dollar City, Shepherd of the Hills Fish Hatchery, Table Rock Lake and State Park, Dewey Short Visitor Center, Lake Taneycomo, and College of the Ozarks; scenic views, hiking, camping, fishing (including trout), boating, swimming, spring and fall colors, and country music and entertainment.

Location: Western Ozarks. The drive begins at Springfield off of U.S. Interstate 44.

Drive route numbers: U.S. Interstate 44, U.S. Highway 65, and Missouri Highways 13, 248, 76, 165, 265, and V.

Camping: Table Rock State Park has over 165 campsites, including basic, improved, and full-hookup sites. Facilities include modern restrooms, hot showers, a coin-operated laundry, and trailer dumping facilities. The U.S. Army Corps of Engineers has 21 recreation areas around Table Rock Lake with public campgrounds. Most parks have modern and complete facilities. Primitive camping is allowed at Busiek Conservation Area in designated areas. There are plenty of commercial campgrounds in the Branson area. Check the Branson Chamber of Commerce office for locations.

Services: All services at Springfield, Ozark, Branson, and Hollister.

Nearby attractions: Wilson's Creek National Battlefield, Boston Ferry and Drury-Mincy conservation areas, Hercules Glades and Piney Creek wilderness areas, Bull Shoals Lake, Kissee Mills Watchable Wildlife Site, and Ashe Juniper Natural Area.

 The drive

This drive begins in a part of the Ozarks known as the Springfield Plateau. When land was uplifted over a period of time to form the Ozarks, this region of primarily limestone bedrock took the shape of a broad dome. Creeks and streams flow out in all directions from the high point of the

Drive 13: Branson Area

Springfield to Branson, Missouri (north)

To Bolivar

1. 13

To 32

To Buffalo

To Marshfield

2.

To H

65

44

To
Mount Vernon

13 **Springfield**

To Republic 60 *Sunshine*

Glenstone

3.

60 *Campbell*

James

River To
Mountain Grove

River Freeway

4.

Lake

Springfield

James

N

```
0   1   2   3   4   5
```
Miles

★

To Nixa

14 *River*

Finley **Ozark**

14 To Ava

65

SITES

1. Fantastic Caverns
2. Dickerson Park Zoo
3. Bass Pro Shop's
    Outdoor World
4. Springfield Conservation
    Nature Center

Drive 13: Branson Area

Springfield to Branson, Missouri (south)

SITES

5. Busiek State Forest and Wildlife Area
6. Old Downtown Branson
7. Ruth and Paul Henning Conservation Area
8. Shepherd of the Hills Outdoor Theater
9. Silver Dollar City
10. Shepherd of the Hills Fish Hatchery
11. Dewey Short Visitor Center
12. Table Rock State Park
13. College of the Ozarks
14. Shepherd of the Hills Expressway

plateau, which today is about 1,400 feet above sea level. Looking out from the city of Springfield, which sits atop the Springfield Plateau, you will notice the land is relatively broad and level, lacking high hills and deep valleys. This was once prairie country. South of here, the White River and its tributaries have cut into the Springfield Plateau and exposed older bedrock of Ordovician age. Composed of dolomite, the hills are steep-sided with narrow, deep valleys. The slopes are forested, and grassy areas called glades are common on the more exposed south and west aspects of hills. Although much of the Springfield Plateau has been converted to pasture and row crops, the White River section still offers extensive wild areas and tremendous views.

Springfield, with its self-proclaimed cognomen of "Queen City of the Ozarks," has been the trading hub for a vast area, even since pioneer days. It was founded in 1829 by a homesteader from Tennessee named John Polk Campbell. He donated fifty acres for a public square and gave cabins to prospective settlers. In 1833, the settlement became "Springfield," as one story tells it, by way of a bribe of whiskey that was offered to each man to vote for the name. The town grew steadily; in 1858, the Butterfield-Overland stage offered passage to California from a depot on the northeast corner of the square. The Civil War divided the city, with major battles occurring over a two-year period. Just after the war, the town square was the site of the nation's first recorded shoot-out. A dispute over a gambling debt owed by "Wild Bill" Hickok to Dave Tutt ended in a gunfight, with Tutt on the losing end. Because of Hickok's fame as a Pony Express rider, the event made nationwide news. In 1870, the town's success and prosperity were guaranteed when the "Frisco," the St. Louis-San Francisco Railroad, arrived at its new station at Commercial and Benton streets. Springfield is also recognized as the birthplace of Route 66, for it was here, in 1926, that officials first proposed the name of the new Chicago-to-Los Angeles highway. It was the first completely paved transcontinental highway in America, and was finished in 1938.

There are many activities to enjoy in Springfield, the third largest city in Missouri. There are some, however, that stand out above the rest. The first is **Fantastic Caverns**. To reach Fantastic Caverns, which is open year-round, travel on I-44 to MO 13 north and follow the signs to the caverns. The cave was discovered in 1862 by a farmer's dog, which had crawled through an entrance. However, five years passed before the first exploration took place. Twelve women from Springfield answered a newspaper ad seeking explorers and were the first to venture into the cave. Their names remain on a cave wall today. Now, Jeep-drawn trams carry visitors on the mile-long, fifty-minute tour. No walking is necessary in this cave, and the trams easily accommodate wheelchairs. This may sound like an environmentally incorrect way to travel through a cave, however, these Jeeps are

Viewing trout in rearing pools is a popular activity at Shepherd of the Hills Fish Hatchery.

fueled by propane, which emits an exhaust of oxygen and water vapor. Only the front part of the extensive cave is used for tourism, and the water in the underground passages is monitored for pollution. The cave supports unique subterranean wildlife including the endangered Ozark cavefish, the rare cave crayfish, and the grotto salamander. Cave formations include stalactites, stalagmites, columns, soda straws, flowstones, cave pearls, and draperies.

If time permits, a tour of **Dickerson Park Zoo** offers an opportunity to see not only exotic animals but some native ones as well. The Missouri Habitats exhibit features black bear, deer, otter, and others. The zoo also has a bald eagle rehabilitation and breeding center, which worked with the Missouri Department of Conservation to release bald eagles back into the state. The zoo is located at the northeast intersection of I-44 and MO 13.

A good place to stop for outdoor recreational supplies is **Bass Pro Shop's Outdoor World**. Billed as the world's largest sporting goods store, the 150,000-square-foot building contains an incredible selection of merchandise for just about every outdoor activity. This is all showcased in a building studded with aquariums of up to 30,000 gallons, a 30-foot waterfall with stream, and numerous wildlife exhibits. To reach the store, take US 65 south to Sunshine Avenue, go east 4 miles to Campbell Street, turn left, and proceed one block to the parking area.

Another recommended stop is the **Springfield Conservation Nature**

Center. Sitting on 80 acres of woods, glades, and lake-front, nearly 3 miles of hiking trails weave their way through several exceptional habitats right within the city limits. The well-designed building features educational exhibits that give you a quick orientation to Ozark habitats and explains why they are special. It is well worth the time to take a hike, enjoy the outdoor setting, and learn about the Ozarks. The best way to find the nature center is to follow the signs beginning on US 65 south to US 60 west, which goes into Springfield. Turn onto the James River Freeway, and exit on the frontage road, which heads south to the nature center. If you are already in the city, you can reach the center by finding Glenstone Avenue (MO Business Route 65) and heading south to the James River Freeway.

Continue south, taking US 65 to Branson. Just south of Springfield, the highway crosses the upper arm of Lake Springfield. This impoundment is part of the James River, a popular float stream that empties into Table Rock Lake. The best access to the river is off of MO 14 west of Nixa at the Delaware Town Access.

The road continues another 6 miles to the town of **Ozark**. It can be reached by taking MO Business Route 65 east into town. The town was platted in 1843. It received national attention in 1889 when three members of the "Baldknobbers" were hung in the courthouse square. The Baldknobbers were a secretly organized band of vigilantes that formed after the Civil War to combat the lawlessness that swept the region. Because the group met on the treeless tops of nearby mountains, known as "bald knobs," they became known as Baldknobbers. Today, bald knobs are called glades. The well-intentioned Baldknobbers eventually became a band of night-raiders conducting murders, whippings, and general disorder. They eventually disbanded after their leader, Nathaniel Kenney, was shot in 1888.

US 65 crosses over Finley River, a small but popular float and smallmouth bass fishing stream that is a tributary of the James River. In another 4.5 miles, the four-lane highway narrows to two lanes and begins to enter the White River section of the plateau. The relief now becomes more pronounced and the road begins to cut into the hills and valleys, exposing more bedrock. This Mississippian rock, called the Reeds Spring Formation, is layered with beds of white limestone and chert. Deep in the valleys an older, more solid rock appears called the Cotter Formation. It is a dolomite of Ordovician age and is characteristic of the White River section. The most dramatic valley lies 5 miles from the beginning of the two-lane section of highway. The highway spans a 2-mile-wide valley in a straight line, dropping 340 feet into the valley and up again. This feat of engineering makes this road the longest, straightest span of highway constructed across a valley in either the Ozarks or the Ouachita Mountains, and probably in the entire Midwest, for that matter.

At the bottom of the valley, the 2,505-acre **Busiek State Forest and**

Wildlife Area offers primitive camping, hiking, self-guided nature trails, opportunities for nature study, and birdwatching as well as fishing, hunting, and horseback riding. The area, which is on both sides of US 65, contains typical Ozark features including streams, extensive forests, glades, and meadows.

As you travel south along US 65 notice that, although there are still plenty of forested hills, several of the hilltops are being cleared for pastures and homesites. This is increasingly evident the closer you get to Branson. There also seems to be no limit to the number of billboards; Busiek Valley is probably the only stretch that is billboard-free.

A new bypass around **Branson** is being developed, called the Ozark Mountain Highroad. It is designed to relieve traffic in Branson by offering an alternative route to the west side of town. When the road is completed, it will be an optional route on this drive, but it will be harder to reach the following highlights from it. The drive should be experienced, however, because if the Missouri Highway Department delivers what it has proposed, you should see a more environmentally sensitive highway with scenic pullouts and landscaping with native Ozark plants instead of traditional fescue, crown vetch, and lespedeza.

Branson began like most Ozarks towns, with a post office and country store, in 1882. About twenty-five years later the railroad came to town, bringing the first tourists to the area. In 1914, the first dam on the White River was completed, backing up water to form Lake Taneycomo. This triggered an influx of tourist and fishing camps, hotels, and boat docks along the new shoreline at Branson. The following decades were filled with gradual growth and change as the nearby towns of Hollister and Rockaway Beach became centers of tourism. The focus shifted back to Branson with the completion of Table Rock Lake in the 1950s. This new dam transformed the downstream Lake Taneycomo into a cold water impoundment. Taneycomo's waters now came from the bottom of Table Rock Lake, and the water's temperature of 48 degrees Fahrenheit was too chilly for swimmers and skiers. Such water recreation shifted to Table Rock Lake, and anglers found the new lake to be an outstanding source of bass, crappie, and other panfish. Meanwhile, Lake Taneycomo was stocked with trout by the Missouri Department of Conservation, and soon became a popular lake for coldwater fishing.

Country music came to Branson in 1960 when the Baldknobbers began performing on the Taneycomo lakefront in town. They were joined in 1967 by the Presleys, who built a theater on West MO 76 in Branson, then the Foggy River Boys, the Plummer Family, and so on. Today, there are more than sixty different shows, and Branson is known as "America's Live Entertainment Capital."

To see where it all began, take a side trip off of US 65 and follow MO

65B into **Old Downtown Branson**. This is where the "locals" prefer to shop and eat; some of the historic brick buildings date back to the early part of the century. Since the 1960s, MO 76 west of town has been the center of activity for all modern development.

Of all the drives in and around Branson, the following is most recommended. At the junction of US 65 and MO 248, start on MO 248 west; immediately to the left is the **Branson Chamber of Commerce Information Center**. It is a good place to stop for maps and brochures; knowledgeable staff can answer any questions you might have about activities in the area. Continue on MO 248 west 2.2 miles to Shepherd Of The Hills Expressway. Follow the expressway another 2.2 miles and cross over the Roark Creek Bridge. Continue 1.4 miles and turn right onto MO 76. The large hill along the road is Dewey Bald, a common reference in Harold Bell Wright's classic book "The Shepherd of the Hills."

Follow the highway around Dewey Bald and turn onto the drive to **Ruth and Paul Henning Conservation Area**. The land is named after the producer of the *Beverly Hillbillies*, a popular television program of the 1960s. Mr. Henning purchased this property, where he filmed some of the show's scenes featuring the characters' "Ozark home." Henning later sold the land, with a partial donation, to the Missouri Department of Conservation. The 1,534-acre area contains some of the best examples of glades remaining in the White River Hills today. There are several trails, with one leading up Dewey Bald to an observation deck. Another trail leads to the White River Hills Natural Area to view one of the "balds" that may once have been used by the Baldknobbers. Scenic views, interpretive displays, and a diversity of wildflowers showcase the area's uniqueness. A naturalist is on duty during the busy season to answer questions, lead tours, and give programs.

Just down the road on MO 76, **The Shepherd of the Hills Outdoor Theatre** reenacts the 1907 book written by Harold Bell Wright. The book was so successful that the Branson area became a popular attraction even before Lake Taneycomo was built in 1914. Tourists began to arrive as early as 1910 to see where the book was written and the places and people it was written about. The outdoor evening performance of Wright's story and day-time tours are both popular. A ride up the 230-foot Inspiration Tower provides a commanding view of the White River Hills and Table Rock Lake even though the tower itself detracts from the beauty of the skyline.

Just beyond the intersection of MO 76 and MO 265, a side trip to **Silver Dollar City** will take you back in time to the 1880s. This theme park ranks as one of the nation's most popular entertainment facilities of its kind. Opened in 1960, Silver Dollar City features native craftspeople creating historic crafts that were once commonly found in the Ozarks. Silver Dollar City also has restaurants, specialty foods, free entertainment, and rides. Special festivals are scheduled throughout the year. To avoid traffic and crowds,

An active water mill can be seen at College of the Ozarks.

come early in the day and avoid holiday weekends.

Return to MO 265 and travel 5.5 miles to the junction of MO 165. Turn left and follow the signs to **Shepherd of the Hills Fish Hatchery**. Operated by the Missouri Department of Conservation, the hatchery offers exhibits including aquariums, an introductory film, guided tours, picnicking, trails, and access to Lake Taneycomo for fishing. The hatchery produces between 350,000 and 400,000 pounds of rainbow and brown trout per year. You can also walk around the raceways and view the various sizes of trout before they are released into Lake Taneycomo.

Return to MO 165 and MO 265 and cross over Table Rock Dam. Immediately to the right, the **Dewey Short Visitor Center** offers four-seasons exhibits, a nature trail, a choice of six audiovisual programs in the auditorium, and tours of the Table Rock powerhouse. Just beyond the visitor center is **Table Rock State Park**, which provides access to the 43,000-acre lake. The 356-acre park is a great place for swimming, boating, fishing, hiking, picnicking, and camping. Bald eagles and loons are winter visitors to the area.

After 1.5 miles MO 165 and 265 divide. Turn left onto MO 165, and in 0.7 miles a scenic view overlooks Lake Taneycomo and, unfortunately, a resort development. This fairly new complex serves as a reminder of the rapid and seemingly unregulated housing and commercial development that has occurred in the Branson area over the past two decades. In addition to habitat loss, wastewater treatment cannot meet the needs of the increasing population. Water quality has noticeably declined, affecting the fisheries and other aquatic life in both lakes, especially Lake Taneycomo. As you stand at this overlook, you are on one of the table rocks that gave the larger lake its name.

In another 2.5 miles and just before US 65, turn left on Hollister Road, which is MO V. Proceed about a mile to the entrance of the **College of the Ozarks**. The school was established in 1907 by the Reverend James Forsyth to provide education in mechanical and commercial skills for young people from poor families. It grew in size from a boarding school for youngsters to a high school, then a junior college, and finally, in 1964, it became a fully accredited four-year college of liberal arts. The school continues its strong tradition of having a work-scholarship plan where students work for their tuition in the school dairy, print shop, water mill, museum, restaurant, or other college enterprises. Be sure to visit the working water mill, the Friendship House (which is a gift shop and restaurant), the Ralph Foster Museum, and other special attractions. The Ralph Foster Museum is dedicated to the history of the Ozarks region. The museum houses thousands of objects representing archaeology, natural history, fine arts, geology, and mineralogy. It even houses the car that was used in the *Beverly Hillbillies* television program. A tour map is available at most campus facilities.

14

Prairie Country

Niawathe to Prairie State Park, Missouri

General description: A 42-mile drive beginning 8 miles north of Lockwood on Missouri Highway 97, traveling west through prairie landscapes and the towns of Lamar and Liberal, and ending at Prairie State Park.

Special attractions: Niawathe Prairie Natural Area, Harry S Truman State Historic Site, and Prairie State Park; prairie wildflowers and wildlife, and hiking.

Location: Western Ozarks. The drive begins at the junction of Missouri Highways 97 and E, 8 miles north of Lockwood.

Drive route numbers: Missouri Highways 97, 43, K, E, and P and U.S. Highway 160.

Camping: Stockton State Park has 45 basic campsites and 38 campsites with electrical hookups. The camping area, which is not far from the edge of Stockton Lake, has a dumping station, modern restrooms, showerhouses, and laundry facilities. Prairie State Park has 6 basic campsites and a pit toilet.

Services: All services at Lamar. Gas and food at Liberal.

Nearby attractions: Truman Lake, Schell-Osage Conservation Area, and several public prairies (consult *Public Prairies of Missouri*, available from the Missouri Department of Conservation).

 The drive

The western part of the Ozarks in Missouri and Oklahoma was predominately prairie until the time of European settlement, which began in this region about two hundred years ago. As the prairie was divided and farmed, what was not plowed was overgrazed by cattle or allowed to grow up in trees. Trees were not at home on the prairie. The gently rolling hills and hot, dry, westerly winds provided ideal conditions to carry wildfires. Prairie plants are adapted to fire, because their growing centers are below the soil. The growing points of trees, however, are fully exposed, making them vulnerable to fire. Occasional fires are good for a prairie. The grasses and wildflowers (called forbs) have adapted to the cycle of fire over thousands of years and actually depend upon this natural event for their survival.

Drive 14: Prairie Country
Niawathe to Prairie State Park, Missouri

SITES
1. Stony Point Prairie
2. Pawhuska Prairie
3. Treaty Line Prairie
4. Redwing Prairie

Plains Indians were very keen observers of nature and knew how important fire was in maintaining a healthy prairie. Fire, either ignited by lightning strikes or set by Indians, kept the trees in check and removed the dead leaf litter that can cause a prairie to stagnate. Like thatch in a lawn, if dead plant leaves are allowed to accumulate, they can choke out new growth. With leaf litter removed, the soil is exposed and can better absorb the sun's warmth in the spring, allowing a flush of green growth. The Plains Indians saw that this attracted game, especially bison, which meant more successful hunts.

Missouri has been a leader in prairie protection. The notes of the original land survey indicate that Missouri once contained 15 million acres of prairie, mostly in the northern and western part of the state. Now, much of the prairie is gone from northern Missouri because its deeper soils were well suited to plowing. Western Missouri has characteristically shallow soils over bedrock; grazing or cutting hay for cattle has been the common practice. Of the estimated 70,000 acres of native prairie remaining in the state, about 17,000 acres have been acquired, restored, and protected, in large part by the Missouri Department of Conservation, but also by Missouri State Parks, The Nature Conservancy, and the Missouri Prairie Foundation. For descriptions and maps of the more than sixty prairies write to the Missouri Department of Conservation and request *Public Prairies of Missouri* (see appendix for address).

This drive crosses prairie country on the western edge of the Ozarks' Springfield Plateau and enters a region called the Osage Plains. This allows for a visit to Prairie State Park, which was created to reclaim lost prairie heritage through interpretive exhibits and trails and is situated in the heart of a prairie. The Osage Plains region is distinguished from the Springfield Plateau by its bedrock of sandstone and shale of older, Pennsylvanian age, while the Springfield Plateau is composed of limestone and chert rocks of Mississippian age.

Begin the drive at the junction of MO 97 and E, 8 miles north of Lockwood. Travel west on MO E for a mile and turn right onto a gravel road that continues for about 0.5 mile to a parking lot on the left. This is **Niawathe Prairie**, a 320-acre prairie named for the Osage Indian term for "life-giver." There are no trails, so wander freely across the prairie. As in any grassy area, chiggers may be present; using an insect repellent would be a good idea. During the growing season, you can see the showiest and best variety of wildflowers in the areas west and north of the parking lot. For the best view, walk toward the north end and look southwest. From there a beautiful prairie landscape unravels that is devoid of powerlines, barns, silos, communication towers, and other reminders of civilization. Walking west to the high point provides more extended views of the landscape and its farmsteads.

Looking over the prairie, notice the mounds rising two to three feet

*A naturalist stands ready to guide visitors through the late president
Harry S Truman's first home in Lamar.*

above the ground and up to ten feet across. These mounds are typical of many prairies in western Missouri and eastern Kansas and Oklahoma. Commonly called pimple mounds or Mima mounds (after a site south of Olympia, Washington), their origin is a mystery. There are several possible explanations for the mounds. They could be Indian burial sites, remnants left by wind or water erosion, seismic activity, or glacial outwash. Another popular theory involves pocket gophers—small mammals that dig their burrows by piling excavated soil into mounds. The plains pocket gopher exhibits this mound-building capability, but on a smaller scale than that required to create these mounds. It is possible that a larger pocket gopher once existed but is now extinct. Whatever caused these mounds is a mystery, because new mounds have been created, at least since the beginning of recorded history.

Prairies are remarkable for their diversity of plants and animals. Grasses such as big and little bluestem, Indian, switch, sideoats grama, and prairie dropseed dominate. A high quality prairie is typically home to more than 150 forbs; species in the sunflower, legume, and rose families are the most numerous. You can also find representatives of the iris, orchid, spurge, mint, parsley, figwort, and many other families. Flowering begins on the prairies in April and ends in late October, guaranteeing a show of colors throughout the season. October is especially brilliant when the prairie grasses turn rusty

American bison, once numbering in the millions, can still be seen at Prairie State Park.

red and gold. Although a variety of animals live on the prairies, birds are especially noticeable. Nesting birds include dickcissels, yellowthroats, American goldfinches, eastern meadowlarks, quail, and several types of sparrows. Less common, but still sometimes seen, are northern harrier, short-eared owl, prairie chicken, Henslow's sparrow, and upland sandpiper. Many species of insects inhabit the prairie, including beautiful butterflies such as the monarch and the rare regal fritillary.

Because prairies have drastically declined throughout their former thirteen-state range, many plants and animals that are exclusive to this habitat are also becoming rare. Even with 17,000 acres of prairie in Missouri, animals such as the prairie chicken are losing ground. Less than 3,000 of these birds are left in the state. Public involvement is essential for fostering support for measures that prevent the further decline of prairies. Recently, the Kaelke family, who live about 10 miles south of Niawathe Prairie, set up a bed-and-breakfast on their farm, which contains a booming ground for prairie chickens. During the month of April, when the birds are going through their courtship displays, the Kaelkes host overnight visitors and provide viewing opportunities in the morning, when the prairie chickens are most active. This does not seem to bother the birds, and the public gets to share in a rare and unusual event. (see the appendix for more information.)

From Niawathe Prairie, return to MO E and proceed west for 3 miles to the junction of MO D. A mile north of here is the 640-acre **Stony Point Prairie**. MO E merges with US 160 in 4 miles. Follow US 160 west; in 3 miles a side trip on MO HH leads to the 77-acre **Pawhuska Prairie**. After another 4 miles on US 160, another side trip on a gravel road south leads to **Treaty Line Prairie**, a 168-acre area.

Return to US 160 and proceed into the town of **Lamar**, home of President Harry S Truman and Wyatt Earp. Lamar was settled in 1852 by George E. Ward, who built a sawmill and operated a small general store. Lamar was incorporated in 1867 and was named by Mrs. Ward in honor of President Mirabeau Lamar of the Republic of Texas. The focal point of the town is the large town square. The county courthouse, built in 1888, still functions as the center of county government. The square is the site of the annual Lamar Fair, which is billed as the "Largest Free Fair in the State of Missouri" and has been in continuous operation for one week each August for the past forty-eight years.

Upon entering Lamar, follow the signs to the **Harry S Truman State Historic Site**. This one-and-a-half-story house, built around 1881, is listed on the National Register of Historic Places. Truman's father, John Anderson, and mother, Martha Ellen, bought the house in 1882 for $685. Two years later, on May 8, Harry was born. Six years later, the family moved north to Independence, Missouri, where the future president began his schooling. The United Auto Workers of America bought the house from descendants of the famous Wyatt Earp (who was once the constable of Lamar) in 1957. The house was donated to the state in 1959. The historic site is open to visitors from 10 a.m. to 4 p.m., Monday through Saturday and from noon to 4 p.m., Sunday. An interpreter provides tours of the house, which is decorated with furnishings from the period of the Trumans' occupancy.

The recent Hollywood movies *Wyatt Earp* and *Tombstone* have triggered renewed interest in Earp's days in Lamar. He followed his parents from Illinois in 1869 and became the town's first constable the following year, at the age of twenty-two. For $15 a month, he served warrants, broke up fights, and hauled drunks to jail. Earp left Lamar around 1872, apparently after a barroom brawl with some of his in-laws; he stole a horse and never returned. Later, his legendary status grew in Wichita and Dodge City in Kansas and at the infamous shootout at the O.K. Corral in Tombstone, Arizona, in 1881.

Continue west on US 160 for about 10 miles to the junction of MO 43. Turn right and proceed north 3.5 miles. A 2.5 mile side trip east on a gravel road leads to the 160-acre **Redwing Prairie**. Proceed another mile on MO 43, then turn west onto MO K and continue to the town of **Liberal**. Founded in 1880 by George H. Walser, Liberal was established as a "Free-thinker" town. It was designed to be a place where Free-thinkers could live in a sort of colony and enjoy their beliefs in a quiet, unmolested way. What is more remarkable is that churches and saloons were not allowed within the town limits. At one point, to keep Christians from settling in the town and eventually outnumbering the Free-thinkers, the latter established a high-post, barbed-wire fence around the entire town, including the public highway. When railroad authorities telegraphed that they would remove the depot if the lunacy was not abandoned—it was abandoned. Today, the town of 689 residents exhibits little of its early beginnings. A visit to the Mustard Seed Restaurant for lunch might be a good opportunity to learn more about this unusual town.

Follow MO K for 2 miles west of Liberal and turn south onto MO P and follow the signs to **Prairie State Park**. Covering just over 3,500 acres, the park began with a purchase of 1,500 acres of prairie in 1982. Today, the park supports a visitor center, complete with interpretive exhibits and programs, 7 miles of trails, and naturalist-led walks. Of particular interest is the opportunity to see bison roaming the prairie much as they did more than two hundred years ago. (For your safety, be sure to obey the signs indicating the current location of bison.) The bison, once numbering over 60 million, almost became extinct before a few hundred animals were found and protected by law. Bison were eliminated from Missouri in the 1870s. Now, in addition to bison, the park supports elk, which were also an original component of the prairie.

Ask a park staff member for an animal checklist which lists 150 birds, 23 mammals, 10 fishes, 12 amphibians, 23 reptiles, and 88 butterflies and moths. Observers have also documented more than 350 species of grasses and forbs that live in the park. The once extensive prairies have been carved up, leaving only small isolated patches, causing plants and animals dependent on prairies to suffer. At least 25 plant and animal species listed as rare or endangered are finding refuge at Prairie State Park. Additional efforts to protect prairie across its former range must continue so that future generations can also experience the awe and excitement of this unique ecosystem.

15

Roaring River State Park

Cassville to Eagle Rock, Missouri

General description: A 15-mile drive beginning in Cassville and dropping into the White River Hills to Eagle Rock.

Special attractions: Roaring River State Park and Fish Hatchery, Roaring River Cove Hardwoods Natural Area, Sugar Camp Scenic Drive, and Mark Twain National Forest; hiking trails, trout fishing, glades, wildflowers, scenic views, fall colors, camping, canoeing, horseback riding, and hunting.

Location: Western Ozarks. The drive begins on Missouri Highway 112 in Cassville on the east side of town.

Drive route numbers: Missouri Highways 112, 248, and F, Forest Roads 197 and 1004, and Table Rock Road 86-97.

Camping: Roaring River State Park has a modern 3-story motel, cabins that can accommodate up to 6 persons, and 180 tent and trailer campsites, both basic and with hookups. Facilities in the camping area include two sanitary dumping stations, ice machines, hot showers, modern restrooms, and laundry facilities. Motel and cabin reservations are required and may be made by calling the park's concessionaire's office. The U.S. Army Corps of Engineers' Table Rock Lake has 21 recreation areas with modern campground facilities. Three local Corps of Engineers recreation areas are Eagle Rock, Viney Creek, and Beaver. Primitive camping is allowed in the Mark Twain National Forest.

Services: All services at Cassville.

Nearby attractions: Flag Spring Conservation Area, Piney Creek Wilderness Area, Eureka Springs, Table Rock Lake, Beaver Lake, and Pig Trail and Ozark Highlands Scenic Drives.

 The drive

The first part of the drive crosses the southwestern part of the Springfield Plateau. The hills are only slightly dissected and rolling. This is a transition region, where prairies from the plains once graded into the forests of the rugged Ozarks. The bedrock is Mississippian limestone, known for its sinkholes, caves, and springs. About 4 miles south of Cassville, on the way to Roaring River State Park, the road leaves the plateau and descends into the watershed of the White River section. For millions of years, the White

Drive 15: Roaring River State Park

Cassville to Eagle Rock, Missouri

SITES

1. Lodge
2. Hatchery
3. Roaring River Spring
4. Ozark Chinquapin Nature Center
5. Roaring River Access
6. Roaring River Cove Hardwoods
   Natural Area
7. Stables
8. Roaring River Conservation Area
9. White Cedar Glade
10. Sugar Camp Lookout Tower
11. Onyx Cave Picnic Area

River has been cutting into the Springfield Plateau, creating deep, steep-walled valleys and exposing various layers of sedimentary rock, including limestone, shale, dolomite, and chert. Today, the hilly White River section still contains extensive forests with some clearing for pastures on the broader ridges and wider valleys.

The drive begins in **Cassville**. Originally platted in 1845, the town was once a stop for the Butterfield Overland Mail and briefly served as the Confederate capital of Missouri. During the Civil War, the secessionist governor and Confederate members of the Missouri General Assembly fled Union troops and met here the first week of November 1861. They considered the ordinance of secession, which was approved at nearby Neosho by eleven senators and forty-four representatives. Both the ordinance and the act of affiliation to the Confederate States were signed here, and the Confederate flag was hoisted above the courthouse. During the war, Cassville was attacked several times by both sides. The courthouse, having suffered from its use as a fort and horse stable, was eventually torn down in 1910 and replaced with the existing building in 1913.

Recently named one of the top one hundred retirement areas in America, Cassville (ranked 49th) was one of only two Missouri towns to receive the honor—the other being Branson at 34th. Cassville received high ratings on quality of life, affordability, housing, safety, and law enforcement. The town is a service center for the surrounding farms and settlements, as well as a gateway to Roaring River State Park and the upper portion of Table Rock Lake.

Before leaving Cassville, a good place to stop for information on recreational opportunities on the Mark Twain National Forest is the Cassville Ranger Station. The office is located on the north side of MO 248 just 0.75 of a mile east of the five-highway intersection in midtown. It is open Monday through Friday.

On the east side of town, take MO 112 south to **Roaring River State Park**. After about 4 miles the road drops off the relatively flat Springfield Plateau and begins its descent into the White River watershed. Be careful as you enter the park: the last mile drops four hundred feet into the Roaring River valley, offering some scenic views but no turn-outs. A busy intersection awaits at the bottom of the hill; turn left to go to the lodge, spring, and hatchery. Trout fishing is the most popular activity here, but the deep hollows, extensive forests, and open glades provide an exceptional diversity of plants and animals that can be seen on the six trails that total 9.7 miles. Although elk, bison, and wolves are gone, armadillos, bobcats, and black bears still roam here. Armadillos and other typically "southern" animals such as the painted bunting and roadrunner have been extending their range northward over the past twenty years due to the mild winters. This may be evidence of global warming.

The road up Roaring River Hollow parallels the spring run. At the end of the road, the Missouri Department of Conservation's **Roaring River Fish Hatchery** offers the chance to see trout grouped by various sizes in rearing pools. Guided tours are given, mostly on weekends. Check at the hatchery for information on tour times. A trail leads past the trout rearing pools to **Roaring River Spring**. An average of 22 million gallons of water per day emerges from the base of a grottolike gorge beneath a high dolomite cliff. Ranked as the tenth largest spring in Missouri, divers have measured the vent, which directs the spring upward, to be 215 feet long. At the bottom, there are several cave passageways from which the water collects. It has been said that before the dam was built in 1880 to pool the spring, the waters rushed from the grotto over rocks with a sound and splash that gave merit to the spring's name.

The first mill to use the Roaring River Spring was built in 1836. Another mill was built in 1845 where the lodge now stands; it was destroyed during the Civil War. Rebuilt in 1886, the mill carded wool, ground grain, and sawed logs. When the milling business declined, the building was converted to a hotel. By the early 1920s, it had become a popular vacation spot for residents of Kansas City and St. Louis. The inn was later destroyed by fire. A private resort and trout hatchery were soon established but met an early demise. Finally, in 1928, a wealthy businessman from St. Louis purchased the entire tract of 2,400 acres with elaborate plans to develop the area as a tourist resort. Within a year, he changed his mind and donated the land to the State of Missouri. Today, with additional purchases, the park includes 3,354 acres.

Before leaving Roaring River Spring and the hatchery, the 0.2-mile **Deer Leap Trail**, begins along the spring walkway and leads to a great overlook. From there you can view the hatchery and the spring grotto. The name of the trail comes from an incident in which someone observed a deer being chased by dogs, which leapt to its death from the towering cliff overlooking the spring. The first part of the hike is a strenuous climb up stone steps built by the 1930s Civilian Conservation Corps. The CCC also constructed the attractive stonework around the lodge. The trail takes you along the base of a huge rock cliff with interesting rock slabs that have broken away from the wall. After spending time at the overlook, continue on the trail, which descends and exits by a cabin near the spring pond.

Another trail, the 1.5-mile **Devil's Kitchen Trail**, begins at the small picnic area across from the lodge or can be accessed from the hatchery road near the junction of MO 112. It was named for a huge cavity in a rock outcrop; legend has it that this feature was once used by Civil War bushwhackers. Before them, Native Americans probably used the alcove as a campsite, for they were observed as late as 1830 hunting in this area along the spring-fed river. A self-guided interpretive brochure for this trail is avail-

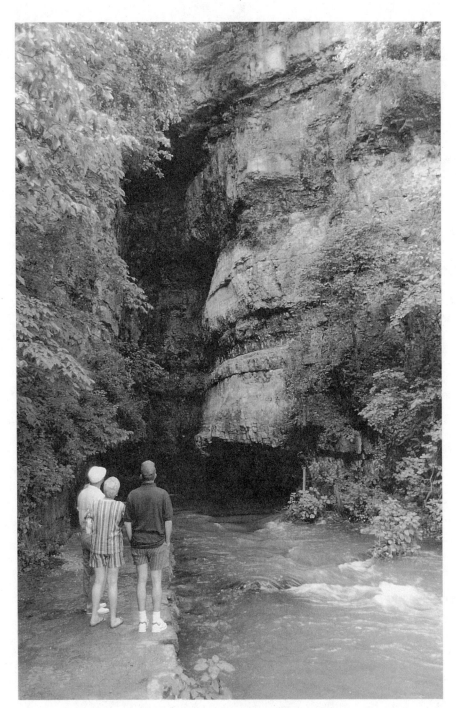

Roaring River Spring issues 22 million gallons of water per day from the base of a towering dolomite cliff.

able at the nature center.

Back on the hatchery road, follow the signs to the **Ozark Chinquapin Nature Center**, which is located just off MO F. The nature center contains exhibits interpreting the natural history of the area. They also have field guides for sale, and be sure to ask for a map showing the hiking trails. In front of the building the staff maintains an excellent display of native wildflowers that can be found growing in the park. The plants have labels for easy identification.

For the more adventuresome, ask about access to the **Roaring River Cove Hardwoods Natural Area**. A 120-acre portion in the northern part of the park was designated in 1978 as a state natural area. The area features old growth, dry upland forest of black oak, white oak, red oak, post oak, and shagbark hickory on rocky chert slopes, with an understory of flowering dogwood and serviceberry. The richer, more protected coves contain basswood, walnut, and sugar maple.

Spring floaters can reach the **Roaring River** off of MO F through campground "C," past the restricted fly-fishing area. The river, which is actually a spring-fed creek, has a permanent flow of 6.5 miles and passes the MO 85 bridge at Eagle Rock before emptying into Table Rock Lake.

Continuing down MO F, the road passes **Roaring River Stables**. Located in the park, its guided one-hour rides leave every half-hour throughout the day. Past the stables and on the right, the 439-acre **Roaring River Conservation Area** contains forest, pasture, and 0.5 mile of the Roaring River. There is no developed access to the river here. The parking lot does offer a convenient place to stop and walk across the highway to see the **White Cedar Glade** restoration project. Trees are being removed and prescribed fire has been used to help restore this overgrown glade and savanna. No trails have been developed yet, so visitors should be prepared for cross-country hiking across the state park and Forest Service land. Walking south along the slope, which parallels MO F, the glade begins to show its true character in about 100 yards. Particularly attractive in the spring and early summer, the glade features an abundance of wildflowers and unusual animals such as collared lizards, or "mountain boomers," tarantulas, scorpions, painted buntings, and roadrunners. The rare white cedar tree also grows here, not to be confused with the more common eastern red cedar, which is one of the main threats to the glade.

Return to the main part of the park and turn onto MO 112 south. You immediately climb a steep hill, passing a scenic overlook after 2 miles. In another mile and on the left, Forest Road 197 starts the **Sugar Camp Scenic Drive**. The 8-mile drive derives its name from a popular activity of the early twentieth century—tapping sugar maples and camping. The well-maintained gravel road is now a popular route, having been featured on a national cable television show and in a recreation magazine. The first vista overlooks Pine

A commanding view from Sugar Camp Lookout Tower.

Hollow and, in the distance, Roaring River Hollow. After 1.7 miles from MO 112, FR 1004, on the right, climbs a short but steep hill to **Sugar Camp Lookout Tower**. The tower, constructed in the 1930s by the CCC, provides a commanding view for many miles in all directions. Use extreme caution if you climb the tower. A picnic area is also provided.

Continuing on FR 197, the road follows a narrow ridge that supports shortleaf pine, white oak, black oak, red oak, hickories, and sassafras. In springtime, the steep, cherty slopes light up with the colors of redbud and flowering dogwood. The next vista overlooks Radium Hollow to the south. The valley derives its name from Radium Spring. Water from the spring was bottled and sent to Germany during the 1930s for medicinal purposes. The site is also said to have been a tomato cannery. Foundations from the old structures can still be found on site.

After about 0.5 mile, **Onyx Cave Picnic Area** overlooks Cedar Creek Valley. A short trail opposite the picnic area leads to Onyx Cave, a crawling-only cave that has about 100 feet of passageway. In 2 miles, passing another vista along the way, the road crosses FR 1051. The flat open areas along the road are actually small limestone glades. The thin soil, with lots of exposed limestone bedrock, supports special plants that are adapted to the harsh conditions. Plants like the prickly pear cactus, glade onion, widow's-cross sedum, Trelease's larkspur, and the fragrant calamint grow here. In another mile, a vista shows a section of the White River as it courses its way to Table Rock Lake. In 1.5 miles, the gravel road comes to Table Rock Lake Road 86/97; turn left, and in 0.1 mile the drive ends at MO 86 and the small community of Eagle Rock.

16

The Christmas City

Anderson to Noel, Missouri

General description: A 9-mile drive along the scenic overhanging bluffs of the Elk River to Noel, the Christmas City.

Special attractions: Elk River, Indian Creek Roadside Park, Mt. Shira Stream Access, and Noel; overhanging bluffs, canoeing, swimming, and fall colors.

Location: Western Ozarks. The drive begins at the intersection of U.S. Highway 71 and Missouri Highway 59.

Drive route numbers: Missouri Highway 59.

Travel season: Year-round.

Camping: Private campgrounds are located along the Elk River. Primitive camping is available at Huckleberry Ridge Conservation Area but no services are provided.

Services: All services at Noel. Food and gas at Anderson.

Nearby attractions: Buffalo Hills Natural Area.

 The drive

This part of the Ozarks is known as the Elk River section. The region is a combination of rolling plains and rugged hills that drain into the Elk River. Historically, there were extensive upland hardwood and pine forests with a few prairie openings, which mostly occurred on the broad, rolling plains. Today, there are still large forested areas, but with fire suppression, pine trees and prairie openings are fewer in number. These are two natural communities that depend on fire to keep them healthy and viable; otherwise they lose ground to hardwood forests. Although the Elk River had lost its namesake by the 1830s, there are reports of 30 or more elk roaming the hills near here having escaped from an elk ranch. Much like the Rocky Mountain elk that were released along the Buffalo River in Arkansas, these elk also seem to be adjusting to the Ozarks.

The drive takes place in McDonald County, a county that gained fame in 1961 by declaring itself the McDonald Territory after the county name was left off the official Missouri highway map that year. Although the county officials have since forgotten their anger, and the added publicity they gen-

Drive 16: The Christmas City
Anderson to Noel, Missouri

To Neosho

To (43)

71

Town Hole
Access

F

Anderson

76

To
Cassville

76

71

71

To
Bentonville

59

Indian Creek

N

0   1   2   3
Miles

To (43)

EE

Lanagan

To 71

*Indian Creek
Roadside Park*

EE

*Mt. Shira
Stream Access*

Elk River

*Overhanging
Bluffs*

To 71

TT

*Shadow
Lake*

H

To
Southwest
City

90

Noel

59

90

To 71

To
Siloam
Springs

Butler Creek

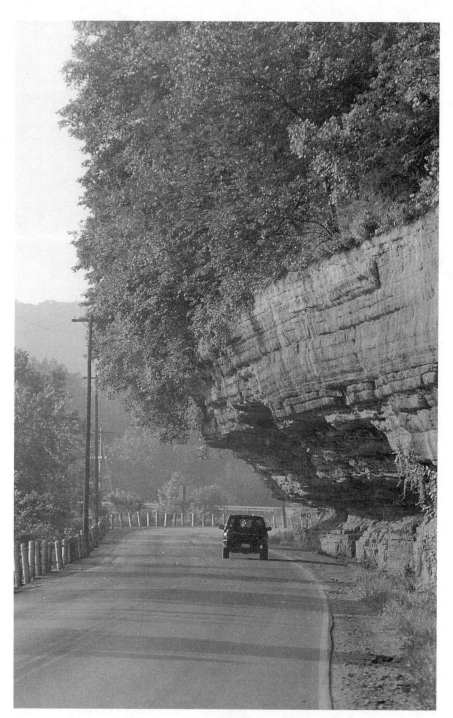

Impressive overhanging cliffs lead to Noel.

erated has declined, the exceptionally scenic overhanging bluffs over the highway endure.

Starting at the intersection of US 71 and MO 59, proceed on MO 59 to **Anderson**. Nestled in the valley of Indian Creek, this small town is a retail and service center for the surrounding farms. Supplies for tourists and outdoor enthusiasts are also an important part of the retail trade. Indian Creek is an excellent fast-flowing run in the spring. The gradient is 8.6 feet per mile with 26 miles of permanent flow. Unlike the Elk River into which it drains, Indian Creek has few developments along the way. Access to Indian Creek is provided at **Town Hole Access**, which is on Main Street in Anderson.

Leaving town, MO 59 follows the Kansas City Southern Railroad, the line that was so instrumental in opening the remote Ouachita Mountains. The road continues down Indian Creek valley to the community of **Lanagan**. Just past Lanagan, the road is forced to take an upland route because the railroad and the creek are already crowded against the bluff, occupying the best route. Once on top of the hill, **Indian Creek Roadside Park** is an interesting stop. Notice the picnic tables made out of huge slabs of limestone rock. They will probably last for thousands of years, making them a permanent fixture of the park.

Proceeding down the hill, the road passes Ginger Blue; though this fishing camp has seen better days, it is one of the oldest in the Ozarks. The restaurant was once known for its excellent cuisine and offered a beautiful view of the Elk River from your dining table.

In less than a mile, turn at the entrance to **Mt. Shira Stream Access**. Since it is the only public access along the drive, this is the best opportunity to get a close-up view of the **Elk River**. The Elk River, along with Big Sugar and Indian creeks, drains much of McDonald County. The Elk flows northwest from Noel and then turns southwest, making its way to Lake of the Cherokees in Oklahoma. With its 22 miles of permanent flow, it is sought out by canoeists and anglers year-round. The best floating is below the mouth of Indian Creek; the scenery is exceptional, with rugged hills, craggy overhanging ledges, and unusually clear water. During the summer season the river receives intensive recreational use. This can be hard on wildlife, because increasing contact with humans causes the animals stress. The fish community in the Elk River section is the most distinctive of the Missouri Ozarks. Unusual fish such as the cardinal shiner, Neosho madtom, Neosho orangethroat darter, and redspot chub are found in this area.

Continue on MO 59, and after 1.5 miles you will be driving under impressive **overhanging bluffs**. Such features are unique to this drive; this craggy limestone bluffline overshadows the highway in dramatic fashion. In the spring and after heavy rains, there is even a small waterfall cascading off the bluff that splatters the windshields of southbound motorists. The overhangs were formed as the Elk River cut into the bluff in the not-too-distant geologic past. The softer, six-foot layer at the base is Chattanooga shale, which is highly erodible. This shale, which is derived from mud, and the massive overlying limestone, which originated from shell fragments, were deposited more than 340 million years ago in a vast sea. Over millions of years, the accumulations of mud and shell fragments were compressed by the weight of additional layers to form rock. Land animals had not yet appeared, but trees, ferns, and other plants were flourishing. In the oceans, primitive fish, sharks, and amphibians were abundant. It is difficult to find a pull-off along here from which to observe the overhangs in more detail, but midway down there is a shoulder wide enough to pull over. Also, just south of the bluffline, there is an area sufficient to park three or four cars.

It is easy to imagine the attraction these shelters held for the early inhabitants of this region. These overhangs and nearby caves were used by Ozark Bluff Dwellers during a period from 500 to 2,500 years ago. A 1922 expedition of archeologists from the Museum of the American Indian in New York found numerous objects in excellent condition, crafted from bone, clay, stone, plants, and feathers. In the 1930s, scientists from the University of Arkansas explored the bluff shelters and found baskets and mats woven of reeds, and also small quantities of acorns and corn that were used for food. To learn more about the life of these early people, visit the commercially-operated Bluff Dweller's Cave and Browning Museum, located two miles south of Noel on MO 59. It offers cave tours and displays of Indian artifacts.

In another mile, the road leads to **Noel**, one of the oldest resort centers in the Midwest. The Elk River in Noel forms Shadow Lake, due to a low-lying dam about 0.5 mile downstream from here. After crossing the Elk River, turn left and you will be approaching a rather spectacular bluff overhang. This setting, especially from the opposite direction, has been the location for many travel brochure photos.

Noel is known as "The Christmas City." Each year the town receives widespread publicity when the post office is deluged with more than a half million Christmas cards to be postmarked with the town's yuletide name. As an added decoration to the "Noel" cancellation, a tiny Christmas tree is stamped in green ink on every piece of mail by volunteers. To receive this special postmark, package up your Christmas cards and mail them to Postmaster, Noel, MO 64854. Children who send their Christmas letter to "Santa Claus," Noel, MO 64854, along with a self-addressed, stamped envelope, will receive a personal message from Old Santa himself.

17

Two Mountains

Mountain Home to Mountain View, Arkansas

General description: A 59-mile drive starting at Mountain Home, traveling south to the scenic river hills of the White River, and ending at Mountain View.

Special attractions: Blanchard Springs Caverns, Ozark Folk Center State Park, Norfork National Fish Hatchery, Norfork Lake, North Fork and White rivers, and Ozark National Forest; scenic views, hiking, canoeing, swimming, fishing (including trout), hunting, cave tour, camping, and horseback riding.

Location: Southeastern Ozarks. The drive begins on Arkansas Highway 5 in Mountain Home and heads south.

Drive route numbers: Arkansas Highways 5, 9, 14, and 177.

Camping: Norfork Lake and Bull Shoals Lake have several modern camping sites. The Sylamore Ranger District of the Ozark National Forest has campsites at the Blanchard Springs (32 sites), Gunner Pool (27 sites), and Barkshed (5 sites) recreation areas.

Services: All services found in Mountain Home, Mountain View, and Calico Rock. Food and gas at Norfork.

Nearby attractions: Bull Shoals Lake, Buffalo National River, and Leatherwood and Lower Buffalo wilderness areas.

 The drive

This area of the eastern Arkansas Ozarks has a lower elevation than its western counterpart. The White River and its tributaries have been carving into this region of the Ozark uplift for more than 100 million years, exposing prominent dolomite cliffs, sandstone outcrops, rugged wooded hills, and canyonlike valleys.

The drive begins at **Mountain Home**, one of the fastest growing communities in northern Arkansas. Most of this growth has been stimulated by tourism and recreation developments associated with Norfolk and Bull Shoals lakes. The town was first called Rapp's Barren for 1839 settler "Rapp" Talburt, who settled in an area barren of trees. Another early settler, Colonel Orrin L. Dodd, came into the area in the early 1850s and developed a plantation along the White River. Accompanied by his slaves, Dodd traveled back and

Drive 17: Two Mountains

Mountain Home to Mountain View, Arkansas

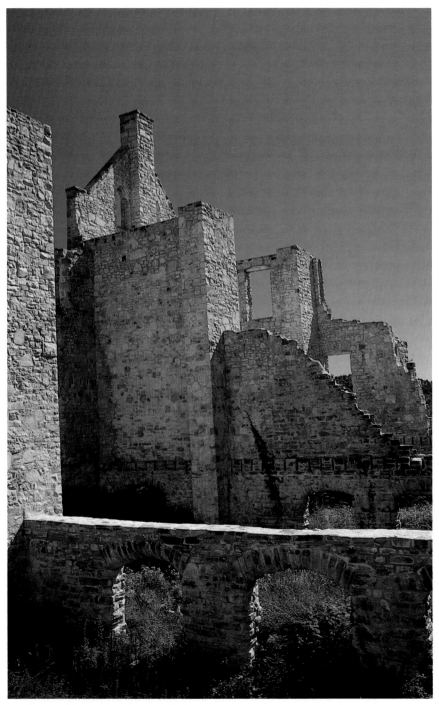

Castle ruins at Ha Ha Tonka State Park, Drive 8

Top: Greer Spring, Drive 11
Bottom: Alley Spring and mill, Drive 9

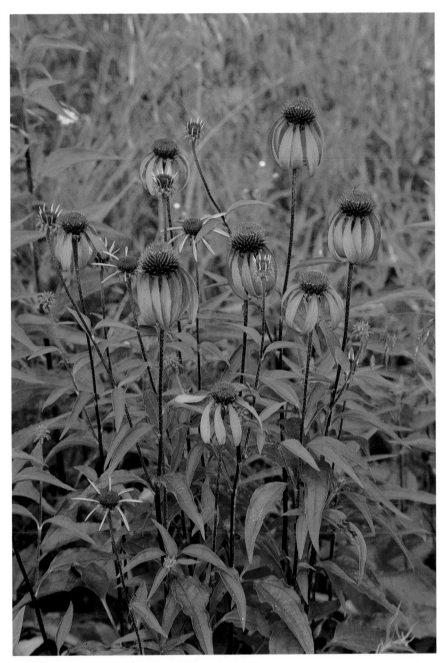

Purple coneflowers in summer, Drives 9, 11, and 18

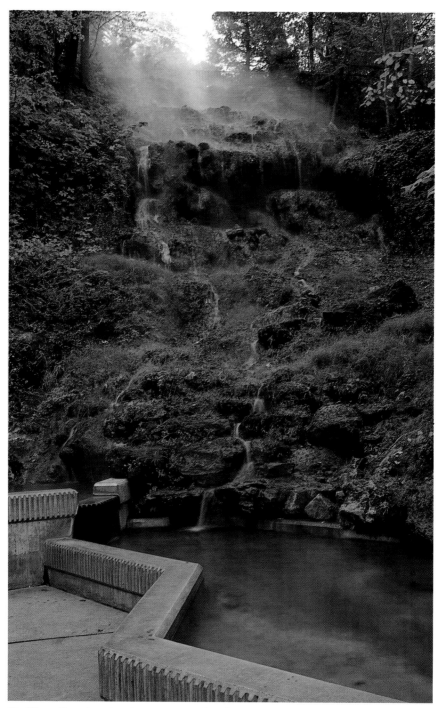

Hot Water Cascade at Hot Springs National Park, Drive 25

Top: A working water mill at College of the Ozarks, Drive 13
Bottom: Morning fog in Current River hills, Drive 9

Fall colors of sassafras and flowering dogwood at Trail of Tears State Park, Drive 1

Top: *Snow geese can be seen wintering at Holla Bend National Wildlife Refuge, Drive 22*
Bottom: *Spring flowering bloodroot grows in rich, wooded valleys, Drives 1, 5, and 18*

Top: Fog shrouds a gnarly, white oak and lichen covered rocks, Drive 28
Bottom: American alligators occur as far north as the Arkansas River, Drive 22

forth from his Augusta, Arkansas, home in the Mississippi River bottoms to his place at Rapp's Barren. Along the journey, Dodd's slaves talked about returning to their "mountain home." When the post office was established in 1857, its name was officially listed as Mountain Home. The town was incorporated as the county seat in 1888.

Leaving Mountain Home, head south on AR 5 for 11 miles and turn east onto AR 177 at the small town of Salesville. Proceed 2 miles to the **Norfork National Fish Hatchery**, which is below Norfork Dam. The federal hatchery, one of the largest of its kind east of the Rockies, was established in 1957 to produce trout for restocking the cold tailwaters below Norfork, Bull Shoals, and other dams. The water in these reservoirs is over 100 feet deep at the dam and the lower depths average between 44 and 56 degrees Fahrenheit. This temperature is ideal for raising trout. The hatchery supplies more than 1.5 million trout of catchable size annually. Dry Run Creek, which runs just outside the fenced-in area of the hatchery grounds is the site of a catch-and-release program for properly licensed disabled individuals and those under sixteen years of age. A wheelchair-accessible ramp, paved walk, and picnic tables are located in this area. Hatchery hours are from 7:00 a.m. to 3:30 p.m. daily and tours are available.

Follow the road signs to **Norfork Lake**; the road offers overlooks of the lake and the dam that was completed in 1944 to hold back the North Fork River. Built for flood control and the generation of hydroelectric power, the project provided jobs and boosted the economy of a region that was still reeling from the depression. Recreational opportunities on the 22,000-acre lake include fishing, boating, skiing, swimming, and wildlife viewing. Below the dam, the North Fork River courses through wooded hills for 4 miles before joining the White River at the town of Norfork. Along this stretch, rainbow trout in the 15-pound class can be caught.

Return to AR 5 and continue south for 2 miles to **Norfork**. One of the oldest settlements in Arkansas, the town was founded at the junction of the North Fork and White rivers during the riverboat days. Because of the shoals and rapids where the two rivers joined, only flat-bottomed boats could navigate beyond that point. Although steamboats could later ascend the White River to Forsyth, Missouri, Norfolk remained the normal unloading point. From here, loads of salt and other goods were freighted over the "Old Salt Road," which led northwest along the White River to Branson, and then north to Springfield. In Norfork, the Wolf House, which was built in 1809, is worth a visit. Guided tours, given seven days a week in May through October, reveal more than four hundred antiques and items of historical interest.

Leaving Norfork, the road climbs steeply and offers dramatic views of the surrounding hills and river valley, which is often shrouded with morning fog. Continue on AR 5 about 12 miles to the town of **Calico Rock**. Many

Anglers try their luck fishing for trout in Blanchard Springs Caverns' Mirror Lake

of the buildings here are built into the hill above the White River, making for a picturesque setting. Like many other points along the river, Calico Rock was named by boatmen prior to any settlement. They often referred to the "calico rock" landmark well before the town was established on the bluff. At one time, multihued mineral stains on the bluff's sandstone face looked similar to calico, the multicolored fabric used to make dresses and shirts. Unfortunately, the original face of the bluff was blasted away to make room for a railroad bed. Centuries from now, with the continual leaching of minerals onto the face of the bluff, the calico effect will probably once again be evident.

Calico Rock affords good views of the **White River**. This stretch of the White River below Bull Shoals Lake is almost always floatable due to daily power generation and has become one of the most famous trout streams in the world. This is one of the positive aspects of the many impoundments upstream from this point. The most powerful and destructive miles of the White are now impeded by a chain of dams forming lakes Beaver, Table Rock, Taneycomo, and Bull Shoals. Flood control and recreation benefited, whereas Ozark plants and animals and their habitats along the river were eliminated.

Although the river's straight-line distance from its source near Boston (in northwest Arkansas) to where it empties into the Mississippi River is

225 miles, its natural meandering causes the water to travel more than 800 miles to complete the same journey. The White River was named by the early French explorers in the 1730s, who called the river *La Riviere au Blanc* referring to the foaming whitewater shoals that, prior to impoundment, were common along the river.

After crossing the White River, AR 5 enters the Sylamore Ranger District of the **Ozark National Forest**. The next 26.5 miles to Blanchard Springs Caverns is designated as a National Forest Scenic Byway. For this national program, the Forest Service has selected exceptional stretches of highways across the nation that offer scenic drives and recreational opportunities on Forest Service land. The Sylamore Scenic Byway, from Calico Rock to Blanchard Springs Caverns, has such a designation. The 175,000 acres in the Sylamore Ranger District offer several recreational opportunities, including an 89-mile trail for horseback riding, hiking, and mountain biking. Most of the trail is located on maintained forest roads. Maps and descriptions of the four horse trails are available at the Blanchard Springs Caverns Visitors Center and at the Sylamore District Office in Mountain View.

After 16 miles, the road crosses over Sylamore Creek just before the creek enters the White River. Turn right onto AR 14 in Allison and begin a steep, 6-mile climb to the **Blanchard Springs Caverns** entrance. Note that the dolomite and sandstone outcroppings seen from Mountain Home to Calico Rock have changed to chert and limestone rock. The latter bedrock is more recent in geologic history and thus higher in elevation. Also, notice more pine trees along this drive; they favor the acidic, cherty soils. Below the chert, the permeable limestone bedrock harbors caves, springs, and openings to sinkholes, and hence the formation of Blanchard Springs Caverns.

For a general orientation to the area, be sure to stop at the visitors center. Follow the road signs off of AR 14 leading down a steep hill to the visitor's center on the right. A guided tour of the caverns and two trails are available. The Dripstone Trail is wheelchair-accessible and no more than 0.7 mile long. However, inclines are steep, and strong assistants are needed to control wheelchairs. The trail passes through two huge rooms filled with an incredible abundance of crystalline cave formations including sparkling flowstone, towering columns, and delicate stalactites. The Discovery Trail follows the path of the first explorers through water-carved passages, under the natural entrance, and along the cave stream. The longer, more strenuous tour is 1.2 miles long, with nearly 700 stairsteps. Do not take this trail if you have walking, heart, or breathing difficulties. The Discovery Trail is open from Memorial Day weekend through Labor Day.

The visitors center also has a bookstore, interesting exhibits, and information on other activities on the recreation area. For hiking, be sure to ask about the North Sylamore Creek Trail. The trail is 15 miles long and can be accessed at Barkshead, Gunner Pool, and Blanchard Springs campgrounds,

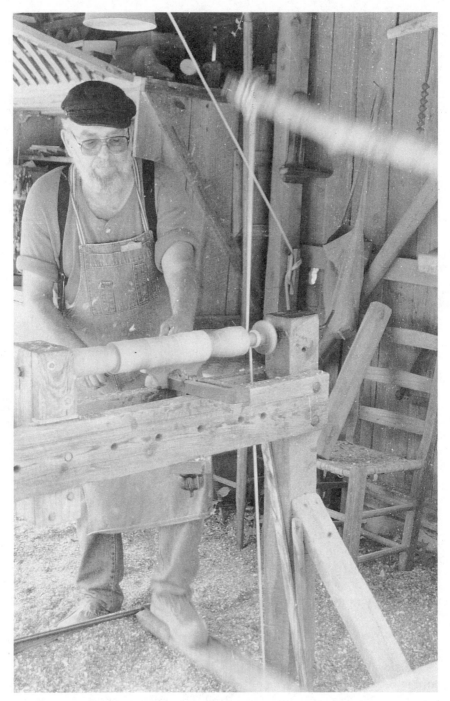

A craftsman at The Ozark Folk Center carves a wooden chair leg.

and at the main trailhead, off AR 14 near Allison. This is one of the most scenic backpacking or day-hiking trails in Arkansas. It follows North Sylamore Creek, a crystal-clear, spring-fed stretch of water winding past impressive limestone bluffs and large trees. Canoeing is possible on this proposed Wild and Scenic River, but only when most other streams are in flood.

Before leaving the recreation area, follow the road to Blanchard Springs, passing by Mirror Lake, a trout-fishing area built by the Civilian Conservation Corps. Proceed to a parking area and walk the short, level trail to a deck overlooking Blanchard Springs. The spring tumbles out of an opening in the limestone wall. Here, in 1971, scuba divers entered to explore the watercourse all the way to the natural cave entrance, which is a large sinkhole half a mile up and on the other side of the mountain, some 4,000 feet away from the spring outlet.

Return to AR 5 and head south 6 miles to the entrance road to **Ozark Folk Center State Park**. The center is a unique facility that works to preserve the heritage and way of life of the Ozark mountain people. Over twenty pioneer skills and crafts are demonstrated to a background of live mountain music. A gift shop, restaurant, and lodging are also available. The season extends from May through October.

Nearby, the town of **Mountain View** is appropriately named for the precipitous bluffs hovering over it 2 miles to the south. The "view" is of the Boston Mountains, the highest and most dramatic part of the Ozarks, which extend westward into Oklahoma. Mountain View offers a variety of activities, primarily around the courthouse square. Weekend afternoons and evenings offer jam sessions by folks who bring both instruments and lawn chairs to hear or make music, dance, and visit. The nearby shops sell antiques, crafts, musical instruments, iron-forged products, and flour from a working mill. A scenic hiking trail, far removed from the busy highway, leads from the city park (north of the square) to the Ozark Folk Center.

18

Scenic 7 Byway North
Harrison to Russellville, Arkansas

General description: An 84-mile drive from Harrison south to Russellville through the picturesque Boston Mountains.

Special attractions: Buffalo National River, Pruitt River Access, Koen Interpretive Trail, Mystic Caverns, Scenic 7 Byway, Alum Cove Natural Bridge, Pedestal Rocks and Long Pool recreation areas, Buffalo River Trail, Ozark Highlands Trails, and Arkansas Grand Canyon; scenic views, fall colors, hiking, horseback riding, canoeing, camping, fishing, hunting, and swimming.

Location: Southern Ozarks. The drive begins on Arkansas Highway 7 at Harrison.

Drive route numbers: Arkansas Highways 7 and 16 and Forest Roads 1206, 1801, 1804, and 1838.

Camping: Ozark, Erbie, and Hasty offer camping on the Buffalo National River. Long Pool, Haw Creek Falls, Richland Creek, and Fairview recreation areas provide camping in the Ozark National Forest.

Services: All services at Harrison, Jasper, and Russellville.

Nearby attractions: Hurricane Creek and Richland Creek wilderness areas, and Haw Creek Falls, Sam's Throne, Twin Falls, and Dismal Hollow recreation areas (in the Ozark National Forest); and Lost Valley, Steel Creek, Kyles Landing, and Tyler Bend Visitor Center (on the Buffalo National River).

 The drive

On April 5, 1994, Arkansas's first National Scenic Byway was dedicated at a ceremony in Russellville. Called the Scenic 7 Byway, AR 7 has long enjoyed a reputation as one of the nation's most scenic drives. Meandering from its origin at Bull Shoals Lake near Diamond City, through the Ozark Mountains to the spa city of Hot Springs and the pine forests of the Ouachitas, the attractions along the highway are as varied as the scenic views. Because of this, the 153 miles of the byway are divided into two separate drives; the first begins at Harrison, which is considered the best place to start. For information on **Harrison**, refer to Drive 19.

Drive 18: Scenic 7 Byway North

Harrison to Russellville, Arkansas (north)

To Branson

To Diamond City

412
62
65
7

To 62
372

Harrison

To Ponca
43

62
65

To 43
206
206
To 65

Mystic Caverns

Dogpatch
Mill Creek

Harp Creek

O Z A R K
N. F.
Buffalo River

Pruitt Ranger Station
Buffalo River Trail

Pruitt River Access

Koen Interpretive Trail

To Ponca
74

Jasper
74

Roundtop Mountain

To Vendor

Little Buffalo River

Buffalo National River

374
To Mount Judea

Arkansas Grand Canyon

N

0 2 4 6 8 10
Miles

O Z A R K
N A T I O N A L   F O R E S T

1206
7

Alum Cove Natural Bridge Recreation Area

Deer
Cowell
To Mount Judea

To 21
16

123
Ozark Highlands Trail

Lurton

Fairview Recreation Area

Drive 18: Scenic 7 Byway North
Harrison to Russellville, Arkansas (south)

Lurton

Fairview Recreation Area

1838

123   16   To Ben Hur

To Hagarville   Pelsor

Pedestal Rocks Recreation Area

7

Rotary Ann Recreation Area

Big Piney Creek

Moccasin Gap Horse Trail

1805

Long Pool Recreation Area

1801

1804

To 21

OZARK NATIONAL FOREST

164

Pleasant Valley

To Scottsville
27

To Augsburg   333

164   To Moreland

Dover

Illinois Bayou

7

To Fort Smith

40

To Conway

Lake Dardanelle

Russellville

Arkansas River

To Hot Springs

Begin the drive on AR 7 on the south side of Harrison. The road travels across the Springfield Plateau from Harrison to Jasper. The broad valleys and low hills were once covered by prairie and grassy woodlands that have been converted to pastures, row crops, and forest. Thanks to the efforts of the Arkansas Natural Heritage Commission, a prairie remnant on the west side of Harrison is now protected. Future generations will be able to see and learn about what the region was once like. See Drive 19 for directions to Baker Prairie.

Located about 8 miles south of Harrison, **Mystic Caverns** offers a commercial tour of two caves at one location. First discovered in 1968, the caves were opened for public viewing in 1982. The caves have been gradually carved out of limestone, which is the principle bedrock of the Springfield Plateau. Interesting features include calcium deposits of soda straws, flowstone, rimstone, an eight-story crystal dome, and large underground chambers. The tour is available beginning at 9 a.m., daily, from March through November.

Continuing on AR 7, you will notice the recently closed theme park called Dogpatch, U.S.A. Conceived in 1967 by Harrison businessmen, the 825-acre tract was built around Al Capp's comic strip "Li'l Abner." Although Dogpatch was a popular attraction at one time, the meteoric rise of Branson as a major tourist stop undoubtedly took its toll on the theme park, together with unsuccessful business investments. On the west side of the highway, just past the entrance to Dogpatch, a historical marker commemorates the Arkansas marble that was taken from this site in 1836, which was used to help build the Washington Monument in Washington, D.C.

After another 5 miles, you cross the **Buffalo River**. Just beyond the bridge, turn right and park at the **Pruitt Ranger Station**. Information is available on naturalist programs, places to hike and camp, and river floating opportunities. Walk the path that leads to the Buffalo River for a good view of the river with its pools, riffles, and gravel bars against a backdrop of a cedar-covered dolomite cliff. Notice the cedar trees with the old man's beard lichen hanging from the branches. From a distance, this lichen closely resembles Spanish moss, which is commonly found in the more warm and humid southern states.

The Pruitt Ranger Station picnic area is the trailhead for the **Buffalo River Trail**. The 25.5 mile one-way trail to Ponca Access traverses the scenic Buffalo National River hills and valleys. Several access points along the way allow for shorter hikes. Information on trail conditions and hiking opportunities, including shorter hikes, is available at the ranger station.

A shorter trail can be reached by heading north on AR 7, crossing over the Buffalo River, and turning right at the entrance to the **Pruitt River Access**. Follow the road to the parking lot where the 2.2 mile **Mill Creek Trail** begins. A relatively easy walk along Mill Creek valley leads past old homesites, a cemetery with headstones dating back to the 1860s, and opportunities to see wildlife along a bottomland hardwood forest. An interpretive map can be obtained either at the Pruit Ranger Station or the superintendent's office in Harrison.

Drive another 2.5 miles on AR 7 to the Erbie Access road, on the right. Follow the gravel road 0.3 mile and turn right, following the signs to the **Koen Interpretive Trail**. This trail is part of the Ozark National Forest's Henry R. Koen Experimental Forest. The experimental forest was established in 1950 to develop scientific principles for forest management and to define and evaluate land management concerns in the Forest Service's Southern Region. Henry R. Koen is known as "The Father of Forestry" in the Arkansas Ozarks. Once the forest supervisor of the Ozark National Forest, his active conservation career spanned four decades in the first half of this century. The Koen Interpretive Trail provides an opportunity to see and identify more than 40 native and non-native trees and shrubs planted along the 0.5-mile, wheelchair-accessible trail.

Return to AR 7 and proceed south to **Jasper**. Just before Jasper and on the right, the Visitor Information Center of the Buffalo Ranger Station, Ozark National Forest, can supply you with maps, books, and specific information on activities in the forest. Jasper lies in a cove at the base of the Boston Mountains escarpment to the south. Jasper is the county seat of Newton

Arkansas Highway 7 is rated as one of the top ten scenic byways in the nation.

Fascinating sandstone rock formations await hikers visiting Pedestal Rocks Recreation Area.

County, the only county in Arkansas that has never had a single mile of railroad track. Because of its rugged topography, Newton County supports a tremendous diversity of plants and animals. With more than half of its total area devoted to public lands, this mountainous area is renowned for being the home to more than 1,500 species of plants, 65 species of mammals, 79 species of amphibians and reptiles, 90 species of fish, and 190 species of birds.

The Jasper/Newton County Chamber of Commerce is very active in promoting and supporting festivals and events; write for their directory to help plan your trip. Also, the Newton County Resource Council sponsors the development of ecotourism as a means of improving the local economy. Guided tours include such activities as photography, birding, nature hikes, genealogy, and visits to historic sites. For more information on how to contact these organizations, consult the appendix.

Leave Jasper and begin a long, steady climb up Roundtop Mountain, which is the beginning of the Boston Mountains. A side trip on AR 374 offers great scenic views as the road descends Judea Mountain. This drive is especially rewarding in October, when the leaves turn their fall colors. Returning to AR 7, the next stop is Cliff House Inn and a view of the **Arkansas Grand Canyon**. A remarkably steep drop of more than six hundred feet and an expansive view of several miles across Big Creek valley give this site its reputation. The quaint restaurant is especially known for its desserts and biscuits.

Within a couple of miles, two scenic overlooks offer more views of Big Creek valley. The first pullout provides picnic tables and, in addition to a nice view, the second pullout shows interesting layering of sandstone and shale in the roadcut. This rock dates back to a time before the Ozark Mountains were uplifted, to the Pennsylvanian Period over 300 million years ago. This was when great coal-forming swamps flourished and reptiles began to appear. Dinosaurs would not evolve for another 70 million years.

Continue south, and after about 5 miles, notice the Ozark National Forest **Scenic 7 Byway** sign. The next 36.3 miles has been designated by the Forest Service as part of the national system of National Forest Scenic Byways.

The next stop is the **Alum Cove Natural Bridge Recreation Area**. Turn right onto AR 16, which is 14 miles south of Jasper. Proceed west for about a mile and turn right onto FR 1206 for 3 miles to the entrance road to the recreation area. Picnic tables and a restroom are provided, but no overnight camping is allowed. The 1.1-mile round-trip trail leads to the natural bridge and other points of interest along the bluff line, including a wet weather waterfall. The natural bridge is 130 feet long and 20 feet wide. The formation is actually a natural arch that was carved from the rock bluff when a fracture was gradually widened by the forces of wind, rain, and ice. Natural bridges are formed from the erosive force of water cutting through cracks in the rock's interior and usually have streams flowing through the opening.

The forest is rich with spring wildflowers growing under stately American beech trees spread out over the canopy. The rare umbrella magnolia can be observed along the trail, especially at the natural bridge. Look for whorls of large leaves up to eighteen inches long and eight inches wide clustered at the ends of branches. Wild azaleas bloom in mid-to-late April at about midslope on the trail.

Return to AR 7 and proceed 12 miles to the **Fairview Recreation Area**. Along with providing 11 campsites, the campground is the crossing for the **Ozark Highlands Trail**, rated one of the top ten trails in the United States. The 160-mile national recreation trail follows a scenic east-west route. A portion of the trail can be hiked for five miles west of here to the Hurricane Creek Wilderness Area, or for about 17 miles east through Richland Creek Wilderness Area to the Richland Creek Campground.

Continue on AR 7 to Pelsor and the intersection with AR 16 east. A side trip down AR 16 east for a little over 5 miles leads to FR 1838 and **Pedestal Rocks Recreation Area**. The newly established trails offer two loops to some unique sandstone bluff formations. Because there are bluffs, care should be taken with small children. The left trail loop passes scenic overlooks and large sandstone pedestals that stand apart from the bluff line. The right loop trail comes out on the top of Kings Bluff and offers a good view of a wet-weather waterfall nearly one hundred feet high. A total of 4.3 miles of trail are available if you hike both loops.

Back on AR 7, the road crosses Piney Creek Wildlife Management Area, home to deer, turkeys, black bears and ruffed grouse. The next pullout is the **Rotary Ann Recreation Area**, which offers a great view of Indian Creek valley and the surrounding mountains. Picnic tables and a restroom are provided.

Continuing on AR 7, the road passes **Moccasin Gap Horse Trail**, a series of loops totaling 28 miles through Forest Service land. A horse camp with seventeen graveled parking spurs, pit toilets, and well water for horses is also provided. A map and more information are available from the Bayou Ranger District.

Proceed 2 miles for a side trip to the **Long Pool Recreation Area**. Follow FR 1801 and 1804 to the recreation area on Big Piney Creek. Long Pool offers picnicking, a swimming beach, canoe access, restrooms, and nineteen campsites. **Big Piney Creek** received congressional designation in 1992 as a National Scenic River. Considered one of the most popular bait-fishing and swimming streams in Arkansas, the 67-mile Big Piney Creek National Scenic River is also a popular float stream. One of the more challenging streams in Arkansas, the paddler can experience rapids up to class III in difficulty. An interpretive sign at the river explains what to expect based on the current water level. (The recreation area can also be reached by following signs for 8 miles starting on AR 164.)

Return to AR 7 and begin the long descent out of the Boston Mountains of the Ozarks to the Arkansas River valley, which is considered a subsection of the Ouachita Mountains. After 10 miles, the road crosses the Illinois Bayou. "Bayou" is a deceptive name, since it is a whitewater stream for most of its length as it courses through the Boston Mountains. The stream becomes slow and silt-laden as it flattens out in the Arkansas Valley, eventually emptying into the backwaters of Lake Dardenelle.

Continue on to **Russellville**. For information on Russellville and the Arkansas River valley of the Ouachita Mountains, see Drive 23.

19

Buffalo Hills

Harrison to Jasper, Arkansas

General description: A 39-mile drive starting at Harrison, heading southwest into the rugged Buffalo River hills, and ending at Jasper.

Special attractions: Baker Prairie, Gaither Mountain, Boxley Valley, Buffalo River, Lost Valley, Buffalo River Trail, Ponca Access, Steel Creek, Kyles Landing, and Ponca Wilderness Area; scenic views, hiking, canoeing, camping, fishing, and hunting.

Location: Southern Ozarks. The drive begins on Arkansas Highway 43 on the south side of Harrison and heads southwest.

Drive route numbers: Arkansas Highways 43 and 74.

Camping: Lost Valley, Steel Creek, and Kyles Landing offer camping on the Buffalo National River.

Services: All services at Harrison and Jasper. Food at Ponca.

Nearby attractions: Alum Cove Natural Bridge, Arkansas Grand Canyon, Boxley Historic District, Ozark National Forest, Tyler Bend Visitor Center, Upper Buffalo Wilderness Area, Scenic 7 Byway North, and Ozark Highlands Scenic Drive.

The drive

The rugged hills of the Buffalo River offer scenic views and places to hike along the northern edge of the Ozarks' Boston Mountains. Of the four scenic drives in the Boston Mountains, this drive offers the most dramatic transition from one major landform to another. The drive starts on the southern edge of the Springfield Plateau, with elevations varying from 500 to 1,500 feet. The bedrock is primarily limestone. The road then climbs onto the northern edge of the Boston Mountains, with a pronounced elevation ranging from 1,500 to 2,300 feet. Composed of sandstone and shale, much of the area is very rugged, with several sections reaching more than 1,000 feet in local relief. Relatively level land is confined to the valleys and to the mountaintops, which are remnants of the old plateau surface.

The drive starts in **Harrison,** a town that was named for surveyor M. L. Harrison. He laid out the town in 1870 and, in lieu of payment, the town was named for him. A map and a self-guided walking tour of downtown

Drive 19: Buffalo Hills

Harrison to Jasper, Arkansas

Harrison leads to twelve historic buildings, some more than one hundred years old. The tour begins at the Boone County Courthouse, which is located on Main Street and Stephenson Avenue. The tour map is available at the courthouse or from the Boone County Heritage Museum at the corner of Central and Cherry Streets. Five miles north of Harrison on US 65, the Harrison Tourist Information Center is operated by the Arkansas Department of Parks and Tourism. This is a nice rest stop with picnic facilities. Numerous brochures of attractions throughout the state are available and the friendly staff will provide routing assistance. The facility is open year-round.

AR 43 begins on the south side of Harrison. Proceed west 2 miles onto AR 43 and turn right onto AR 397. Then travel 1 mile and turn right on AR 392. After slightly less than a mile, turn left onto Goblin Drive and, after 0.5 mile, look for Harrison High School on the right (east) side of the road. Park in the lower parking lot (north) and walk downslope and onto **Baker Prairie**, which is located on both sides of the road. Designated in 1992, Baker Prairie is a state natural area owned by the Arkansas Natural Heritage Commission. This 71-acre tallgrass prairie is a remnant of a much larger prairie, that once covered much of Boone County. A variety of prairie grasses and wildflowers (called forbs) are on display throughout the growing season, with different flowers coming into bloom about every two weeks. Take time to explore the prairie and examine the diverse array of plants and animals. Because of its location within Harrison, this prairie offers an excellent opportunity for environmental education. Return to AR 43 by taking Goblin Drive and turning right onto AR 392, then left onto AR 397, and finally, turn right onto AR 43.

As you head west, notice the prominent outcrop known as **Gaither Mountain**. After 3 miles, the road steeply ascends the eastern flank of the mountain. Notice the bands of shale and sandstone, characteristic of the Boston Mountains. A pull off on the left offers a great view of Harrison Valley, which was once covered with prairie and grazing bison. The town of Harrison is to the left, just out of sight.

Continue another 9 miles, driving through the small community of **Compton**. This region has been getting considerable attention since July, 1992, when a United States Department of Agriculture employee found a male gypsy moth in a trap just west of Compton. This was the first recorded outbreak of gypsy moths in Arkansas. The gypsy moth is one of the most notorious pests of hardwood trees in the eastern United States. Since 1980, the gypsy moth has defoliated close to a million or more forested acres each year. Trees that are defoliated two to three years in a row weaken and often die. The gypsy moth is not a native insect. It was introduced into the United States in 1869 by a French scientist living in Massachusetts, who was interested in developing a disease-resistant silkworm. Since then, the moth has

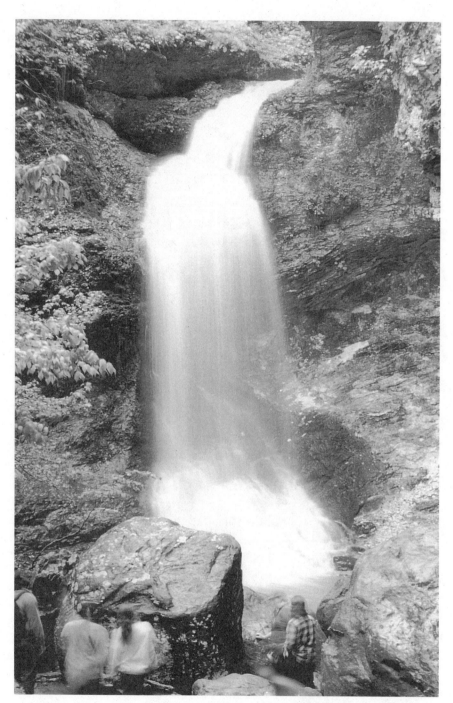

A short trail at Lost Valley leads to Eden Falls, which comprises a series of four falls ending at this forty-foot drop into a plunge pool.

Dolomite cliffs tower above the tree-shrouded Buffalo River at Steel Creek Campground.

spread throughout the Northeast and, more recently, into Utah, Oregon, Washington, and California.

After the initial discovery of a male gypsy moth, a visual survey of the Compton area revealed an active breeding population producing an estimated 10,000 gypsy moth egg masses per acre. This 25-acre core area was well established and probably dated back to an introduction in the mid-1980s. In 1993, additional trapping revealed male moths over a 200-square-mile area. Treatment with an insect growth regulator and a biological insecticide is being used to control the spread of this major threat to the Ozark forest.

About 3 miles past Compton, AR 43 skirts the 11,300-acre **Ponca Wilderness Area** at the Center Point Trailhead, located 3.5 miles north of Ponca. This is one of three wilderness areas on the Buffalo National River. All have developed trails for hiking or horseback riding. No motorized vehicles are allowed. Maps and trail information are available at the Buffalo National River superintendent's office in Harrison or at the Pruitt Ranger Station, 8 miles north of Jasper on AR 7.

Follow AR 43's steep descent into the Buffalo River valley to the community of **Ponca**. Sharing the narrow valley with the river, the village of Ponca is now a collection of canoe outfitters and lodges serving visitors to the Buffalo National River.

South of Ponca is the "Big Buffalo Valley," also sometimes referred to as **Boxley Valley**. The valley is a distinctive cultural landscape, and as such, it was included in the National Register of Historic Places in 1987. More than two hundred structures of historical significance—houses, barns, a gristmill, and a community building—are "fine examples of regional vernacular architecture." Many date from the last century. Just past the intersection of AR 43 and AR 74 and on the right, the pre-Civil War log house of Beaver Jim Villines stands. Interpretive signs provide the history of this renowned trapper.

Just beyond Villines's cabin, follow the signs to **Lost Valley**, a National Park Service campground. In the campground, a 3.5-mile round-trip trail passes waterfalls, Clark Creek, cliffs, a large sandstone bluff shelter, and a natural bridge. The trail deadends at a cave that can be accessed (with a flashlight) for 200 feet. The cave ends in a large room with a 35-foot waterfall. Plan on spending two or three hours hiking the trail. The first mile is level and easy hiking, then the trail climbs steeply to the cave. It is a special trail that offers a variety of features and is well worth the visit.

Return to AR 43 and head north to Ponca. Just before the junction of AR 43 and AR 74, a road on the right leads to **Ponca Access**. Watch for elk in a field to the right of the gravel road. This access is a popular starting point for those canoeing the **Buffalo River**. It also offers a good view of the upper reaches of the river. The Buffalo River, which is about 150 miles long, flows entirely in Arkansas from its origins near Fallsville in the Boston Mountains to its confluence with the White River near Buffalo City. Here, at its upper reaches, the river courses through steep drops, hairpin turns, and swift chutes. Averaging a drop of ten feet per mile, this stretch of the Buffalo River is primarily a springtime float. Below Pruitt, the lower stretch of the river drops three feet per mile and can be floated year-round. The Buffalo River, named for the buffalo (or bison) that roamed this area prior to 1820, is one of the few unchannelized and dam-free streams in the Ozarks. After several years of threats to contain its flow, in 1972, the river won enough public support to convince the government to authorize the creation of the Buffalo National River. Because of its protected status and its natural beauty, it is considered one of the most popular rivers in the United States.

Just across the low-water bridge, and on the other side of the Buffalo River, the **Buffalo River Trail** begins. This 25.5-mile one-way trail now goes to Pruitt but will eventually run most of the length of the Buffalo National River. Plans call for the trail to someday connect with the Ozark Trail and go across Missouri all the way to St. Louis. When all the trails in the two states are completed, there will be more than 1,000 miles in one connected trail system. Information on the Ponca-to-Pruitt trail can be obtained from the Buffalo National River office or from Tim Ernst's hiking books, listed at the back of this book. When hiking this trail, it is not recommended that you leave vehicles at the trailhead overnight—rising floodwaters have been known to sweep them away. It is safer to park in Ponca.

Return to AR 43 and turn right onto AR 74. Drive with caution: this 14-mile stretch to Jasper is narrow and winding. After 1.3 miles a road to the left leads to **Steel Creek**, a campground and access to the Buffalo River and the Buffalo River Trail. The steep and winding gravel road to the river valley is worth the effort to see the grand, towering cliffs carved by the river. (Because of the narrow and sometimes steep descent, motorhomes and travel trailers should not try this road.) Elk can sometimes be seen in the open valley that parallels the river. The eastern elk, a subspecies that lived along the Buffalo River, was overhunted, and by 1840 became extinct in Arkansas. Between 1981 and 1985, a total of 112 Rocky Mountain elk were stocked at five release sites in Newton County by the Arkansas Game and Fish Commission. There are 300 to 350 elk presently living in or adjacent to the Buffalo National River corridor.

The campgrounds at Steel Creek and Kyles Landing can be extremely crowded during spring weekends due to those floating the river at this optimal time of the year. Both campgrounds provide pit toilets, fire pits, and water. **Kyles Landing** can be reached by returning to AR 74 and driving 7.4 miles to the gravel road entrance on the left. The 3-mile drive is slow-going, becoming very steep as it descends into the river valley. (Motor homes and travel trailers should not try this road.) About a mile down the gravel road, bear left at a fork in the road. (The road to the right leads to a Boy Scout camp.) Although not as dramatic as the road to Steel Creek, this road does offer another view of the Buffalo River valley.

Returning to AR 74, continue another 4.5 miles to **Jasper** and the end of the drive. For information on Jasper, refer to Scenic Drive 18, Harrison to Russellville.

20

Ozark Highlands
Eureka Springs to Clarksville, Arkansas

General description: A 95-mile drive beginning at historic Eureka Springs, crossing the Boston Mountains, and ending at Clarksville.
Special attractions: Kings River, Eureka Springs, Boxley Valley, Upper Buffalo Wilderness, Buffalo National River, Ozark Highlands Scenic Byway, Ozark Highlands Trail, and Ozark National Forest; fall colors, scenic views, hiking, canoeing, fishing, hunting, and camping.
Location: Southern Ozarks. The drive begins in Eureka Springs on U.S. Highway 62 to Berryville and south on Arkansas Highway 21.
Drive route numbers: U.S. Highway 62 and Arkansas Highway 21.
Camping: Lost Valley, Buffalo National River; Ozone Recreation Area, Ozark National Forest; Spadra Park, Lake Dardanelle.
Services: All services at Eureka Springs, Berryville, and Clarksville. Gas and food at Boxley, Fallsville, and Ozone.
Nearby attractions: Beaver Lake; Lost Valley; Alum Cove and Haw Creek Falls recreation areas; Lake Dardanelle; and Mount Magazine, Buffalo Hills, and Pig Trail scenic drives.

The drive

The northern part of the drive is in a region underlain by limestones and dolomites. For over hundreds of thousands of years, water seeping into cracks in the bedrock dissolved minerals in the rock, creating caves, sinkholes, and springs. This type of region is named "karst," after a similar area in the former Yugoslavia near the Adriatic Sea. The Ozarks are one of the best-known of karst regions worldwide, with over 7,000 caves. Leaving the karst region, AR 21 just beyond Kingston climbs into the Boston Mountains, the highest part of the Ozarks. Composed of sandstone and shale, this rugged landscape offers great variations in elevation (from 1,500 to 2,300 feet) creating panoramic views and deep, moist valleys rich in wildflowers and crystal-clear streams.

The drive begins in **Eureka Springs**. There has been much recent development along US 62, which follows a ridge along the south side of town. Modern hotels, motels, restaurants, and stores line the highway; however,

Drive 20: Ozark Highlands

Eureka Springs to Clarksville, Arkansas (north)

Drive 20: Ozark Highlands

Eureka Springs to Clarksville, Arkansas (south)

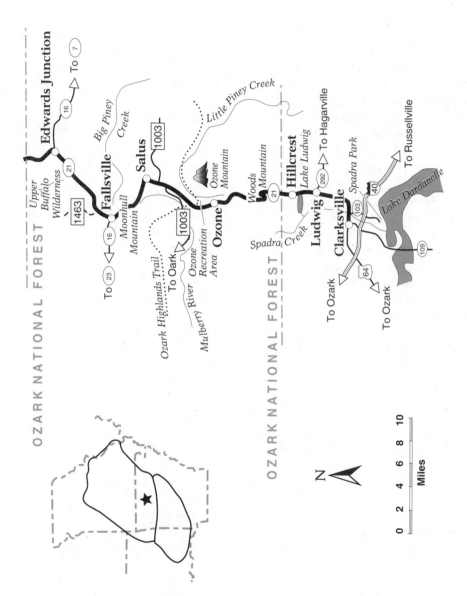

the attractions that spawned their growth lie in the narrow valleys that drop off the ridge to the north. From US 62, take AR 23 north along the historic loop through the old part of Eureka Springs. One of the first buildings encountered is the Eureka Springs Historical Museum, on the west side of the road. It is worth the stop for a general orientation to Eureka Springs.

It is said that the Native Americans knew about the "great healing spring," but few early European settlers visited it. However, in 1856, a Dr. Alvah Jackson found the spring and believed its waters cured his long-standing illness. The "Indian Healing Spring" was also known as Basin Spring because the water flowed into a small natural stone basin. Be sure to visit Basin Spring in Basin Circle Park on Spring Street. During the Civil War, Dr. Jackson treated the wounded from both armies, and many believed it was the curative waters of the spring that brought them back to health.

The spring's healing powers remained relatively unnoticed until 1879, when Dr. Jackson convinced the ill L. B. Saunders, a prominent judge from nearby Berryville, to sample the waters. The judge was so delighted by the relief he obtained that he proclaimed the news of his healing far and wide. People began coming in droves—by horseback, in carriages, and by simple farm wagons, and, in a few months more than 4,000 people were camped nearby. At a meeting on July 4, 1879, the people decided that the judge's young son Burton Saunders's suggestion of "Eureka Springs" was a fitting name for the new community. After only eight months, daily newspapers heralded the news of a city of healing waters that already contained ten to twelve thousand residents. By May 1880, there were two thousand dwellings plus daily mail service, churches, schools, and thirty physicians.

From 1885 until 1910, the town was at the height of its popularity as a health resort. It attracted thousands of visitors who arrived on the Eureka Springs Railroad, which scheduled six trains a day. Health spas, motels, theaters, shops, and homes mushroomed to accommodate the health-seekers. However, many of these wood frame buildings were destroyed by a series of four fires and rebuilt again over a ten-year period. It was not until the last fire, in 1893, that the next stage of the city's development ensured it against more than fire. Native stone quarried near the White River was used to build more permanent structures, which are still seen today, along with miles of attractive retaining walls that border the streets.

By 1904, the permanent population was five thousand, with fourteen doctors and six dentists. The health spas, however, began to decline because people began putting more trust in surgery and medicine than in the healing powers of the spring water. Gradually, the visitors shifted from health-seekers to those seeking rest and relaxation. From 1907 through World War II Eureka Springs barely kept alive. But tourism increased and funds became available for restoration of the many fine old Victorian homes, businesses, and public buildings. In fact, the entire town is listed on the Register of Historic Places.

The narrow city streets were laid out to accommodate pedestrians, horseback riders, and wagons—they are not multilanes for automobile traffic. To fully appreciate the Historic District, it is best to park and walk the streets, which are lined with shops, galleries, artists' studios, craft workshops, restaurants, and hotels. Open-air trolleys are available to take you through the Historic District. Information on their routes and a detailed brochure of things to do in Eureka Springs and the surrounding area are available at the Eureka Springs Chamber of Commerce (see Appendix). The Visitor Information Center is located on US 62 west, past the intersection of AR 23 north.

Proceed east on US 62 towards Berryville. In 6.6 miles you cross over **Kings River**, a floatable stream from April to June, which empties into Table Rock Lake to the north. The river originates near the town of Boston, as do the Mulberry and White rivers. Kings River's water quality is considered above average, and there is a greater feeling of wilderness on the Kings River than on the more heavily used rivers nearby.

Continue on to **Berryville**, which was founded in 1850 by Blackburn Henderson Berry of Alabama. During the Civil War, the town, except for a few houses, was burned by both sides. Two attractions of particular interest are the Saunders Memorial Museum and the Heritage Center Museum. The former, which is located just off the town square, was established with funds provided by C. Burton Saunders, who is credited with naming Eureka Springs. A world-champion sharpshooter by 1910, Saunders toured the country with Buffalo Bill's Wild West Show. He also traveled the world collecting antiques and firearms and bequeathed his collection, along with money to build a museum in his hometown of Berryville. Weapons on display include those used by Jesse James, Billy the Kid, Belle Starr, Buffalo Bill, Wild Bill Hickok, and Annie Oakley, to name a few. Besides its famous gun collection, the Saunders Museum has a great variety of other artifacts, including Native American relics.

Located on the town square, the Heritage Center Museum houses hundreds of historical items including a moonshiner's still, a pioneer schoolroom, a barbershop, and an undertaker's office. The museum is located in the 1881 courthouse, which is on the National Register of Historic Places.

Leaving Berryville, head south on AR 21 for about 20 miles and enter the Kings River valley. The valley is flanked on both sides by the Boston Mountains as you proceed 4 miles to **Kingston**. Continuing past Kingston, the road leaves the Springfield Plateau and climbs Logan Mountain. After a couple of miles, following the crest of the mountain, the road descends steeply for 3 miles into the community of Boxley at the intersection of AR 21 and 43.

Boxley was first settled in 1838, when it was named "Whiteley." After the Civil War, a merchant, D. Boxley, moved to the site. In 1883, he established another post office, and the community later took his name. Just north of Boxley a grist mill was established in 1870 to replace an 1840 mill. The mill was closed in 1960 after serving the community for almost a century. It is now a part of the Buffalo National River system, and there are plans to restore it someday. A side trip north on AR 43 leads to Lost Valley, Villines Cabin, the Buffalo River Trail, and Ponca. For more details see Drive 19.

Continuing on AR 21, the road crosses the **Buffalo River** a mile south of Boxley. The river is seasonally dry at this location because it is close to its headwaters. The 150-mile river is floatable in the spring from Ponca to Pruitt and year-round from Pruitt to the White River. The Buffalo River, because of its protected status and natural beauty, is considered one of the most popular floatable rivers in the United States.

In 4.5 miles, AR 21 enters the boundaries of the Ozark National Forest and the **Ozark Highlands Scenic Byway**. For the next 35 miles, this scenic byway traverses some of the highest elevations of the Ozarks and offers several panoramic views. A National Forest Scenic Byway, its special status helps provide funding for hiking trails, scenic overlooks, camping and picnic areas, brochures, and interpretive displays.

Just west of here the boundaries of the 11,094-acre **Upper Buffalo Wilderness** begin. Protecting the headwaters of the Buffalo River, the wilderness contains extensive hardwood forests with scenic sandstone outcrops, mountainous terrain, and nineteen waterfalls. Access is best off of Forest Road 1463, a mile north of Fallsville on AR 21.

The scenic byway continues south through **Edwards Junction**, where AR 16 joins AR 21 for 8.5 miles. There is a roadside scenic view along the east side of the highway, 0.5 mile north of Fallsville. The road runs along high ridges through **Fallsville**, paralleling Moonhull Mountain and the headwaters of the Mulberry River, which has premier canoeing farther downstream, beginning in Oark.

Eleven miles south of Fallsville and just before Ozone Recreation Area, AR 21 crosses the **Ozark Highlands Trail**. Parking is on the west side of the road. The trail begins at Lake Fort Smith State Park on the western edge of the national forest and travels eastward 165 miles to the Buffalo National River. At the Ozone Campground Trailhead, the westward trail goes 29 miles to Lick Branch Trailhead. This is the longest section of the Ozark Highlands Trail. The trail crosses the Mulberry and Little Mulberry Rivers and passes a number of waterfalls, valleys, and steep hills. The trail east goes 20 miles to Big Piney Trailhead. A mile-long walk from the trailhead leads to Little Piney Creek and in another mile crosses the creek. Moss-covered boulders and bluffs add interest along the way.

Ozone Recreational Area provides eight campsites. It was a Civilian

Unique and attractive stone and brick buildings await exploring along the narrow streets of historic Eureka Springs.

Conservation Corps camp during the 1930s and foundations from the original buildings remain.

Continuing on AR 21, the road passes through **Ozone**, over Woods Mountain, and leaves the boundaries of the **Ozark Highlands Scenic Byway**. Leaving the Boston Mountains of the Ozarks, the road eventually levels out in the Arkansas River valley, which is part of the Ouachitas. The Ozark Forest Visitor Information Center is located just south of **Ludwig**. Maps, brochures, books, and information on recreational opportunities on the national forest are provided. AR 21 and, thus, the scenic drive ends at Clarksville.

Clarksville was incorporated in 1848. Once the third largest coal-producer in Arkansas, it also has natural gas reserves. The Johnson County Courthouse contains one of the most impressive and best preserved courtrooms in Arkansas. Built during the Great Depression, the second story courtroom accurately reflects the look and atmosphere of the 1930s. The Walton Fine Arts Center has exhibits and shows at the University of the Ozarks, which was founded in 1834. Among special events, the Johnson County Peach Festival, held in July, has the distinction of being the oldest continuing outdoor festival in Arkansas, dating back to July 1936. Just south of Clarksville on AR 103, the U.S. Army Corps of Engineers' Spadra Park offers camping, picnicking, restrooms, showers, electrical hookups, and access to Lake Dardanelle.

21

Pig Trail

Ozark to Eureka Springs, Arkansas

General description: A 78-mile drive from Ozark north across the rugged Boston Mountains to Eureka Springs.

Special attractions: Pig Trail Scenic Byway, Ozark Highlands Trail, Ozark National Forest, White Rock Mountain Recreation Area, Mulberry River, White River, and Reed Mountain Park; fall colors, scenic views, hiking, canoeing, fishing, hunting, and camping.

Location: Southwestern Ozarks. The drive follows Arkansas Highway 23 north from Ozark.

Drive route numbers: Arkansas Highway 23 and Forest Roads 1003, 1505, and 1504.

Camping: Ozark National Forest campgrounds at Redding, Shores Lake, and White Rock Mountain recreation areas; Withrow Springs State Park has 25 campsites, 17 of which have water and electrical hookups. Aux Arc Park, at Ozark Lake Dam Site 13, has campgrounds, water, and comfort stations.

Services: All services at Ozark and Eureka Springs. Food and gas at Huntsville. A small store, gas, and canoe rental at Turners Bend.

Nearby attractions: Mount Magazine, Ozark Highlands, and Roaring River State Park scenic drives; Haw Creek Falls Recreation Area; Upper Buffalo Wilderness; Buffalo National River; Arkansas River; and War Eagle Mill.

 The drive

Climbing out of the Arkansas River valley, AR 23 scales the rugged Boston Mountains, offering breathtaking views of a densely forested, seemingly never-ending landscape. This region is the highest and most deeply dissected of the Ozarks, with local relief sometimes exceeding 1,500 feet. Sandstone bedrock forms bluffs and rocky slopes that favor shortleaf pine, the Ozark region's only native pine. In sheltered deep ravines, moist, cool conditions provide habitat for such uncommon trees as American beech and umbrella magnolia. In the lush understory, ferns, orchids, and spring wildflowers carpet the ground.

This section of AR 23 is known as the Pig Trail. Those traveling this

Drive 21: Pig Trail

Ozark to Eureka Springs, Arkansas (north)

Drive 21: Pig Trail

Ozark to Eureka Springs, Arkansas (south)

route in the autumn should be prepared to encounter football fans, especially from Little Rock and Hot Springs, driving to Fayetteville to attend games of the University of Arkansas Razorbacks. Do not be surprised to see carloads of fans wearing bright red hog hats, yelling, "Wooo-pig-sooee" out of their windows as they drive by.

The drive begins in **Ozark**, which is the northernmost point of the Arkansas River. There are several explanations for the name "Ozark," which is said to be derived from the French *Aux Arc*. In 1909, Professor Marinoni of the University of Arkansas theorized that "Ozark" was derived from the French *Aux Arkansas*, which he translated to mean, "from amongst the Arkansas." The French called the Indian tribes in this area the *Arkansas* or the shortened name *Arcs*. Professor Marinoni felt that the French named this area after its inhabitants.

In his publication *Geography of the Ozark Highlands*, Carl O. Saure theorized that this word comes from the French phrase *pays aux Arcs*, or "land belonging to the Arcs [Indians]."

Aux Arc can also be translated to mean "the big bow." French explorers reported that the Indians in this area carried extra-large hunting bows. According to this interpretation, "Ozark" comes from the large hunting bows used by the Indians.

Another explanation of "Aux Arc" is that the translation means "the big bend" or "the big bow" of the Arkansas River. This is in reference to the sharp bend that the Arkansas River makes at the town of Ozark.

Although it is not certain what the French meant by "Aux Arc," the "Ozark Mountains" appeared on maps long before the settlement of Ozark was established in 1838 along the Arkansas River.

Two miles east of town on US 64, **Reed Mountain Park** offers a scenic overlook, picnic and playground facilities, and the mile-long River Bluff Nature Trail. From US 64, turn south on the Ozark Lock and Dam and Reed Mountain Park entrance road. Follow the signs to the park. Reed Mountain was named after Randall Reed, a former slave who purchased the land from Fort Smith Railroad Company in 1880. For those wanting a closer look at the lock and dam, follow the road down to the Arkansas River, where there is an observation platform.

Returning to town, proceed north on AR 23. The office of the Boston Mountain Ranger District is located on the north end of Ozark. Its staff can provide information and maps on recreational opportunities in the Ozark National Forest. In another 4.5 miles the road passes under Interstate 40. While crossing White Oak Creek valley, you will have a good view of the Boston Mountains lying straight ahead.

In about 6 miles, the **Pig Trail Scenic Byway** sign marks the boundary of the Ozark National Forest. The next 19 miles of highway are designated as a National Forest Scenic Byway. This special designation helps provide funding for hiking trails, scenic overlooks, camping and picnic areas, brochures, and interpretive displays.

After a steep climb over Douglas Mountain, the road drops into the Mulberry River valley. The **Mulberry River**, known by some as the state's "wildest" river during spring, pours over ledges, shoots through willow thickets, and whips around sharp turns. Much of its 70-mile run to the Arkansas River has been given a Class II/III (medium to difficult) rating by its floaters. Just before the Mulberry River bridge, **Turner Bend** store offers canoe rentals, shuttles, camping, and groceries.

Cross the bridge and after 0.3 mile, FR 1501, on the left, offers a side trip to **White Rock Mountain Recreation Area**. Because of the narrow roads, recreational vehicles are not recommended beyond the Shores Lake Recreation Area. The 18-mile distance is easily forgotten when you drive right up

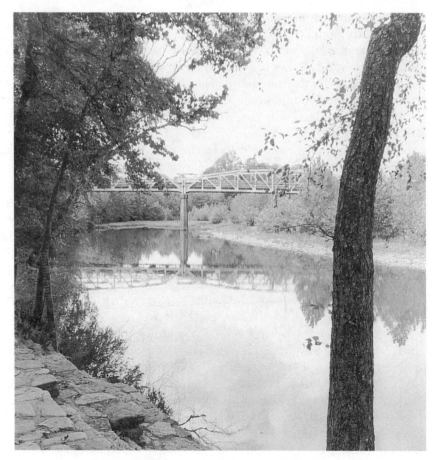

Turner Bend offers access to the scenic Mulberry River.

on top of one of the highest mountains in the Ozarks (2,260 feet). White Rock Mountain is named for the white lichen found growing on the sandstone rocks. Whether you take the 2.1-mile Rim Walk Trail or the shorter 1-mile loop, the views are some of the finest in the Ozarks. Four stone-and-timber shelters along the trail provide scenic picnic areas. There are three cabins and a lodge that can be reserved by calling the White Rock Mountain Concessionaires (see Appendix). Camping spaces are also provided, and there is a trailhead for the Ozark Highlands Trail on White Rock Mountain.

Before reaching White Rock Mountain, FR 1501 goes to **Shores Lake Recreation Area**. This 82-acre lake, built by the Civilian Conservation Corps in the 1930s, provides swimming, fishing, camping facilities, and picnic areas. A 14.4-mile loop trail runs from Shores Lake past several nice waterfalls, up to White Rock Mountain, and then returns to the lake through the Salt Fork drainage. This would be a nice weekend hike, especially if you reserve a cabin at White Rock Mountain.

Continue one mile on AR 23 to the small community of **Cass**. Settled by Elias Turner and called "Turner's Bend" until the 1850s, from 1915 to 1920, Cass reportedly produced more wooden wagon wheels than any other place in the world. Today, the Cass Job Corps Center and canoe outfitters produce income for the community. The Cass Job Corps Center trains more than two hundred young people a year in various occupational skills such as carpentry, plumbing, masonry, painting, and heavy equipment operation. Visitors may tour the facilities.

The next Forest Service road to the east, FR 1003, goes 3 miles to **Redding Recreation Area**, another side trip. This is a popular access point for floaters on the Mulberry River. An 8.8-mile trail to Spy Rock is also available. For a shorter trip to Spy Rock take FR 1504, just past the turnoff to Redding Recreation Area. Follow FR 1504 approximately 2.5 miles to a trail on the left. It may be difficult locating the trailhead that leads up to **Spy Rock**. Contact the Boston Mountains Ranger District Office for directions and trail conditions. Legend has it that Spanish gold was buried in this area and that a lookout was stationed at Spy Rock while others buried the gold. Spy Rock offers a nice view of the Mulberry River valley.

Proceeding on AR 23, the road climbs up and over Whiting Mountain; just 4 miles before you reach FR 1003, the **Ozark Highlands Trail** crosses the road. Parking for the trail is on the east side of the road. The 165-mile trail begins at Lake Fort Smith State Park, on the western end of the national forest, and goes out the northeastern edge of the forest to the Buffalo National River. Rated as one of the top ten trails in the United States, the trail offers great vistas, enchanting streamside walks, bluffs, boulders, rich forests, and hundreds of waterfalls. Eventually, the Ozark Highlands Trail will join the Buffalo River Trail, go across to the Sylamore Ranger District, then go along Lake Norfork, join the Ozark Trail through Missouri, and end

Prominent sandstone cliffs rim White Rock Mountain Recreation Area.

up at St. Louis for a total of 1,000 miles of hiking experience. If you wish to walk a portion of it going east, a steep climb goes to Cherry Bend Hollow and broad vistas. West of the road, the trail is easier and goes around the mountain past an old rock house beneath a bluff 0.25 mile from the road.

Just north of the Ozark Highlands Trail, the road crosses **Fly Gap**, which is the highest spot on the drive at an elevation of 1,953 feet. In 4 miles the scenic byway portion of AR 23 ends at the Ozark National Forest boundary at AR 16.

After 3.3 miles, AR 23 crosses the headwaters of the **White River**. Just east of here at the community of Boston, the White River begins. The river starts its 225-mile journey by flowing west toward Fayetteville and then north, where its flow is checked by lakes Sequoyah and Beaver. It then continues north into Missouri, where it is impounded by the Table Rock and Taneycomo Lake dams. It then flows into Bull Shoals Lake and, after emerging below the dam in Arkansas near the community of Mountain Home, it cuts a winding path south to the Mississippi River. In spite of all the alterations it is considered one of the finest fishing and floating streams in the Ozarks.

After 20 miles, the road crosses **War Eagle Creek**. Rising just east of Boston, it flows northwest to Beaver Lake. For most of its length it is considered a Class II (moderate) floating stream. War Eagle Creek is named after an Osage Indian, Hurachis the War Eagle, who signed treaties with the federal government during the 1820s.

In 3 miles, the road passes through **Huntsville**, the "Crossroads of the Ozarks," according to the sign. It was named by pioneers from Huntsville, Alabama. The town was platted and made the permanent county seat in 1839. Mostly destroyed during the Civil War, it was incorporated in 1877.

North of Huntsville, the road leaves the Boston Mountains and enters the Springfield Plateau. This region is not as dramatic; its elevations vary from only 500 to 1,500 feet. The bedrock is limestone, with caves, springs, and sinkholes contributing to the Ozark landscape.

In 4 miles, after you again cross War Eagle Creek, **Withrow Springs State Park** appears on the west side of AR 23. This 786-acre park was named after an early settler, Richard Withrow, who came west from Tennessee in 1832 and established the first grist mill in the area. The park has three trails; one, the War Eagle Trail, is a 2-mile round-trip hike. The trail runs along War Eagle Creek, offers a chance to enter a cave, and climbs 150 feet to the top of a bluff overlooking the river and countryside.

Continue on to Eureka Springs, which is 20 miles away. For details on Eureka Springs, see Drive 20.

22

Eastern Ouachitas
Little Rock to Holla Bend, Arkansas

General description: A 75-mile drive from Little Rock along the eastern edge of the Ouachita Mountains to the Arkansas River valley and Holla Bend National Wildlife Refuge.

Special Attractions: Pinnacle Mountain State Park, Ouachita National Recreation Trail, Ouachita National Forest, Winona Auto Tour, Lake Sylvia Recreation Area, Petit Jean State Park, and Holla Bend National Wildlife Refuge; hiking, scenic views, fall colors, camping, swimming, hunting, fishing, crystal prospecting, and birdwatching.

Location: Eastern Ouachitas. The drive begins on Arkansas Highway 10 on the west side of Little Rock and heads west.

Drive route numbers: Arkansas Highways 10, 9, 154, and 155 and Forest Roads 132, 152, and 324.

Camping: The U.S. Army Corps of Engineers' Maumelle Park contains 111 campsites with water and electrical hookups, tables and grills, pavilions, hot showers, and a dump station. Petit Jean State Park has Mather Lodge with 24 guest rooms, swimming pool, gift shop, and a full-service restaurant; 19 fully equipped cabins; and 127 campsites with water and electrical hookups. Lake Sylvia Recreation Area has 19 camping units with electricity, 9 basic camping units, picnic areas, restrooms, showers, and swimming.

Services: All services at Little Rock and nearby Morrilton and Russellville. Food and gas at Perryville, Perry, and Oppelo.

Nearby attractions: Mount Nebo State Park, Lake Dardanelle, Lake Maumelle, Flatside Wilderness Area, Arkansas River, Lake Winona, and Scenic 7 Byway.

 The drive

The drive, which begins just west of Little Rock, is on the extreme eastern edge of the Ouachita Mountains. These mountains began to form more than 300 million years ago, when the continental plates of South America and Africa began pushing from the south, uplifting the Ouachitas and the Ozarks at the same time. This uplifting, folding, and faulting lasted millions of years, producing the dramatic shapes and sizes of mountains

Drive 22: Eastern Ouachitas

Little Rock to Holla Bend, Arkansas

unique to the Midwest. Over the last half of the drive, the road follows the Arkansas River valley, which is considered part of the Ouachitas. Here, backwater areas provide habitat for more "southern" plants and animals such as bald cypress trees and alligators.

AR 10, on the western edge of **Little Rock**, begins the drive. Little Rock, with a population of more than 180,000, is the largest city and the capital of Arkansas. North Little Rock, located on the north side of the Arkansas River, is the third largest city in the state, with more than 63,000 people. Historical accounts indicate that Little Rock's name originally referred to a moss-covered rock jutting out from the south bank of the Arkansas River. French explorers in the early 1800s noted that the location of this rock marked the transition from the broad lowland plains to the rugged mountainous region. In 1821, Little Rock was established on a bluff at the intersection of two major transportation routes: the Arkansas River and the Southwest Trail. Little Rock grew as successive waves of travelers passed through it. In 1836, there was a flood of migrants to the newly created state of Texas; then came the California gold rush of 1849 and the arrival of the Cairo and Fulton Railroad in 1870. Because of the city's accessibility, Little Rock grew to become the state's center of finance, education, transportation, industry, medicine, and government.

Traveling west on AR 10 from the intersection with I-430, you pass the entrance road to Maumelle Park after 2 miles. The park offers camping facilities and access to the Arkansas River. Continuing on AR 10, the prominent mountain lined with communication towers on the left of the highway is Crystal Mountain. At 1,085 feet above sea level, it is the highest mountain in the eastern Ouachitas. After 3 miles, turn right onto AR 300 and follow the signs to the entrance to **Pinnacle Mountain State Park**. Pinnacle Mountain, to the east of AR 300, is 1,011 feet above sea level. Although its cone shape suggests a volcanic origin, it is actually part of a ridge of the massive Jackfork sandstone formation, which has been gradually isolated by streams cutting through it. The main part of the ridge, called the Fulk Mountain chain, lies to the east.

For an orientation to the park, take Pinnacle Valley Road east 1.8 miles, turn left, and follow the road north to the visitors center. Upon entering the lobby, you will notice a huge stuffed alligator. These reptiles were once common in the southern half of Arkansas, but poaching for hides reduced their numbers until alligators were declared endangered in the state. Although they are now protected, habitat destruction continues to keep their population in low numbers. Alligators require quiet waters such as swamps, bayous, and lakes. Grassy Lake, west of Hope, Arkansas, is such a place, and it is one of the few areas in the state where alligators are known to breed. Individual animals have been sighted as far north as the Arkansas River, having migrated or been transplanted from the southern part of the state. Be

*An impressive roadcut just north of Perry gives testament to the massive forces
that uplifted and formed the Ouachita Mountains.*

sure to ask the naturalist if there is an opportunity to see one of these incredible living fossils in the quiet waters around the park.

Pinnacle Mountain State Park was established in 1977 and is Arkansas's
first state park adjoining a major metropolitan area. Although not open to
camping, the recreation area at the base of the mountain has shaded picnic
tables, grills, water, a playground, restrooms, and a large, open-air pavilion.
Boat ramps allow access to the Big and Little Maumelle rivers that border
the park. The many trails lead you into bottomland hardwood forests, shaded
boulder-strewn valleys, along cypress-lined rivers, and windswept
mountaintops. The trail up and over Pinnacle Mountain, the steepest trail
in Arkansas, offers a spectacular panoramic view of the Ouachitas, Lake
Maumelle, and the Arkansas River. The other trails vary in difficulty from
level, paved, and barrier-free to moderately difficult. Consult the trail map
brochure and the knowledgeable staff at the visitors center. While at the
center, be sure to walk to the scenic overlook just off the parking lot.

At the lower parking lot, the **Ouachita National Recreation Trail** begins its 225-mile route to Talimena State Park in Oklahoma. The Ouachita
Trail is the longest trail in Arkansas, traversing mountains, valleys, lake and
river overlooks, bottomlands, and pine/hardwood forests, with many plant
and animals surprises along the way. The first segment of the trail, which is
managed by Pinnacle Mountain State Park, extends 34 miles west to Lake
Sylvia. A trail map is available at the visitor center.

Return to AR 10 and proceed west, crossing **Lake Maumelle** after 7 miles. This 9,000-acre lake formed after the damming of the Big Maumelle River in order to provide an adequate water supply for Little Rock. The lake also provides boating and fishing and includes a disabled-accessible area just off the right side of the bridge.

Continue on AR 10 for 11 miles to the junction with AR 9. A 3-mile side trip south on AR 9 will take you to FR 132 and the beginning of the **Winona Auto Tour**, which includes the **Lake Sylvia Recreation Area**. A self-guided interpretive brochure for the scenic drive is available at the Winona Ranger District Office at Perryville or by writing the Supervisor's Office, Ouachita National Forest, in Hot Springs. The 26-mile Winona Auto Tour features mountain vistas, quartz crystal hunting, displays of spring and fall color, lush forests, and wilderness experiences, and ends at AR 7. For a shorter drive that loops through Lake Sylvia Recreation Area, also take FR 132, 3 miles south of the intersection of AR 9 and 10. While traveling south on AR 9, you cross over the Maumelle River and the Ouachita National Recreation Trail. Turn west on FR 132, proceed about 4 miles, driving through the Chinquapin Mountain Walk-in Turkey Hunting Area, and turn right on FR 152. In about a mile, the road crosses the Ouachita Trail. After another mile, a parking lot to the right accesses a 0.5-mile disabled-accessible interpretive trail. A side road just beyond the parking lot leads to the campground and to additional trails. Continuing on FR 152, another side road leads to a swimming area and bathhouse overlooking Lake Sylvia, a 16-acre Forest Service lake. FR 152 now becomes FR 324 and continues for 4 miles, ending at the junction of AR 9 and AR 10.

Continue on to **Perryville**, passing the Harris Brake Lake and Wildlife Management Area and the Fourche LaFave River. Be sure to stop for information and maps at the **Winona Ranger District Office** in Perryville on the west side of town.

Proceed 3 miles north on AR 9, over Perry Mountain, to Perry. On the north side of town, notice the roadcut on the right. Instead of horizontal rock strata, the layers are vertical, attesting to the tremendous pressures that squeezed the once-level landscape together like an accordion to form the Ouachita Mountains. This roadcut is one of the best in the Ouachitas that illustrates how the mountains were formed. After another 4 miles, turn west onto AR 154 at Oppelo. While driving across the Arkansas River valley, notice the prominent mountain straight ahead—this is the 1,100-foot Petit Jean Mountain. After 5 miles the road begins the climb to the mountain's plateau. After 2 miles, a road to the right leads to **Petit Jean's Gravesite**. Petit Jean, whose name has been given to numerous features in the region, was said to have lived during the period of French exploration of the New World. Legend has it that she disguised herself as a cabin boy so she could secretly accompany her fiance, a sailor, to the New World. Because of her diminutive size, the crew called her "Petit Jean" ("little John"). After exploring the region, she became fatally ill and requested to be buried on this mountain, which now bears her name.

After another 2 miles, you will reach the visitor information center of **Petit Jean State Park**. Be sure to stop, view the exhibits, and ask about recreational opportunities in the park. Set aside as parkland in 1923, before there was a park system, Petit Jean is considered one of the finest state parks in Arkansas. Interesting historic features add to the exceptional natural beauty of the mountain. A mountaintop motor tour brochure, available at the visitor information center, guides you to interesting stone structures built by the CCC, scenic overlooks, exceptional geologic features, and cultural landmarks. The drive takes a minimum of two hours, depending on the length of stay at each stop.

There are seven trail systems at Petit Jean State Park. Be sure to visit the Cedar Falls Overlook if you do not have time to hike one of the trails. From the overlook, Cedar Creek can be seen as it plunges one hundred feet into a box canyon. Depending on the time of year and the amount of rainfall, Cedar Falls can be spectacular. The Cedar Falls Trail, which begins at Mather Lodge, is a 2-mile round-trip hike into the canyon. This is the most popular trail in the park, even though the hiking difficulty is moderate to hard because of its steep descent into the deeply incised sandstone canyon. There is a great variety of vegetation in the canyon. The south-facing slopes are more exposed and provide habitat suitable for more drought-tolerant plants such post oak, blackjack oak, shortleaf pine, and hickory. The more protected north-facing slopes have red oak, white oak, sweet gum, and red maple. Two unusual plants, Ozark chinquapin and yellow ladyslipper orchid, inhabit the canyon.

The unspoiled beauty of Seven Hollows Trail inspired the establishment of Petit Jean as Arkansas's first state park. In the early 1900s, executives of the Fort Smith Lumber Company, who owned the Seven Hollows area, recognized that it should be preserved for everyone to enjoy. The 4.5-mile Seven Hollows Trail is moderate to hard in difficulty. Sites along the way include a natural bridge, grotto, turtle rocks, bluffs, and desertlike sandstone glades. (Another place to see turtle rocks, which are weathered sandstone shaped like the backs of turtles, is along the Rock House Cave Trail.) Turtle rocks exhibit a variety of colors and weathering patterns because of the varying iron deposits in the sandstone.

A shorter, easier, 0.25-mile walk is the Bear Cave Trail, named for the last bear killed on Petit Jean Mountain. Piles of huge sandstone boulders, rock shelters, and monoliths allow visitors to walk under, around, through, and over these erosional features. A map showing the location of Bear Cave and the other trails in the park is available at the visitors center.

When leaving Petit Jean State Park, visit the Palisades Overlook oppo-

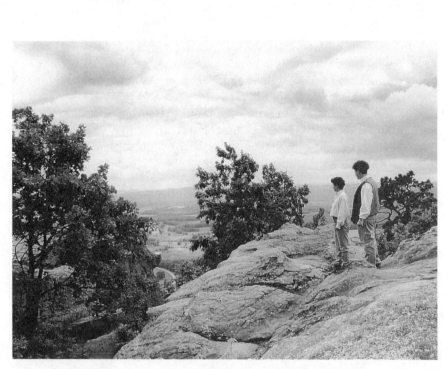

Massive sandstone outcrops provide spectacular views of the Arkansas River valley near Petit Jean's gravesite atop Petit Jean mountain.

site the intersection of AR 154 and 155. A commanding view of Cedar Creek Canyon, the towering Red Bluff above the canyon, and the vast Arkansas River valley lay before you. Continuing on AR 154 after 4 miles, the road passes Pontoon Park, which is maintained by the U.S. Army Corps of Engineers as an access to the Petit Jean River.

After another 3.5 miles, a gravel road on the south leads to **Petit Jean Wildlife Management Area**. Managed by the Arkansas Game & Fish Commission, the 15,000-acre area is best known for its duck hunting. There are additional opportunities to see wildlife at Kingfisher Lake, located at the headquarters, and Pelican Pond, which is reached by a gravel road that eventually leads to AR 7.

Continue on AR 154, turn north onto AR 155 for 3 miles, and take the entrance road into **Holla Bend National Wildlife Refuge**. A per-vehicle entrance fee is required for all visits. Be sure to stop at the office for information and a map of the area. The staff can suggest special wildlife viewing opportunities; these change depending on the season. The winter months offer viewing of up to fourteen species of ducks, four species of geese, and bald eagles. The numbers of these birds peak in December and January. Any time of year, especially during early morning and evening hours when wildlife are most active, may yield sightings of white-tailed deer, eastern cottontail and swamp rabbits, gray and fox squirrels, red fox, raccoon, beaver, coyote, bobcat, opossum, nine-banded armadillo, muskrat, and river otter. Refuge personnel have also identified 240 species of birds on the refuge. A checklist is available for your reference.

The refuge provides an 8-mile auto tour that is one of the best ways to see wildlife and learn about the refuge and its management practices. A self-guided tour brochure is available at the information station; there are also interpretive signs along the route.

23

Scenic 7 Byway South
Russellville to Hot Springs, Arkansas

General description: A 69-mile drive south from Russellville across the Arkansas River valley, into the Ouachita Mountains, and ending at Hot Springs.

Special attractions: Lake Dardanelle, Dardanelle Rock, Mount Nebo, Ouachita National Recreation Trail, Ouachita National Forest, Scenic 7 Byway, Winona Auto Tour, Flatside Wilderness Area, Buffalo Gap Auto Tour, Iron Springs Recreation Area, and Hot Springs; scenic views, camping, hiking, mountain biking, horseback riding, swimming, crystal prospecting, fall colors, fishing, and hunting.

Location: Eastern Ouachitas. The drive begins on Arkansas Highway 7 at Russellville and heads south.

Drive route numbers: Arkansas Highways 7, 7s (a side road off 7), and 22 and Forest Roads 132 and 11.

Camping: Lake Dardanelle, Mount Nebo, Petit Jean, Lake Catherine, Lake Ouachita, and DeGray Lake Resort state parks; Lake Dardanelle and Nimrod Lake of the U.S. Army Corps of Engineers; South Fourche and Iron Springs recreation areas in the Ouachita National Forest; and Gulpha Gorge in Hot Springs National Park.

Services: All services are available at Russellville, Dardanelle, and Hot Springs. Gas and food at Centerville, Ola, Fourche Junction, Hollis, Jessieville, Blue Springs, and Hot Springs Village.

Nearby attractions: Long Pool Recreation Area; Holla Bend National Wildlife Refuge; Petit Jean and Galla Creek wildlife management areas; Petit Jean State Park; and Eastern Ouachitas, Mount Magazine, Hot Springs National Park, and Crystal Trail scenic drives.

The drive

The drive begins in the Arkansas River valley, which is considered a subregion of the Ouachitas. The valley occupies a band running from 25 to 35 miles wide, separating the Ozarks to the north from the Ouachita Mountains to the south. Although it is composed primarily of the floodplains and terraces of the Arkansas, Fourche LaFave, Petit Jean, and Poteau rivers and their tributaries, several ridges rise conspicuously above the valley floor.

Drive 23: Scenic 7 Byway South

Russellville to Hot Springs, Arkansas (north)

Drive 23: Scenic 7 Byway South
Russellville to Hot Springs, Arkansas (south)

To Onyx — 314 — **Hollis**

South Fourche LaFave River

Flatside Wilderness

132

South Fourche Recreation Area

Crystal Mountain

7

Deckard Mountain

Walk-In Turkey Area

Winona Auto Tour

114

11

OUACHITA N. F.

122

Buffalo Gap Auto Tour

Iron Springs Recreation Area

Ouachita National Recreation Trail

Middle Fork Saline River

Jessieville Ranger Station

To Story — 298 — **Jessieville**

Blue Springs

Hot Springs Village

Mountain Valley

To Benton

5

Fountain Lake

To 30

Hot Springs

To Mount Ida — 270 — 70 — To 30

7 — 270

70

To Glenwood

To Arkadelphia

Examples include Mount Magazine, Mount Nebo, and Petit Jean Mountain; Mount Magazine, at 2,753 feet, is the highest point in Arkansas as well as the Midwest.

This part of AR 7, from Russellville to Hot Springs, is a continuation of the nationally designated Scenic 7 Byway—one of the nation's most scenic drives. The northern section of Scenic 7 Byway is described in Drive 18.

Russellville is the starting point for this drive. Incorporated in 1835, the town was named for Dr. T. J. Russell, a British-born and -educated physician, who immigrated here in 1835. Russellville, the largest town between Little Rock and Fort Smith, is experiencing steady population growth due to its well-developed manufacturing sector. The headquarters for the Ozark National Forest is located here and is a convenient stop for those wanting advice and information on the national forest. The Ouachita National Forest headquarters are located in Hot Springs, the destination of this drive.

There are several places to view and access **Lake Dardanelle** on the west side of Russellville, but for the best orientation to the lake's history and recreational uses, visit the U.S. Army Corps of Engineers' Arkansas River Visitor Center. Follow AR 7 to the south side of Russellville and turn right on AR 7s, a side road that heads west to Old Post Road. Follow the signs to the visitors center and take the time to view the interpretive exhibits. Information is available on recreational opportunities in the area, including several hiking trails maintained by the Corps. The area just below Dardanelle Lock and Dam is a favorite winter feeding location for large numbers of bald eagles. Eagles can be seen in the park most mornings between sunrise and 10 a.m. during December, January, and February.

Dardanelle Rock is visible from the visitors center looking south. A geologic natural area owned by the Arkansas Natural Heritage Commission, Dardanelle Rock has been a major landmark on the Arkansas River since the days of earliest exploration. Although the craggy sentinel offers some limited hiking, it is best viewed from the visitor center because the graffiti sprayed on its massive rock face is lost in the distance.

Return to AR 7, cross over the Arkansas River, and drive to the town of **Dardanelle**. The town's name stems from the resemblance of the landmark rock to the Strait of Dardanelles in Turkey. Originally established as a trading post, the settlement that grew up beside Dardanelle Rock in the early 1800s was one of the first in the Arkansas valley.

Proceed south on AR 7 to the intersection with AR 22. Turn right and then left on AR 155 and follow the signs to **Mount Nebo**, which rises 1,350 feet above the valley. A spectacular view of the 34,000-acre Lake Dardanelle, the Arkansas River, and the surrounding mountain ridges can be obtained from **Mount Nebo State Park**. Because of the steep climb up the mountain, no trailers or RVs over 15 feet in length should be used. Seven trails and several overlooks draw the visitor to such places as Sunrise Point, Fern Lake,

Nebo Springs, and Sunset Point.

Return to AR 7 and continue south across the Arkansas River valley. Patches of woods seen along the way are dominated by bottomland hardwoods such as sweet gum, willow oak, water oak, pin oak, and persimmon. Along the route, you will find access points to Holla Bend National Wildlife Refuge by way of AR 155 and 154. See Drive 22 for details.

Pass through **Centerville**; the next town is **Ola**. Situated in the Petit Jean River valley, the community is sustained by forest-related industries and providing services to the nearby farmers and ranchers. South of Ola, AR 7 climbs out of the Arkansas River valley to the summit of Ola Mountain. A pull-off with picnic tables offers an expansive view across Nimrod Lake and the Fourche LaFave River valley.

Ola Mountain marks the northern boundary of the rugged Ouachita Mountains. These east-west trending mountains are unique in the United States as a result of folding when another continent from the south collided with the North American continent more than 300 million years ago. The mountain-building lasted million of years forming the Ouachita Mountains and the Ozarks. The Ouachita Mountains are composed of sandstone and shale and rise as much as 1,500 feet above the valley floor. Their more acid and well-drained soils are favored by shortleaf pine and upland hardwoods.

Continue on to **Fourche Junction**, which is on the eastern edge of

Dardanelle Rock has been a major landmark along the Arkansas River since the days of earliest exploration.

Nimrod Lake, an 18,300-acre lake built in 1942 for flood control of the Fourche LaFave River that also provides recreational opportunities. The lake is a popular fishing site for largemouth bass, white bass, crappie, and large channel catfish. There is a public duck-hunting area and a 1,200-acre waterfowl refuge.

Proceeding on AR 7, the road enters the boundary of the Ozark National Forest. For the next 24.3 miles, this segment of **Scenic 7 Byway** is part of the national system of National Forest Scenic Byways. This designation promotes special emphasis on varied recreational facilities such as hiking trails, camping and picnic areas, and lakes for boating and fishing; development of scenic overlooks and drives; and production of brochures, interpretive displays, and visitors centers on Forest Service land.

After 10 miles, the road crosses the South Fourche LaFave River; immediately to the left is the **South Fourche Recreation Area**. Camping and picnic areas are provided with easy access to the river.

About another 7.5 miles on the left, FR 132 marks the beginning of the 26-mile **Winona Auto Tour** between AR 7 and 9. This side trip offers an opportunity to get off the main road and see some of the backcountry. The route takes about one hour, one-way. The gravel road is two-lane, but caution is advised when you approach oncoming vehicles and curves in the road. Be sure to pick up an auto tour interpretive booklet, available from the Jessieville or Winona Ranger District offices, or from the Ouachita National Forest headquarters in Hot Springs. The route provides scenic mountain vistas and a chance to hunt for Arkansas "Diamonds," which are veins of white quartz crystal considered to be the best-quality white quartz in the world. Surface collecting of a small amount of quartz is allowed on Crystal Mountain. Much of the road parallels Flatside Wilderness, a 10,105-acre forested expanse featuring small creeks, panoramic views, rugged terrain, and a section of the Ouachita National Recreation Trail.

Back on AR 7 and across from the entrance to FR 132, another side trip, on FR 11, leads west to **Deckard Mountain Walk-In Turkey Area**. Two trails, the 9-mile Buffalo Gap Mountain Bike Ride and the 36-mile Bear Creek Horse Trail, have been developed. Maps are available at the Jessieville Ranger District office.

FR 11 also begins the 9-mile **Buffalo Gap Auto Tour**. A tour brochure is available at the Jessieville Ranger District office. The gravel road offers overlooks of Deckard Mountain, Blue Ouachita Mountain, and Buffalo Gap.

Continuing south on AR 7, in 0.6 miles the **Ouachita National Recreation Trail** crosses the highway. This trail spans 225 miles from Talimena State Park in Oklahoma east to Pinnacle Mountain State Park, west of Little Rock. A shorter, 4.3-mile trail called Hunts Loop can be accessed here, or from an easier trailhead 1.3 miles down the road at **Iron Springs Recreation Area**. This moderately difficult trail leads to panoramic views from Short

Mountain Vista, interesting rock outcrops, and valleys lush with ferns and spring wildflowers. Plan on three to four hours with stops along the way. The recreation area offers campsites, picnic areas, and places to wade and explore the clear-flowing Middle Fork Saline River. The National Forest Scenic Byway ends just south of Iron Springs Recreation Area.

After another 4 miles down AR 7, the **Jessieville Ranger Station** maintains a visitor information center with staff to answer your questions plus an extensive supply of brochures on recreational opportunities in the area. Also, a 0.7-mile trail called the Friendship Barrier-Free Trail is marked with interpretive signs and a paved trail that winds through a mature pine and hardwood forest. This path offers everyone a good opportunity to relax in a natural setting before proceeding on to Hot Springs.

Along the next 14 miles of AR 7, you may notice a gradual increase in the amount of tourist attractions and traffic as you approach **Hot Springs**. For details on Hot Springs and Hot Springs National Park, see Drive 25.

24

Mount Magazine

Paris to Havana, Arkansas

General description: A 28-mile drive from Paris, to the top of Mount Magazine, and down to Havana.

Special attractions: Mount Magazine (highest point in Arkansas), and Cove Lake; scenic overlooks, hiking, camping, fall colors, fishing, and hunting.

Location: Northern Ouachitas. The drive begins on Arkansas Highway 309 at Paris.

Drive route numbers: Arkansas Highway 309 and Forest Road 1606.

Camping: Cameron Bluff and Cove Lake recreation areas, both in the Ozark National Forest, have picnic tables, drinking water, fire grates, and pit toilets.

Services: All services at Paris. Food and gas at Havana.

Nearby attractions: Blue Mountain Lake, Lake Dardanelle, Mount Nebo State Park, and Scenic 7 Byway.

 The drive

Mount Magazine, at 2,753 feet above sea level, is the highest point in the Midwest. Only the Appalachians to the east, the Rockies to the west, and mountains in western Texas attain higher elevations. Standing approximately 2,300 feet above the surrounding valley floor, it is truly an impressive site. From the top of the mountain there are scenic views of the surrounding Arkansas River valley, the Boston Mountains to the north, and the Ouachita Mountains to the south. Because of its exceptional scenery, AR 309, the highway that takes travelers up and over Mount Magazine was designated as an Arkansas Scenic Byway in 1994. WARNING: Low-flying clouds and fog can sometimes cause visibility to be poor. Ice can form on the roads in winter.

Begin the drive in **Paris**, a community that was settled about 1820 on the Old Military Road that connected Little Rock and Fort Smith. This road later became the Butterfield Overland Mail route. The village was incorporated in 1879 and was named for Paris, France. A side trip east on AR 22 takes you to the Magazine Ranger District, located on the south side of the

Drive 24: Mount Magazine
Paris to Havana, Arkansas

highway. Information and brochures on recreational opportunities in the national forest are available at the district office.

A few miles south of Paris on AR 309, you enter the Mount Magazine District of the Ozark National Forest. The next 24.9 miles are designated as the Mount Magazine Scenic Byway, which is part of the national system of National Forest Scenic Byways. This designation recognizes special scenic drives through national forest land and emphasizes the development of special recreational opportunities such as trails, picnic and camping areas, and scenic overlooks.

The road begins to climb, and in about 3 miles, **Cove Lake Recreation Area** comes into view. There are 28 campsites, restrooms, and showers available in the summer. Cove Lake also has picnicking, swimming, fishing, a 3-mile loop hiking trail, and a boat-launch ramp. Interpretive programs are offered by naturalists in the summer.

Across the highway from the entrance to Cove Lake Recreation Area is the head of the Mount Magazine Trail. This moderately difficult, 14.2-mile trail climbs to the top of Mount Magazine, offering spectacular scenic views, dense stands of hardwoods and pine trees, glade openings, beautiful wildflowers, and strolls along picturesque streams. For shorter hikes, there are two other trailheads along the way that can be reached by Forest Service roads. The Magazine Ranger District has a trail map and can advise you on trail options.

Travelers from Texas have come to view the fall colors from the top of Mount Magazine.

From Cove Lake, AR 309 continues the climb up **Mount Magazine**. This flat-topped mountain would be called a mesa in the West. Named by French hunters, the shape of Mount Magazine reminded them of a barn or warehouse—*magasin*, in French. The mountain is composed of layers of sandstone and shale with a very resistant cap of Savannah Formation sandstone that was deposited about 300 million years ago. Steep bluffs circling the top of the mountain form cliffs up to 200 feet tall. Mount Magazine truly has the character of a mountain with its summit sometimes shrouded in low-lying clouds and its temperature averaging 6 and sometimes 25 degrees cooler than the surrounding valleys. Wild and rugged, Mount Magazine has the most confirmed sightings of mountains lions in the Ozark and Ouachita regions combined.

Although the odds of seeing a mountain lion are extremely slim, there are plenty of opportunities to see other kinds of wildlife. Forest inhabitants include deer, bobcats, foxes, raccoons, opossums, skunks, and squirrels. A variety of bird species also inhabit the area, including northern cardinal, whippoorwill, indigo bunting, Carolina chickadee, tufted titmouse, and a variety of woodpeckers. Rare sightings of painted buntings, scarlet and summer tanagers, and rufous-crowned sparrows in open areas along the cliff tops are possible.

One especially noteworthy animal that has found a home on Mount Magazine is the black bear. Sometimes seen at night around the Cameron Bluff campground, black bear sightings are becoming more frequent in the rugged mountains of the Ozarks and the Ouachitas. This has not always been the case, however. At one time, black bears were common in Arkansas and, until 1923, Arkansas was known as "The Bear State." That year, the state's General Assembly changed it to "The Wonder State," probably because of the disappearance of the black bear. In 1927, all bear hunting was banned. By 1940, less than 50 black bears remained in the state, with most occurring in southeast Arkansas. With the establishment of the Ozark and Ouachita national forests, the black bear's habitat improved, so the Arkansas Game & Fish Commission began restoration. Between 1954 and 1968, 254 black bears were trapped in Minnesota and in Manitoba, Canada, and released on Forest Service land. The restoration effort was first thought to be a failure, for few bears were being sighted. This, however, was probably due to their secretive nature and the remoteness of the rugged mountains into which they had been placed. But by 1973, there were an estimated 700 animals; and now approximately 2,000 black bears are living in Arkansas. As their population increases, the black bear's range is expanding into Missouri and Oklahoma. Although sightings of black bears are considered very rare, when encountered they should be treated with respect and from a distance.

A variety of natural features are found on Mount Magazine. Dense forests, glades, bluffs, springs, and streams provide habitat for a variety of

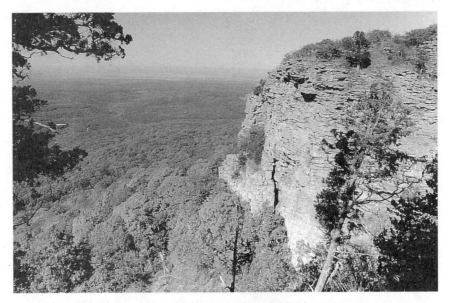

Views of impressive cliffs and vast expanses are afforded from Mount Magazine, the highest point in the Midwest.

plant life. Dry, exposed sandstone cliffs and glades support stunted trees, grasses, and sun-loving wildflowers. Meanwhile, shaded north slopes and ravines provide habitat for orchids, ferns, and spring blossoms. The mountain is rich in plant diversity; more than 600 plant species have been found on its upper elevations alone. Unusual plants growing on the mountain include the maple-leaved oak, a variety of Shumard Oak with maple-like leaves, which is found only on Mount Magazine on shaded north slopes. Growing near the oak, the Rocky Mountain woodsia fern is also found nowhere else between the Rocky Mountains and the Appalachians. Other interesting plants include pipewort, hay-scented fern, and bottle gentian.

Near the top, two pull-outs offer impressive views looking east. On top of the mesa, FR 1606 leads to the Cameron Bluff overlook and campground. Be sure to hike the Signal Hill Trail, which is across from the entrance to the campground. The ten-minute hike up the last two hundred feet of the mountain assures you that you are standing on the highest point in the Midwest. The Mount Magazine Trail can also be accessed at the campground. The road continues around to the south side of the mountain, where Mount Magazine Lodge once stood. It burned in 1971. There are future plans to build a state park on Mount Magazine but, hopefully, it will not take away from the rugged character of the mountain.

Returning to AR 309, the drive passes the East End Picnic Area and another scenic overlook before the long descent down the mountain. The drive ends at **Havana**, located in the Petit Jean River valley.

25

Hot Springs National Park
Hot Springs, Arkansas

General description: A 5-mile drive in Hot Springs National Park with scenic views, historic sites, interesting rock outcrops, and hot springs.

Special attractions: Hot Springs, Bathhouse Row, Hot Springs Mountain Drive, West Mountain Drive, Hot Springs Mountain Tower, and National Park Aquarium; scenic views, hiking, camping, and hot springs bathing.

Location: East-central Ouachitas. The drive begins and ends on Arkansas Highway 7 on the north side of Hot Springs.

Drive route numbers: Arkansas Highway 7.

Camping: Gulpha Gorge Campground, located on the east side of Hot Springs National Park, has 43 tent and trailer sites. Water, comfort stations, and a dumping station are provided; however, there are no showers and no water or electrical hookups. There are also campsites at the nearby national forest, U.S Army Corps of Engineers' Lake Ouachita, and Lake Ouachita State Park.

Services: All services at Hot Springs.

Nearby attractions: Scenic 7 Byway and Crystal Trail scenic drives, Ouachita National Forest, Lake Ouachita, Mid-America Museum.

 The drive

Hot Springs National Park is located in the middle of a series of mountains called the Zig-Zag Mountains. These long, linear mountains, spaced from 1 to 3 miles apart, are the result of giant folds produced during the mountain building of the entire region. The angle of these tilted layers of bedrock and the type of rock itself account for the unique occurrence of hot springs in this area. Although hot springs are found in a few locations in the Appalachian Mountains and are much more common in the West in places such as Yellowstone, in the Midwest they occur only at Hot Springs, Arkansas.

Geologists believe the hot springs originate in the valley north of Hot Springs National Park, which is traversed by AR 7, Park Avenue, and Whittington Avenue. Rainwater is collected in the broad valley and flows downward through extensive cracks and fractures in a hard, brittle rock

Drive 25: Hot Springs National Park
Hot Springs, Arkansas

To Russellville

To Little Rock

Indian Mountain

Gulpha Gorge Campground

Gulpha Creek

Goat Rock Trail

North Mountain

North Mountain Loop

Hot Springs Mountain Tower

NATIONAL PARK

Mountain Drive

Fountain Street

Hot Springs

Mt. Drive

Hot Springs

Reserve Ave.

Street

Bathhouse Row
Fordyce Bathhouse Visitor Center
Arlington Lawn
Grand Promenade
Peak Trail
Dead Chief Trail

70

270

To Lake Catherine

National Park Aquarium

Spring

Hot Springs

Central Avenue

7

To Arkadelphia

Whittington Ave.

HOT SPRINGS

West Mountain Drive

Summit Drive

West Mountain

Sunset Trail

270

70

To Mount Ida

N

0   0.5   1
Mile

180

called Bigfork chert. By using the carbon 14 dating technique on representative water molecules, scientists have estimated that the water, which travels to a depth of from 6,000 to 8,000 feet, takes about four thousand years to complete that journey. At that depth, the temperature is several degrees hotter than at lesser depths; this heat is produced by the natural radioactive decay of particles in the earth's crust. The heated water, being lighter and under pressure, rises upward through the cracks and fractures in the chert, taking a year to reach the surface. Along the way, the 143-degree-Fahrenheit water dissolves minerals and salts from the surrounding bedrock, giving the water an odorless, yet distinctive taste that was once thought to have curative powers.

The drive begins at **Hot Springs National Park**, which is located on the north end of Hot Springs. Central Avenue, which is also AR 7, is the principal road. Parking is available along Central Avenue or on the adjoining streets near Bathhouse Row. Finding a space is more difficult on weekends and during the summer tourist season. Arriving early or using the pay lots alleviates the hassle of searching for a parking space in this popular but concentrated area. A visit to the **Fordyce Bathhouse Visitor Center**, located along Bathhouse Row, is a good place to get oriented. The visitor center contains exhibits and a film explaining the history of the area and of thermal water bathing. A tour through the restored bathhouse is like stepping back into the 1920s, when the popularity of Bathhouse Row as a travel destination was at its peak. Today, traditional thermal baths are available at the Buckstaff Bathhouse on Bathhouse Row and at some of the hotels and medical facilities located near the park. Inquire at the visitor information desk for more details. In back of the Fordyce, a thermal fountain is displayed, one of the few outlets that was not capped to divert water to the bathhouses. Another uncapped hot spring, Maurice Historic Spring, can be seen on the north side of the Maurice Bathhouse, which is next to the Fordyce.

From Fordyce Bathhouse, walk north along Central Avenue and Bathhouse Row to **Arlington Lawn**, just before the corner of Central Avenue and Fountain Street. Against the bluff, hot springwater flows down the Hot Water Cascade into concrete pools in which visitors seem to be compelled to soak their sidewalk-weary feet. To the left of Hot Water Cascade, DeSoto Rock marks what some believe to be the site visited by Hernando de Soto and his men in the Spanish Expedition of 1541. The text of his chapter of narratives describing this part of his expedition were lost, but the title was titled "Hot Rivers and Salt Made from Sand." It is not known whether the conquistadors actually visited the hot springs, which are actually freshwater springs, or one of the several warm, salty seeps that are known elsewhere in the region. Evidence shows that thousands of years before Europeans first set site on the hot springs, Indians were bathing in the warm, healing waters. The Caddo Indians believed that their people originated in the waters of the

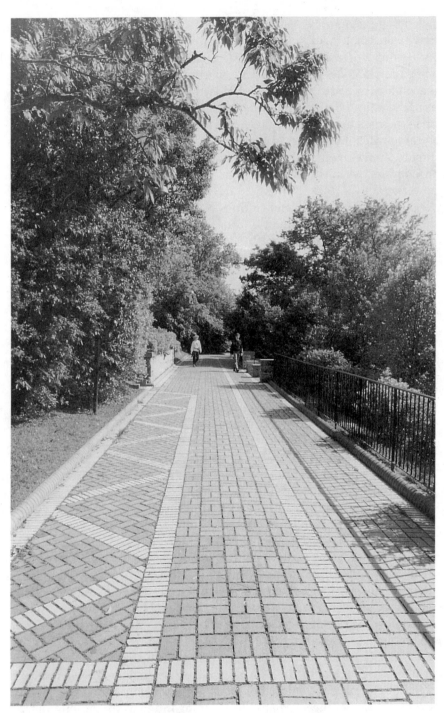

Above Bathhouse Row, one can take a leisure stroll along the brick-lined Grand Promenade.

hot springs.

The French followed the Spanish into Arkansas. Although there is little written record left from these early trappers and hunters, they were surely aware of the hot springs. In 1803, the United States purchased the Louisiana Territory from France. President Thomas Jefferson, wanting to learn more about these new lands, sent expeditions into the region west of the Mississippi River. One of these parties, led by William Dunbar and Dr. George Hunter, traveled from the Mississippi River up the Red and Black rivers to the Ouachita River. Navigating up the river, they unloaded their boats at a point where Gulpha Creek enters the Ouachita. Traveling 9 miles overland, they entered the valley of the hot springs and found a deserted cabin and a few shelters. The valley was an impressive site, with springs bellowing up steam along the hillside issuing from low cones of tufa, a calcareous rock stained various shades of orange and red by traces of iron oxide. Today many of the springs have been capped, and the tufa deposits covered up with soil. DeSoto Rock is one such remnant that was made of tufa that broke away from the nearby cliff. Another place to see tufa is Hot Water Cascade, where tufa is still being formed.

Upon returning home, Dunbar and Hunter communicated their findings to President Jefferson; their news generated much interest in the "Hot Springs of the Washita." Visitors began to seek out the soothing springs; some stayed and built cabins. The first hotel was established in 1828. The U.S. government recognized the significance of the area and set aside the hot springs and immediate surroundings as a federal reservation in 1832. In 1921, the area was designated as a national park. Hot Springs slowly began to grow with bathhouses, saloons, doctor's offices, and stores. The first two decades of the twentieth century were a time of rapid growth and change, despite a devastating fire that swept through fifty blocks of residences and businesses in 1913. As the twentieth century progressed, the medical profession increasingly doubted the water's healing powers, which resulted in less interest and visitation by the public. Today, Hot Springs is thriving due to the development of its other attractions. However, the historic character of Hot Springs and the Victorian buildings along Bathhouse Row continue to appeal to tourists and those who continue to believe in the water's special healing and therapeutic powers.

The **National Park Aquarium** is located just past the Arlington Hotel on Central Avenue. This building houses both fresh- and saltwater aquaria and more than 250 species of tropical, native, and saltwater fish. Of particular interest is the 50-year-old, 150-pound alligator snapping turtle that is native to backwater areas in the delta region of Arkansas.

Before leaving Bathhouse Row, take a walk along the **Grand Promenade**. This level, brick-lined pavement cuts across the lower flank of Hot Springs Mountain and parallels Central Avenue and Bathhouse Row. The

0.5-mile promenade can be accessed from either end of Bathhouse Row or from behind Fordyce Bathhouse. It is wheelchair-accessible from the north end or from behind the Fordyce. The promenade is a good place to observe birds such as mockingbirds, catbirds, cardinals, and thrushes. A bird checklist for the park is available at the visitor center. It is also the main access for Peak Trail and Dead Chief Trail. The Peak Trail starts midway down the promenade. This 0.5-mile, moderately strenuous trail leads to the summit of Hot Springs Mountain and the Mountain Tower. The Dead Chief Trail is located at the south end of the promenade. This 1.4-mile trail is strenuous (at the start) and leads to Gulpha Gorge Campground. In all, there are twenty trails with a total of 22 miles available for hiking at Hot Springs National Park. Unfortunately, a trail guide book has not yet been developed describing the routes. Two more trails will be discussed later.

There are two scenic drives within Hot Springs National Park. The first, **Hot Springs Mountain Drive**, is reached by driving north along Central Avenue and turning right on Fountain Street. Follow the signs to the entrance. The 4.5-mile one-way loop first stops at **Hot Springs Mountain Tower**, a site with a picnic area, water, and restrooms. This commercially operated, 216-foot observation tower offers an outstanding panoramic view of Hot Springs and the surrounding Ouachita Mountains. The second level of the tower contains exhibits and a glass-protected view. On pleasant days, the third level affords an open-air experience.

A drive to the upper loop, called **North Mountain Loop**, leads to a scenic view and a 0.7-mile hike to Goat Rock, a massive Arkansas novaculite outcrop. Just before reaching Goat Rock, the trail crosses rare grassy openings called novaculite glades, which harbor a diversity of wildflowers and sun-basking lizards.

The second scenic drive, **West Mountain Drive**, can be reached by following Central Avenue north to Whittington Avenue and turning left. After about 0.5-mile, turn left again at the "West Mountain Drive" sign and begin the tour. After about a mile, take the Summit Drive road to the top of West Mountain. There are scenic pullouts along the way. As the road circles the crest, notice the large white rock outcrop in the center just off the parking lot. This is Arkansas novaculite, a dense rock composed of fine silica that is prized around the world for its qualities as a sharpening stone. Indians crafted arrowheads, spearpoints, tools, and implements using this rock. One novaculite pit on Indian Mountain, which can be reached opposite the Gulpha Gorge Campground, measures 150 feet in diameter and 25 feet deep. The shaping of arrowpoints was rarely done at the quarry; the rock was carried in blocks back to villages, where it was chipped and flaked into the desired shapes. Arkansas novaculite can be seen in outcrops on the crests and upper slopes of the mountains in and around Hot Springs National Park and along Scenic Drive 27. Rock shops in the Hot Springs area sell the

This large outcrop at the end of West Mountain Drive is Arkansas novaculite, which is known worldwide for its use as a sharpening stone.

"Arkansas Stone" individually or in gift packages.

Also at the parking lot is the start of the Sunset Trail, a 8.5-mile trail that follows the ridges of West Mountain, Music Mountain, and Sugarloaf Mountain. After 2.2 miles, the trail reaches the top of Music Mountain, which, at 1,450 feet above sea level, is the highest point in the park. There are several great views and interesting rock outcrops along the way.

26

Crystal Trail

Hot Springs to Page, Arkansas/Oklahoma

General description: A 91-mile drive beginning at Hot Springs; traveling westward through the heart of the Ouachita Mountains where beautiful quartz crystals abound; and ending at Page, Oklahoma.

Special attractions: Hot Springs, Mount Ida, Ouachita National Forest, Hickory Nut Mountain Recreation Area, Crystal Vista Auto Tour, Big Brushy Recreation Area, Ouachita Trail, Womble Trail, Lake Ouachita, Black Fork Mountain Wilderness, and Mid-America Museum; scenic views, hiking, crystal prospecting, canoeing, camping, fishing, and hunting.

Location: Central Ouachitas. The drive begins on U.S. Highway 270 on the west side of Hot Springs and ends at Page, Oklahoma.

Drive route numbers: U.S. Highway 270, Arkansas Highway 227, and Forest Road 50.

Camping: There are 6 national forest campsites; 16 U.S. Army Corps of Engineers' Lake Ouachita campsites; and additional campsites at Lake Ouachita and Queen Wilhelmina state parks.

Services: All services at Hot Springs, Mount Ida, and Mena. Food and gas at Royal and Crystal Springs. Gas at Hurricane Grove and Pencil Bluff.

Nearby attractions: Hot Springs National Park; Scenic 7 Byway; Little Missouri Falls; Crystal Vista; Heavener Runestone State Park; Talimena Scenic Drive; and Poteau Mountain, Caney Creek, Upper Kiamichi River, Dry Creek, and Flatside wilderness areas.

The drive

While the Ozarks are flat-topped mountains, the Ouachitas are long, narrow ridges running from east to west. Both mountain regions began forming during the Paleozoic Era, about 300 million years ago, when the continents of South America and Africa collided with the southern end of North America. The Ozarks were uplifted into a high, flat plateau, while the Ouachitas, being closer to the point of collision, were wrinkled and folded into long ridges. This mountain-building process occurred over millions of years and added a couple of inches of height per year, then abruptly stopped. Since then, the mountains have been eroded by rain and wind to their present shape. This east-west trending chain of mountains is unique in the United

Drive 26: Crystal Trail

Hot Springs to Page, Arkansas/Oklahoma (east)

States. Most mountain ranges, like the Appalachians, Rockies, and Sierra Nevada, have a north-south alignment due to past continental collisions from the east (forming the Appalachian mountains) or from the west (forming the Rocky and Sierra Nevada Mountains). This tour along US 270 takes you through the heart of the Ouachitas and provides excellent opportunities to see the results of this ancient mountain-building process.

The drive begins on the west side of **Hot Springs**. For details on Hot Springs, see Drive 25. Where US 270 and AR 227 meet, a side trip on AR 227 takes you to Lake Ouachita and Blakely Dam, Lake Ouachita State Park, and the **Mid-America Museum**. Follow the signs to this privately owned museum. For a small fee your family can explore interactive exhibits about science, nature, and the arts. The museum, nestled in twenty-one acres of forest, also has a restaurant and gift shop. From Memorial Day to Labor Day it is open daily from 9:30 a.m. to 6:00 p.m. The winter hours are from 10:00 a.m. to 5:00 p.m. and the museum is closed on Mondays. For more information, see the Appendix.

AR 227 continues on to **Mountain Pine**, a lumber milling town, established in 1928. In another mile, you can see Blakely Mountain as well as Blakely Mountain Dam, which formed **Lake Ouachita**, the largest lake in Arkansas. The dam was constructed across the Ouachita River in 1952. The rock exposures on either side of the dam contain layers of sandstone and shale. The layers were originally horizontal, but intensive geologic forces millions of years ago pushed and folded these layers over on themselves. These phenomena are best seen here and along roadcuts along the route. If you are boating on the lake, the U.S. Army Corps of Engineers has developed a unique boating trail, called the Ouachita Geo-float Trail, which has interpretive stops along a water route explaining geologic features. Ask for it at the Corps' office just beyond the dam. Lake Ouachita was built by the Corps of Engineers for flood control, recreation, and the production of hydroelectric power. At normal pool, the lake extends up the Ouachita River valley a distance of 30 miles and has a surface area of approximately 40,000 acres. Fishing is popular on the lake; its tributary arms are especially good for crappie, largemouth bass, white bass, and catfish. Adding to the popularity of the lake is the surrounding beautiful, heavily forested, mountainous terrain.

Six miles north of Mountain Pine on AR 227, **Lake Ouachita State Park** provides camping, a swimming beach, a marina, and a visitors center with a store, gift shop, and cafe. Interpretive programs and guided hikes are offered, or you may also hike the two trails on your own. The 4-mile Caddo Bend Trail meanders through the forests and along the lakeshore peninsula. The Dogwood Trail is a casual, 0.25-mile loop beginning near Camp Area C. Be sure to visit Three Sisters Springs, which has been a popular attraction in the area since the late 1880s. The water welling up from these springs is said to have curative powers for different ailments. An exhibit on the springs is located in the visitors center.

Return to US 270 and proceed west for 3 miles, crossing over the upper end of **Lake Hamilton**. Completed by the Arkansas Power and Light Company in 1931, Hamilton Lake is 24 miles long and covers 9,000 acres. The lake, which impounds the Ouachita River, is privately owned and was built before the U.S. Army Corps of Engineers' lakes, which accounts for the hundreds of private homes, restaurants, and tourist attractions around Lake Hamilton. The main part of the lake lies along the south side of Hot Springs. Many rocky points and sheltered coves provide varied habitats for such fish as crappie, largemouth bass, bream, channel catfish, and, more recently, walleye. Trout are stocked in the upper part of the lake, where cool water is released from Lake Ouachita, and the Arkansas Game & Fish Commission maintains a trout hatchery just below the dam.

Along US 270 you will notice several Corps of Engineers public use areas and Forest Service recreation areas. Many offer camping and access to the lake. Maps and brochures can be obtained by writing or visiting their offices, which are listed at the start of this drive. This drive leads you to some of the more interesting areas.

Continue on US 270 to **Crystal Springs**, a 1930s recreational area named for a clear spring flowing from the base of Crystal Mountain to the north. From here to Mount Ida, roadside stands selling crystals become more evident. The sandstone in this region of the Ouachitas holds veins of quartz crystals; some of the crystals can be two or three feet long. Most, however, form porcupinelike clusters up to six feet in diameter. Roadside stands sell the crystals for rock gardens and interior ornaments. Smaller pieces are fashioned into costume jewelry.

After another 5 miles on US 270, a side trip on FR 50 leads to a spectacular view of Lake Ouachita and the surrounding mountains. The 4-mile gravel road goes to **Hickory Nut Mountain Recreation Area** and just beyond that **Lake Ouachita Vista**. From the overlook, Lake Ouachita can be viewed 800 feet below.

Returning to US 270, proceed west and in 3.5 miles cross the Denby Arm of Lake Ouachita. Just before Mount Ida, the Womble Ranger Station, on the left, is a good place to stop for Forest Service maps and information. Ask about the **Crystal Vista Auto Tour**, which is a self-guided drive featuring the best of the Winona District, including Crystal Vista where you can collect quartz crystals.

Mount Ida was founded in 1836 when Granville Whittington, a Massachusetts immigrant who, a year earlier, had helped to draft a petition requesting Arkansas statehood, built a general store in the area. Mount Ida was incorporated in 1854, and for more than one hundred years it was a

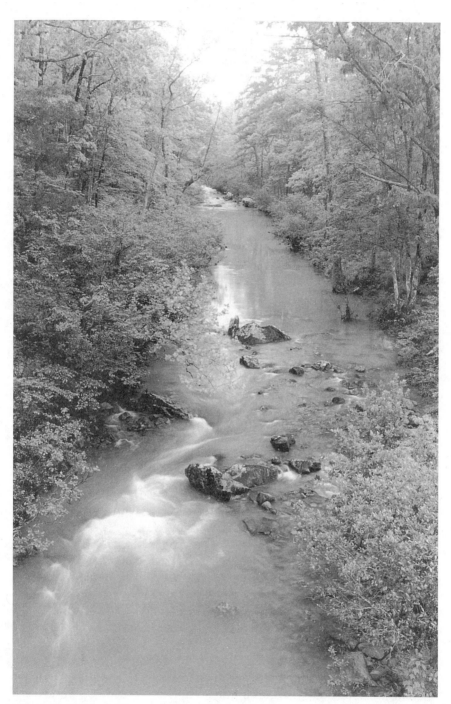

A bridge at Big Brushy Recreation Area offers a view of the tranquil waters of Brushy Creek.

center for extensive crystal mining. Today the town is known as the "Quartz Crystal Capital of the World." Taking millions of years to form, these crystals are transparent or translucent six-sided prisms that terminate in six-sided pyramids. They are used for thousands of products ranging from sandpaper to crystal balls. The area has many dig-it-yourself mines and a few mineral museums. An annual event in mid-October, the Quartz, Quilts, and Crafts Festival, offers music, food, displays, and a crystal dig. In 1994, 123 entrants from twenty-seven states and 2 diggers from Canada competed in local mines for prizes awarded to those with the best crystals.

Note on the map the town of Washita, about 10 miles north of Mount Ida on AR 27. The town is named with an Indian word meaning "good hunting ground." The French explorers spelled the sound of Washita as "Ouachita," which became the common spelling for the region.

Continuing west on US 270 for about 4 miles, the road crosses the 39.5-mile **Womble Trail**, the third longest trail in Arkansas. The Womble Trail was once proposed to be a part of the Ouachita National Recreation Trail. However, when it became too difficult to extend the Ouachita Trail west of Gaston Mountain, this trail became the Womble. The Ouachita Trail was relocated north of here. From this access, the Womble Trail goes west, crossing a couple of nice streams, then climbs Mauldin Mountain, passes Gaston Mountain, and ends at North Fork Lake for a total distance of 14.2 miles. East of US 270, the trail goes 25.7 miles, joining the Ouachita Trail towards its end. This stretch of the trail meanders along the scenic shores of Lake Ouachita and offers breathtaking views and lots of large trees along the way.

The highway continues west, crossing over the **Ouachita River**. The Ouachita is the largest and longest river within the Ouachita mountain region. It begins as a mountain stream in the Acorn Basin, northwest of Mena, and meanders eastward through the heart of the Ouachita National Forest to a point just west of Hot Springs, where its flow is checked by three man-made dams. The river then flows southward into Louisiana. There are nine camping areas and landing points along the river above Lake Ouachita that can be reached by Forest Service roads. The river float is not too difficult; the paddler has a chance to experience the remoteness of the area in the upper stretches, and a chance to fish in the sections closer to the lake. Information on river floats, access points, and camping areas can be obtained from the local ranger district office or from Forest Service headquarters in Hot Springs.

Continue on US 270 to **Pencil Bluff**. A side trip on AR 88 west for 5 miles will take you to the Oden Ranger Station, where you can obtain maps and information about activities in the Ouachita National Forest. Also ask about hiking the nearby 1-mile Serendipity Loop Interpretive Trail.

Five miles from Pencil Bluff on US 270, the road climbs Blowout Mountain; in another mile, it crosses the Ouachita National Recreation Trail or **Ouachita Trail**. This 223-mile trail from Talimena State Park in Oklahoma to Pinnacle Mountain State Park near Little Rock, Arkansas, contains many challenges to go along with its beautiful streams, extensive forests, and outstanding vistas. Unlike the Ozark Trail, which goes up and down all day long, the Ouachita Trail will climb a hogback ridge and stay there for hours, following the east-west trending mountains. Just beyond the trail and on the south side of US 270, **Big Brushy Recreation Area** provides access to the Ouachita Trail. In the campground, another trail, the **Brushy Creek Loop Trail**, provides a 6.9-mile hike along scenic Brushy Creek, joins the Ouachita Trail, passes Brushy Mountain (with some great views along the way) and ends back at Big Brushy Recreation Area. Just before reaching the recreation area a 0.5-mile hike up Brushy Mountain offers nice views during winter, when the trees are bare.

Proceed up Mill Creek valley on US 270; Fourche Mountain is on the south and Mill Creek Mountain is on the north. The road passes **Mill Creek Recreation Area**, which provides camping (including equestrian campsites), swimming in Mill Creek, and a 0.75-mile interpretive trail to a scenic overlook. Beginning at the recreation area, the Mill Creek Equestrian Trail heads south, crosses US 270, and branches out into a network of 30 miles of equestrian/hiking trails. A map is available at the nearest Ranger District office.

Proceed on to **Y City**. Just beyond Y City, on US 270, the road follows Johnson Creek for about 6 miles before turning south as it climbs through a gap in Fourche Mountain and crosses the Ouachita Trail again. If you are interested in hiking this section of the trail, finding the parking lot can be a bit difficult. To locate the trailhead parking area, travel 1.5 miles south along US 270 from the Polk County sign marker. There is an unmarked pull-off on the west side of the highway that is difficult to see. From the parking lot, the trail goes east 26.4 miles to US 70 along a high, dry section (so carry plenty of water). The westward trail goes 16.5 miles to Queen Wilhelmina State Park. A mile-long leisure walk on the trail west from the parking lot passes several waterfalls that flow most of the year.

About 2 miles down US 270, AR 76, to the left, leads another 2 miles to **Iron Fork Mountain Lake**. This is a small fishing lake managed by the Arkansas Game & Fish Commission in cooperation with the city of Mena. No camping facilities or trails are provided.

US 270 continues through the small community of **Acorn**, where the Big Creek and other creeks combine to form the upper reaches of the Ouachita River. Just past **Eagleton**, the highway crosses the Ouachita Trail again and goes by the **Black Fork Mountain Wilderness Trailhead**. A parking lot is on the north side of the road. The trail south and west up Rich Mountain goes a distance of 5.1 miles to Queen Wilhelmina State Park. The trail north is steep and goes up Black Fork Mountain 1 mile, where the Ouachita Trail breaks east and the Black Fork Mountain Trail heads west. There is an incredible view from the top of Black Fork Mountain. The trail is 11.6 miles round trip. The hike climbs gradually and passes through an area that burned in 1963. The fire covered about 13,000 acres and was caused by a spark from a passing train. After 2.3 miles, the trail enters the 13,579-acre Black Fork Mountain Wilderness. Along the top of this 15-mile-long mountain, severely stunted post oak, blackjack oak, and black oak trees are usually less than eight feet tall and resemble large shrubs. This habitat receives maximum exposure to the winds, which distort their branches and cause the thin, rocky soil to dry very quickly. Also of interest are the rock flows or "glaciers." Loose, unstable rocks are continually moving downslope, creating perilous conditions for plants trying to maintain a foothold on life. These rock glaciers are unique to this part of the Ouachita Mountains and to the Midwest. More examples can be seen along the Talimena Drive just south of here (see Drive 28).

Continue on US 270 to the community of **Rich Mountain**; then, a side road, AR 272, goes south and up Rich Mountain to Queen Wilhelmina State Park and connects with Talimena Scenic Drive. US 270 proceeds west, paralleling Big Creek and the Kansas City Southern Railroad, crosses the state line into Oklahoma, and enters **Page**, a small village nestled in the heart of the Ouachita National Forest. The west side of Black Fork Mountain Wilderness can be reached by traveling 2 miles north out of Page on FR 1040 to a parking area that provides space for equestrian trailers. There are no official trails on this side of the wilderness area. Contact the Mena Ranger District Office for access information.

27

Caddo Gap

Glenwood to Langley, Arkansas

General description: A 52-mile drive beginning at Glenwood, traveling west through Caddo Gap, and featuring crystal country, scenic overlooks, mountains of Arkansas Stone, and Little Missouri Falls.

Special attractions: Caddo Gap, Caddo River, Collier Springs, Crystal Recreation Area, Crystal Mountain Scenic Area, Crystal Vista, Little Missouri Falls, Albert Pike Recreation Area, and Ouachita National Forest; hiking, scenic views, camping, canoeing, swimming, fishing, hunting, and crystal prospecting.

Location: Central Ouachitas. The drive begins on Arkansas Highway 8 at Glenwood and travels west, ending at Ouachita National Forest's Albert Pike Recreation Area.

Drive route numbers: Arkansas Highways 8, 27, and 369, and Forest Roads 25, 43, 73, 177, and 539.

Camping: Forest Service campsites are available at Crystal, Albert Pike, Shady Lake, and Bard Springs recreation areas and also at the U.S. Army Corps of Engineers' Lake Greeson, which has 13 campgrounds.

Services: All services at Glenwood. Gas and food at Norman, Black Springs, and nearby Mount Ida.

Nearby attractions: Lake Greeson, crystal shops at Mount Ida, Caney Creek Wilderness Area, Cossatot River State Park Natural Area, and Daisy and Crater of Diamonds state parks.

 The drive

This region, known as the Central Ouachitas, offers dramatic views of mountains that have been pushed and folded over on themselves creating narrow ridges, steep slopes, and deep valleys. This drive will explore the Crystal, Caddo, and Cossatot mountains and their beautiful views, interesting rocks, clear-flowing streams, and unusual plants and animals that are characteristic of this region.

The drive begins on the west side of **Glenwood** on AR 8. Glenwood grew up around a sawmill on the Missouri Pacific Railroad. Just south of town along US 70 there is a popular put-in and take-out point for those

Drive 27: Caddo Gap
Glenwood to Langley, Arkansas

floating the **Caddo River**. The river parallels AR 8 all the way to its headwaters in the Missouri Mountains, about 23 miles west of here. That stretch of the river is floatable in the spring; below Glenwood, the river can be floated most other times. The Caddo eventually flows into DeGray Lake, which was completed in 1972 and impounded the Caddo.

Three miles west of Glenwood on AR 8, you will notice a prominent notch straight ahead in Nelson Mountain. This is **Caddo Gap**. Carved by the Caddo River, the opening now also gives passage to the Missouri Pacific Railroad and AR 8. In about 3 more miles, the road climbs into the gap. Before entering the gap, a side trip on AR 240 affords an opportunity to view the Caddo River while driving across the highway bridge. The river here is broad, clear, and very inviting. Return to AR 8 and drive into Caddo Gap. Notice the roadcut along the highway. It is worth finding a place to park along the shoulder on the outside lane. This is a busy highway, so be careful. The roadcut formations evoke wonderment at what powerful forces there must have been to have pushed these once-horizontal layers of rock to their present vertical positions. If you examine them closely, you will see that some layers are folded back over themselves. This small exposure dramatically illustrates the mountain building processes that created the Ouachita Mountains. These cream-to-white layers of rock are Arkansas novaculite, or "Arkansas Stone," which is commonly used to sharpen knives, tools, and other instruments. The nearby town of Caddo Gap has a historical marker that explains the local history of the area. It is said that the narrow pass at Caddo Gap marks the de Soto expedition's most westward journey into North America. The historical site bears a monument to the Tula Indians who fiercely fought the uninvited Spanish expedition in 1541, forcing de Soto and his men to retreat down the Caddo and Ouachita Rivers, eventually to Louisiana, where DeSoto later died.

Proceed on AR 8 for 5 miles to the town of **Norman**. Turn north onto AR 27 and go 0.6 mile. Then, turn east onto FR 177 and go 3 miles to the **Crystal Recreation Area**. This attractive wooded setting along Montgomery Creek offers camping, picnicking, sanitary facilities, drinking water, swimming, and a hiking trail. The trail is a 0.7-mile loop that begins just opposite of campsite #5; it leads to a creek and a spring. The trail continues through stately old trees and along a steep hillside lush with ferns and mosses. Watch for a small waterfall where the trail crosses the creek again on the way back to the parking lot.

Continue on FR 177 for 2.5 miles to **Collier Springs**, a Forest Service picnic area that features a small, clear-flowing spring. Stay on FR 177 for 1 mile, passing the intersection where FR 2237 bears left. Look for the **Crystal Mountain Scenic Area** sign on the right, and park. To the left of the sign, a 0.5-mile trail passes through giant shortleaf pine trees more than three hundred years old, a rare sight today. Pine trees this size are critical for the

Large leaves of the aptly named umbrella magnolia shade the trail to Little Missouri Falls.

red-cockaded woodpecker, which prefers a large diameter pine in which to hollow out a nest cavity. Because of a lack of old-growth pine forests, caused by extensive logging, the red-cockaded woodpecker is now on the federal endangered species list. Leaving some areas of old-growth forest will help this woodpecker and other species that are dependent on these kinds of conditions to survive. The trail also passes by a scenic sandstone bluff and crosses Twin Creek before heading back to the trailhead.

Turn around on FR 177 and head west. Then take FR 2237 east to **Crystal Vista**, about 1.9 miles. From the parking lot, a 1-mile hike up a steep trail leads to the top of Gardner Mountain. A four-acre opening marks the remnants of a former crystal mine that is now open for public rock collecting. Quartz crystals can be collected for personal use but not for re-sale. Only hand tools such as trowels and rock hammers are permitted. The rock before you is Crystal Mountain sandstone. Deposited about 500 million years ago, it is the oldest exposed rock in the Ouachita Mountains. Between the layers of sandstone, quartz crystals slowly grew forming clusters up to six feet in diameter. These larger crystals make popular lawn ornaments; smaller pieces are fashioned into costume jewelry. Called "Arkansas Diamonds," some of the finest crystals, when first cut and polished, closely resemble diamonds; unfortunately, their luster is not as permanent. Continue north past the opening to the top of the ridge for a spectacular view of Lake Ouachita and the surrounding landscape.

From Crystal Vista, FR 2237 continues 4.1 miles to AR 27. If you have the time, a side trip to the Womble Ranger Station on US 270 just east of Mount Ida is worth the effort. They have Forest Service books and maps and a self-guided brochure called the Crystal Vista Auto Tour. The tour route begins 4.5 miles east of the ranger station and provides a more complete tour across the Crystal Mountains, interpreting historic sites and natural features.

Back on AR 27, return to Norman and turn west onto AR 8. After about 7 miles, notice the **Knobby Hills** along the north side of the road. This unusual array of eroded small hills, composed of Polk Creek shale, creates an interesting contrast in sizes and shapes compared to the more resistent sandstones in the surrounding mountains. The road crosses the upper reaches of the Caddo River twice and shortly comes upon FR 43 on the south side of the road.

Turn on FR 43; after about 2.5 miles, the road crosses over the Caddo Mountains through Mosquito Gap. Notice the outcrops of Arkansas novaculite or Arkansas stone. Novaculite is made up of an extremely hard material called chert, which is mostly silica, the same substance found in sand. Chert was prized by Native Americans for making arrowheads and cutting tools. Today, Arkansas novaculite has an international reputation as a sharpening stone for tools and instruments.

At the intersection of FR 43 and 25, go west on FR 25 for a mile to entrance road FR 539 and then another 0.7 mile to **Little Missouri Falls Recreation Area**. A short trail leads to the falls and loops back to the parking area. Along the trail, large American beech trees with smooth white bark spread their broad limbs into the forest canopy. Also along the trail, look for hop hornbeam, white ash, sweet gum, eastern red cedar, and umbrella magnolia. The Little Missouri River cuts through dense novaculite mountains, confining itself to a narrow gorge. In Missouri, such a formation would be called a "shut-in." The Little Missouri River, because of its exceptional condition, is designated as a National Wild and Scenic River. Rising in the Missouri Mountains just west of here, the headwaters area is notable for its spectacular pine-forested ridges and valleys. The river cascades through a series of difficult whitewater gorges, including the extraordinary Little Missouri Falls in its upper reaches, before leveling off for a more leisurely journey into Lake Greeson. It is best for floaters to put in downstream from here at the Albert Pike Recreation Area. The 11.6-mile Little Missouri Trail can be accessed at the parking lot and follows the river downstream with five crossings that can be traversed at normal flow rates. The trail ends by way of FR 10105.

Return to FR 43 and continue 8 miles to the **Albert Pike Recreation Area**. A crystal-clear pool on the Little Missouri River is the major attrac-

The scenic Little Missouri River cascades over resistent Arkansas novaculite at Little Missouri Falls Recreation Area.

tion here. In addition to camping, swimming is allowed and there is a 1-mile interpretive trail. This is a popular put-in for canoeists wanting to float the 8.5 miles to the AR 84 bridge or beyond to the US 70 bridge. The floating conditions are highly dependent upon suitable amounts of rainfall. Rated up to Class IV, the twisting drops, rapids, and standing waves are best reserved for the experienced paddler. As you leave the recreation area on AR 369 and drive toward Langley, notice the vertical rock strata as the road climbs out of the Little Missouri River valley. This spectacular example of mountain folding is one of the best in the Ouachitas.

28

Talimena Scenic Drive

Mena to U.S. Highway 271, Arkansas/Oklahoma

General description: A 54-mile drive beginning at Mena, Arkansas, and winding along mountain ridges with spectacular views.

Special attractions: Queen Wilhelmina State Park and Lodge, Robert S. Kerr Memorial Arboretum and Nature Center, Ouachita Trail, Winding Stair Mountain National Recreation Area, and Ouachita National Forest; fall colors, scenic/interpretive vistas, "dwarf" or "elfin" forests, rock glaciers, hiking, camping, horseback riding, historical sites, and hunting.

Location: Western Ouachitas. The drive begins on Arkansas Highway 88 at Mena and continues to the state line, where it becomes Oklahoma Highway 1 and continues to the intersection with U.S. Highway 271.

Drive Route Numbers: Arkansas Highway 88 and Oklahoma Highway 1.

Camping: Queen Wilhelmina State Park has a lodge offering 36 guest rooms, a restaurant, a private meeting room for up to 50 people, 35 campsites with water, electrical hookups, showers, and 5 tent sites. Talimena State Park has picnic sites, 7 RV sites, 15 unimproved campsites, and a comfort station with shower. The Forest Service's Winding Stair Campground has 27 campsites, water, and flush toilets.

Services: All services at Mena and nearby Talihina.

Nearby attractions: Black Fork Mountain Wilderness, Kiamichi River Wilderness; Heavener Runestone State Park; Three Sticks Monument; John F. Kennedy Memorial; Little Missouri Falls; Crystal Trail, Heavener, Runestone, and Caddo Gap scenic drives; and Cossatot River State Park Natural Area.

 The drive

Talimena Scenic Drive is perhaps the most impressively scenic of all the drives in both the Ozarks and the Ouachita Mountains. This highway was intentionally built as a scenic drive across the long and narrow Rich and Winding Stair mountains because of the dramatic and far-ranging views afforded in all directions. (WARNING: Low-lying clouds and morning fog can obscure views anytime. Ice can form on the roads in winter.) The name

Drive 28: Talimena Scenic Drive

Mena to U.S. Highway 271, Arkansas/Oklahoma

SITES

1. Mena Visitor Information Center
2. Blue Haze Vista
3. Acorn Vista
4. Grandview Overlook
5. Rich Mountain Fire Tower
6. Queen Wilhelmina State Park Lodge
7. State Line Historical Site
8. Chaha Vista
9. Robert S. Kerr Memorial Arboretum & Nature Center
10. Emerald Vista
11. Horse Thief Springs
12. Potato Hills Vista
13. Talihina Visitor Information Center

"Talimena" is derived from blending the names of the towns at either end of the drive, Talihena and Mena. Construction began in June 1964 and was completed in April 1970. Because of its narrow ridges, steep slopes, fog, and ice storms, the construction of the road, according to one highway worker, was challenging and sometimes dangerous. In February 1989, the Talimena Scenic Drive was one of the first scenic highways to be designated a National Forest Scenic Byway.

To gain a true appreciation for the ruggedness of this part of the Ouachitas, visit this drive in early May. In the deep valleys, the leaves are fully out and spring is at its peak. But 2,000 feet above, on top of the Rich, Black Fork, and Winding Stair Mountains, the leaf buds on the oak and hickory trees are just beginning to open. In a five-minute drive, you can pass from early to late spring just by changing altitude. This interesting response of nature to altitude and temperature differences is commonly seen in the Rockies, the Sierras, and the Appalachians; but in the Midwest, it is uniquely found only in this part of the Ouachitas.

The drive begins at **Mena**, which, with 5,475 inhabitants, is one of the larger towns in western Arkansas. The town of Mena was born with the construction of a new railroad line. Turned down by United States investors in 1896 because of a depression, the railroad builder for the Kansas City Southern, Arthur Stilwell, looked to Holland for the three million dollars needed to finish the proposed line from Siloam Springs, Arkansas, to Shreveport, Louisiana. With the word that several Dutchmen would contribute the money to complete this first railroad through the mountains, a tent city of more than 1,000 was created in less than 40 days. The Mena Star newspaper is one business that has operated ever since that first day. The town itself is named for Mena DeGoiejen, the wife of one of the Dutch investors, John DeGoiejen.

There are several historic buildings to see in Mena; information is available from the Mena Depot Center, located in the center of town along the Kansas City Southern railroad. Maintained by the Mena-Polk County Chamber of Commerce, the depot also contains historic displays, railroad memorabilia, and art exhibits. For information on the Ouachita National Forest, the Mena Ranger District office is located in town along US 71 north.

In Mena, follow AR 88 west and you will begin to ascend Rich Mountain, named by early settlers for the very productive soils found on the north slope of the mountain. Leaving town and on the right, the Forest Service's **Mena Visitor Information Center**, which is open daily from April to November, is a good place to obtain maps, brochures, guidebooks, and information on activities from Forest Service volunteers. There are twenty-three vistas and fifteen historic sites along this drive, with most displaying interpretive signs. Only selected stops will be discussed here. However, all the stops are worth a visit, and a more complete guide on this special drive can

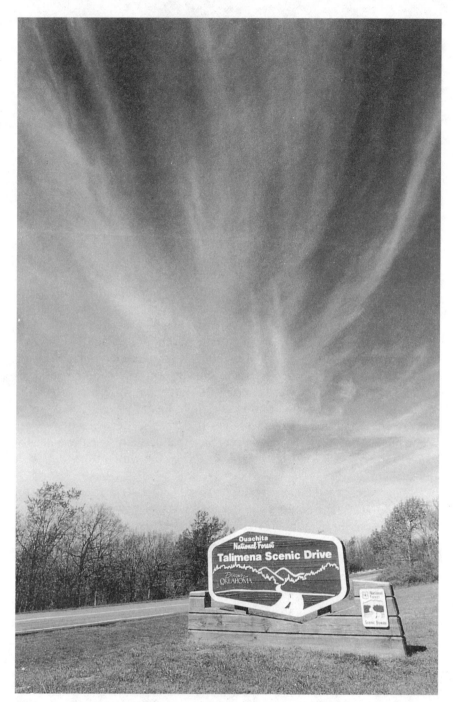

High cirrus clouds provide a dramatic backdrop to the attractive Talimena Scenic Drive sign that marks the boundary between Arkansas and Oklahoma.

be purchased at the visitors centers at either end. There are two trails at the Mena visitors center. The first is the Mountain Settler Interpretive Trail, which is a short, easy loop. The second is Earthquake Ridge Loop, named for a rock formation found not far off the trail. This is a more vigorous, 2.1-mile hike that parallels AR 88 up and down the east flank of Rich Mountain. There are some great views, large trees, a small spring, and several rock formations along the way. Leaving the visitors center, the road continues to climb, and after 2 miles, it reaches the **Blue Haze Vista**, which overlooks the Ouachita River valley. In another 0.6 mile, **Acorn Vista** offers a view of the community of Acorn. The town's original name, "Gourd Neck," was descriptive of the shape of the valley, with the "handle" of the gourd lying between Fourche and Rich mountains. This is a good overlook for viewing sunrises across the Ouachita River valley. For the next 0.5 mile of the drive, the road snakes along an exposed section of the Jackfork Group, showing layers of sandstone and shale in an interesting pattern.

Six miles from the beginning of the drive, **Grandview Overlook** provides a commanding view of the south slope of Rich Mountain and a large portion of the Mountain Fork River basin; to the west are the Kiamichi and Winding Stair mountains in Oklahoma. From this point, spectacular sunsets that backlight rows of mountains can capture the photographer's eye. Above the roadcut at the parking lot, a very good example of a "dwarf" or "elfin" forest can be viewed. Here, post oak and blackjack oak trees take on a stunted appearance due to their environmental conditions. Located on the narrow crest of a tall mountain, these trees are exposed to extremes in heat and cold. The shallow, poor-quality soils, coupled with the trees' exposure to high winds, ice storms, severe winter temperatures, and summer drought, greatly slow their growth. A hundred-year-old tree could be only eight feet tall.

In about 3.5 miles, a steep road leads to the **Rich Mountain Fire Tower**. The Forest Service began operating this tower in 1907, though it is no longer used. Air patrols now take the place of fire spotters. The altitude here is 2,681 feet. This is only 72 feet below the peak of Mount Magazine, the highest point in the Midwest. The tower is open during the summer months at selected hours.

Continue on to **Queen Wilhelmina State Park**. The original lodge was built in 1896 by investors in the Kansas City Southern Railway as an unusual resort retreat for passengers on the line. The three-story lodge became known as the "castle in the sky." Since the railroad was largely financed by Dutch interests, the new resort was named in honor of Holland's Queen Wilhelmina, who is reputed to have had some of her personal funds invested in the project. Unfortunately, because of its remoteness, the lodge closed after three years and fell into disrepair. It was not until the 1960s, after the area became a state park, that the lodge was reconstructed. It was destroyed by fire in 1973 and rebuilt as a modern lodge in the same basic style, using much of the original stone.

On the east side of the Queen Wilhelmina Lodge, the Lover's Leap Trail winds its way through woods and rock outcrops to a large, exposed cliff at the head of a steep ravine, a hiking distance of 0.3 mile. Beyond this great view, the trail becomes strenuous at times, and ends back at the lodge after a total of 1.1 miles. The first section of this trail is part of the **Ouachita Trail**, which originates 51 miles west in Oklahoma and ends 171 miles east at Pinnacle Mountain State Park, this side of Little Rock. The Ouachita Trail breaks off just beyond the Lover's Leap Trail, crosses over the scenic drive, and drops down the north side of Rich Mountain. It then crosses over the Ouachita River and heads up the east end of Black Fork Mountain. After dropping down to Eagle Gap, it then goes up and along Fourche Mountain eventually to US 71, a distance of 16.5 miles. West of Queen Wilhelmina State Park, this section of the Ouachita Trail crosses the length of Rich Mountain and part of Winding Stair Mountain for 27.9 miles, the longest section along the Ouachita Trail.

Looking north from the lodge to Black Fork Mountain, notice several white streaks running down the upper flanks of the mountain. They are called "rock glaciers." Their unusual occurrence in this part of the Ouachitas will be discussed later, at Chaha Point.

Continue west 5 miles down AR 88, passing several old homestead sites to the **State Line Historical Site**. A path leads from the parking area to a 1877 survey marker of the 48th mile of the line between Arkansas and the Choctaw Nation. The original survey line, established in 1825, was found to diverge to the west, depriving the relocated Choctaws of some of their new land. The original home of the Choctaw Indians was central and northern Mississippi. Having been influenced by the Spanish and the French for several years, they were adapting to living with the white settlers until the latter's greed for more land forced the Choctaws to move westward. Today, they still make up a large part of the citizenry of southeastern Oklahoma; the Choctaw Nation headquarters are located in Tuskahoma.

In another 8 miles, the **Chaha Vista** (*Chaha* is Choctaw for "mountain higher than others") offers a view of Kiamichi Mountain and the Kiamichi River valley below. East of the parking lot, notice, on the upper slope, an opening in the forest covered with rocks. This is a rock glacier, named for its tendency to move downhill much like an ordinary ice glacier. These rocks, composed of Jackfork sandstone, are prominent features on the Rich and Black Fork mountains. Because of their unstable nature, plants and soils are not able to establish on these exposed rock surfaces.

In 5.7 miles, the **Robert S. Kerr Arboretum and Nature Center** offers the opportunity to see interpretive displays and walk self-guided trails emphasizing the natural world of the forest. Each trail is less than a mile long;

one trail focuses on soil formation, another identifies various plants including trees, while the third explains plant succession and communities.

The road continues west, leaving Rich Mountain, and crosses US 259, which is part of Drive 29. The ascent of Winding Stair Mountain begins with numerous opportunities for far-reaching views and long, swooping stretches of highway make this section possibly the most exciting of all the scenic drives.

The first overlook, **Emerald Vista**, offers a view north to Cedar Lake, Lake Wister, Poteau Mountain, the town of Heavener, and the Poteau River valley. On the horizon, Cavanal Hill, towering above the City of Poteau, is visible some 12 miles away.

Continuing past Winding Stair Campground, several more pull-outs offer tremendous views of the surrounding mountains and valleys. To the right, Cedar Lake Road, or FR 12, leads to Holson Valley and the Cedar Lake Recreation Area. This area contains a 84-acre lake, with camping, showers, boating, picnicking, and hiking trails.

Another 1.7 miles will bring you to the historic **Horse Thief Springs**, a crossing for people moving horses from Texas to market in Missouri. Horse thieves were common along the route; the last group of outlaws were captured near the spring in the early 1900s. A 5-mile trail called Horse Thief Springs Trail starts here and descends Winding Stair Mountain to Cedar Lake.

The **Potato Hills Vista** provides an opportunity to see the Potato Hills, which were named for their likeness to the "hills" or mounds in which potatoes are planted.

The end of the drive is marked by the Forest Service's **Talihina Visitor Information Center**. The center features displays, maps, brochures, and books relating to the region. Knowledgeable volunteers are there to answer questions you may have about activities and weather conditions. The road also intersects with US 271, which is part of Drive 30.

29

Heavener Runestone

Poteau to Three Sticks Monument, Oklahoma

General description: A 35-mile drive starting at Poteau and heading south through the valley of the Viking explorers and over the Winding Stair Mountains to Big Cedar.

Special attractions: Cavanal Hill, Heavener Runestone State Park, Peter Conser Home, Cedar Lake Recreation Area, Ouachita National Forest, Winding Stair Mountains, Ouachita Trail, John F. Kennedy Memorial, Kiamichi River, Kiamichi Mountains, and Three Sticks Monument; scenic views, hiking, equestrian trails, camping, swimming, fishing, and hunting.

Location: West-central Ouachitas. The drive begins on U.S. Highway 59 at Poteau, travels south to U.S. Highway 259, and ends at Three Sticks Monument.

Drive route numbers: U.S. Highways 59 and 259.

Camping: Lake Wister State Park has 5 campgrounds with 172 sites; most offer showers, water, electricity, and RV hookups. Heavener Runestone State Park has day use only. Cedar Lake Recreation Area has 88 campsites. Winding Stair Recreation Area has 27 campsites. Primitive camping is allowed in the Ouachita National Forest.

Services: All services at Poteau and Heavener. Gas and food at Howe and Hodgen.

Nearby attractions: Black Fork Mountain and Upper Kiamichi River wilderness areas; Talimena Scenic Drive; Three Creeks National Scenic Area; and Indian Nations National Scenic and Wildlife Area.

 The drive

The northern part of the drive lies in the Arkansas River valley region of the Ouachitas. Although the Arkansas River is 15 miles to the north, its meandering and flooding over hundreds of thousands of years have influenced the character of the surrounding landscape. Broad, forested floodplains with prairie openings were once common near the river and along its major tributaries such as the Poteau River. On higher ground, rolling hills with scattered trees and a prairie understory provided habitat for elk, bison, and other animals of the open range. Land use changes and overhunting of the animals that once roamed the prairie have destroyed the former ecology.

Drive 29: Heavener Runestone

Poteau to Three Sticks Monument, Oklahoma

To Panama

59

Poteau

Cavanal Mountain

Sugar Loaf Mountain

271

Poteau River

83 ▷ To 71

Wister

To ◁ Red Oak

Lake Wister State Park

59

Lake Wister

Howe

270

Poteau Mountain

Heavener

Heavener Runestone State Park

128

N

Poteau River

Peter Conser Home

Hodgen

OUACHITA N. F.

0 1 2 3 4 5
Miles

7269

Cedar

Creek

Cedar Lake Recreation Area

Holson Valley Road

Indian Nations National Scenic and Wildlife Area

Robert Kerr Arboretum, Nature and Botanical Center

To Talimena State Park

Winding Stair Recreation Area

WINDING STAIR MOUNTAINS

1

259

270

Black Fork Mountain Wilderness Area

Page ▷ To Mount Ida

Rich

Ouachita Trail

Talimena Scenic Drive

1 ▷ To Queen Wilhelmina State Park

Mountain

Upper Kiamichi River Wilderness Area

Pipe Spring Picnic Grounds

To ◁ Talihina

63

Big Cedar

6032

Kiamichi River

John F. Kennedy Memorial

Three Sticks Monument

▷ To Mena

OUACHITA N. F.

259

To Broken Bow

The southern part of the drive enters the west-central region of the Ouachita Mountains. The mountains, with steep slopes and narrow valleys, are still forested today. They provide habitat for a wide variety of plants and animals—some of which are found only in this unique and fascinating landscape. Because the mountains trend to the east and west, there are a number of impressive views as the road climbs up and down its flanks winding its way south.

The drive begins in **Poteau**, which was founded in 1887. Its name, from the French word for "post," was taken from the nearby Poteau River. A post, or stake, was used to mark trade areas in Indian territory. Poteau is nestled in a picturesque valley, with the Sugar Loaf Mountains (2,600 feet in elevation) to the east and the overshadowing Cavanal Mountain (2,369 feet in elevation) on the west. The word "Cavanal" is derived from a French word meaning "cave." The mountain is called the "world's highest hill," because geologists use the term "mountain" only on land forms that rise a minimum of 2,000 feet above the surrounding landscape. Cavanal Mountain happens to rise 1,999 feet above Poteau, technically classifying it as a hill. A 6-mile scenic road to the top of Cavanal Mountain can be reached from US 59 on the north end of town. From US 59 north, find Hughes Drive and turn left, proceed to the first stop sign, and turn left again. Go to the next stop sign and turn right onto Witteville Road. Follow this road for 1.2 miles until you reach a Y in the road. Go left and follow this to the top of Cavanal.

This ancient Viking Inscription at Heavener Runestone State Park is said to have been carved in sandstone more than 1,300 years ago.

Follow US 59 south of Poteau to **Heavener**, about 10 miles away. Notice the commanding mountain northeast of Heavener. This is Poteau Mountain, a 1,200-foot, flat-topped mountain composed of sandstone, shale, and coal seams, which extends for 28 miles eastward with 23 of those miles in Arkansas. The town of Heavener was built in 1896 along the newly laid tracks of the Kansas City, Pittsburg, and Gulf Railway (now the Kansas City Southern Railway).

In Heavener, follow the signs to **Heavener Runestone State Park**, which is situated high up on Poteau Mountain, about 2 miles from US 59. The park was dedicated in 1970 to protect and display ancient Viking inscriptions on a large slab of Savannah sandstone. A Rune is any of the characters of an alphabet used by the ancient Scandinavian and other Germanic peoples. Such rock carvings are known as "runestones." These inscriptions have been dated as early as 600 A.D. and not later than 900 A.D., based on the type of characters used. Similar inscriptions have been found in New England at a settlement on the Atlantic coast by pre-Columbian Norsemen or Vikings. These Scandinavians traveled from their homeland to Iceland, then to Greenland, across Baffin Bay to Canada, and south to New England, where they established a settlement. From there it is speculated that they went down the Atlantic Coast, around Florida, and up the Gulf coast to the Mississippi River. Apparently, they then traveled up the Mississippi River to the Arkansas River and from there to the Poteau River, which leads to within a mile of the runestone.

The Heavener Runestone inscription reads *Glome Dal*, which translates as "valley owned by Glome," indicating that this might have been a boundary marker or land claim. Two other runestones, which were found nearby in 1969, help support the theory of the early Vikings' presence. Replicas of these inscriptions are on display at the state park. Unfortunately, it is reported that additional runestones existed, but were destroyed in the 1940s by treasure hunters.

In addition to a visitors center, Heavener Runestone State Park offers a winding, scenic trail that leads to a cove containing huge sandstone slabs that have broken away from the bluff face. The large sandstone rock with the runic inscription is housed in a small display building to protect it from further deterioration and potential vandals. A drive past the visitors center leads to a picnic area and a spectacular view of the Poteau River valley and the town of Heavener. The state park also has a 1-mile nature trail and two shorter trails that follow the bluff line.

Return to Heavener and head south on US 59. After about 1.5 miles, the Choctaw Visitor's Center of the Choctaw Ranger District, Ouachita National Forest, appears on the right. There, you can obtain information on places to visit, maps, and souvenirs.

At the town of Hodgen, a highway sign marks the way to the **Peter**

Conser Home by directing you to turn west on an unmarked road. After 3 miles you can see a white, two-story, wood-frame house. Tours of the 1894 home built by Peter Conser are available Wednesday through Sunday. Conser, whose mother was Choctaw, became deputy sheriff in 1877 at the age of twenty-five; later, he was a captain of the Choctaw Lighthorse, a mounted police force of the Five Civilized Tribes. They were an effective peacekeeping force in the region. He also served as a representative and senator to the Choctaw Council. He died in 1934, with wealth and social prestige. The Oklahoma Historical Society has renovated the house, returning it to its appearance during the Indian Territory period.

After returning to US 59, notice the mountain range rising to the south, the Winding Stair Mountains. An east-west range typical of the Ouachitas, it features some of the highest and grandest mountains in the region. This drive will soon lead into the midst of these mountains.

Ten miles south of Heavener a road to the right, called Holson Valley Road, goes 2.7 miles to the **Cedar Lake Recreation Area**. This Forest Service area contains an 86-acre lake, swimming beaches, and a fishing pier. In addition to camping, more than 70 miles of marked equestrian trails wind over hills and mountains and through rich river bottoms. These trails are also open to hikers and mountain bikers. One 5-mile trail, Horsethief Springs Trail, begins in the recreation area and climbs up the Winding Stair Mountains to Talimena Scenic Drive.

Continuing on US 59, in 5 miles, take US 259 south and begin the climb up Winding Stair Mountains. In about 4 miles, the road crosses Talimena Scenic Drive. For more details see Drive 28. In another 1.3 miles is the **Pipe Spring Picnic Ground** (five units).

After a little over 2 miles, the highway crosses the **Ouachita Trail**. Parking is on the west side of the road. The trail east crosses a short stretch of the Indian Nations National Scenic and Wildlife Area, runs down the middle of the Upper Kiamichi Wilderness Area, then crosses into Arkansas and ends at Queen Wilhelmina State Park, a total distance of 27.9 miles. The trail west follows the Winding Stair Mountains to the beginning of the Ouachita Trail at Talimena State Park, a total length of 23.7 miles. The entire distance offers beautiful views, steep mountains, lush vegetation, and lots of rocks. The Ouachita National Recreation Trail is the longest trail in Arkansas, extending 225 miles from Talimena State Park to Pinnacle Mountain State Park, just west of Little Rock, Arkansas.

After another mile on US 259, a side trip on FR 6032 leads 3 miles east to the 9,371-acre Upper Kiamichi River Wilderness Area. The Ouachita Trail can also be accessed at the boundary of the wilderness area.

In 0.7 mile on US 259, **Big Cedar**, now a ghost town, once boasted a population of about 50 people in 1910. On the south side of the intersection of US 259 and Oklahoma 63, a monument commemorates President John F.

This monument commemorates the dedication of US Highway 259
by President John F. Kennedy in 1961.

Kennedy's visit to Big Cedar on October 29, 1961, to speak at the dedication of US 259.

Continuing south on US 259, notice the impressive Kiamichi Mountain range ahead. Just 0.6 mile south, the road crosses the **Kiamichi River**, the most popular float stream in the Oklahoma Ouachitas. It originates on the south slope of Rich Mountain, northwest of Mena, Arkansas, near the Ouachita River. The Kiamichi flows west before turning south to eventually join the Red River. The best floating opportunities occur in the spring and fall at higher water levels. Due to several whitewater hazards, it is not recommended for the inexperienced floater.

In 4 miles the road climbs to the summit of the **Kiamichi Mountains**. Kiamichi is derived from the French word *kamichi*, which means "horned screamer," a species of bird. It might have referred to the now-extinct Carolina parakeet, whose call consisted of much yelling and screeching. An observation pull-out provides an opportunity to see **Three Sticks Monument**, which honors several political leaders who were credited with the rapid development of the State of Oklahoma. Their names are inscribed on a plaque at the base of the monument.

30

Spiro Mounds

Fort Smith to Talihina, Arkansas/Oklahoma

General description: A 58-mile drive beginning in Fort Smith, then generally heading south to the Spiro Indian Mounds and ending just beyond the Winding Stair Mountains at Talihina.

Special attractions: Fort Smith Historic District, Spiro Indian Mounds, Cavanal Mountain, Ouachita National Forest, Winding Stair Mountains, Ouachita Trail, and Talimena State Park; scenic views, fall colors, hiking, camping, swimming, fishing, and hunting.

Location: Western Ouachitas. The drive is on U.S. Highway 271 from Fort Smith to Talihina.

Drive route numbers: U.S. Highway 271.

Camping: Lake Wister State Park has 5 campgrounds with 172 sites; most offer showers, water, electricity, and RV hookups. Talimena State Park has picnic sites, 7 RV sites, 15 unimproved campsites, and a comfort station with shower.

Primitive camping is allowed in the Ouachita National Forest.

Services: All services at Fort Smith, Spiro, Poteau, and Talihina. Gas and food at Panama and Wister.

Nearby attractions: Robbers Cave State Park, Talimena and Heavener Runestone scenic drives, and Sardis Lake.

The drive

Heading south out of the Arkansas River valley, this drive climbs over the Winding Stair Mountains and comes within sight of the Kiamichi Mountains. Both of these east-west trending mountain chains are located in the western part of the Ouachita Mountains. In the Fort Smith area, the relatively flat to rolling Arkansas River valley was once characterized by prairie and bottomland hardwood forests. Today it is primarily pasture and cultivated land. The Ouachita Mountains, because of their rugged nature, still contain extensive forests of pine and hardwoods.

The drive begins in **Fort Smith**, the second largest city in Arkansas. The development of Fort Smith can be traced back to the early 1800s, when the Cherokee Indians were forced to move west from their Appalachian

Drive 30: Spiro Mounds
Fort Smith to Talihina, Arkansas/Oklahoma (north)

Drive 30: Spiro Mounds

Fort Smith to Talihina, Arkansas/Oklahoma (south)

homelands. In 1818, the U.S. government gave the Cherokees a large tract in northern Arkansas; however, it was not long before the Cherokees were having trouble with the resident Osage Indians, white hunters, and white squatters trying to settle in Indian territory. In 1817, on orders from Secretary of War Joel R. Poinsett, General Thomas A. Smith detailed Major William Bradford to establish a fort to keep peace. After arriving from Bellefontaine, on the Missouri River north of St. Louis, his small contingent of sixty-four men began work on a military outpost. Five years later, the fort was completed and named Fort Smith after Bradford's commanding officer. However, the presence of the fort did not squelch the conflicts among the Indian tribes and the white hunters and squatters, so the original garrison was moved northwest to Fort Gibson in 1824, closer to the frontier.

Although the initial fort never fulfilled its original mission, it did stimulate the development of the town. In 1841, after much political pressure, a new fort (now a national historic site) was built near the site of the original post to serve as a supply depot for other frontier forts. Two years later the town of Fort Smith was incorporated. The town quickly grew when gold was discovered on the West Coast in 1848; Fort Smith served as a major supplier for the miners heading to California. The arrival of the first Butterfield stagecoach in 1858 caused more people who were traveling from St. Louis to California to pass through Fort Smith, bringing more business to the town.

The arrival of the railroads in 1879 also contributed significantly to the development of Fort Smith. These railroads stimulated coal mining in the region, provided cheap transportation for agricultural products, and encouraged industries to locate in Fort Smith.

Today, Fort Smith provides conveniences and services customarily found in larger cities. Overnight lodging, restaurants, numerous historical and cultural attractions, and shopping opportunities contribute to the city's prosperity. For information on activities in Fort Smith, contact the Fort Smith Convention and Visitors Bureau (see Appendix). Be sure to visit the Fort Smith Historic District, which includes the **Fort Smith National Historic Site**. It can be reached by following AR 22, which is Rogers Avenue, to the west end of the city. When AR 22 turns right onto Garrison Avenue, stay left on Rogers Avenue, which leads to the historic site. The principal building, a former federal courthouse, contains a visitors center with exhibits and items for sale.

To continue the drive, proceed south from Fort Smith joining US 271 from I-540. US 271 crosses over the Poteau River and, in 4 miles, intersects with a road and a sign indicating the direction to **Spiro Mounds State Park**. Follow the road for another 4 miles to the park. Located on 140 acres, the park is the site of an Indian mound-building culture that occupied the area from 850 A.D. to 1450 A.D. Named for the nearby town of Spiro, the mounds are considered one of the most important archaeological sites in the United States. The museum and interpretive center contains fascinating and elegant displays of stone effigy pipes in human and animal forms, shell beads, pottery, copper plaques, basketry, engraved conch shell bowls, and other artifacts. An interpretive trail behind the center leads to twelve mounds, that were built for religious and political ceremonies and burial sites for prominent leaders.

Located on a bend of the Arkansas River, the site was a natural gateway between Indian societies in the southeastern United States and those living in the Great Plains to the west. For several centuries, the Spiro culture exerted much political, religious, and economic influence with their mound construction, political and religious leadership, horticulture, craftsmanship, and trading practices.

Despite their complex and advanced society, the Spiro culture mysteriously disappeared around 1450 A.D. Reasons for abandonment of the Spiro site are unknown, and archaeologists speculate any number of causes including a long period of drought, warfare, internal strife, disease, or a combination of factors.

Although it was known locally as a prehistoric Indian site as early as the late nineteenth century, it was not until 1933 that the Spiro Mounds attracted national and worldwide attention. That year, a group of treasure hunters calling themselves the Pocola Mining Company leased the land containing the mounds and began digging at Craig Mound, which was the largest of the mounds. Unfortunately, thousands of artifacts were either carelessly destroyed or else sold indiscriminately to onlookers or private collectors. Although some of these artifacts did find their way into museums, there was little or no description as to their significance or the context in which they were found. Fortunately, when the mining company's lease ran out in 1935, federal and state agencies and institutions took over and conducted a systematic excavation of the remainder of the Spiro Mounds. Today, the Oklahoma Archaeological Survey carries out excavations at the park and publishes scientific findings and interpretations.

Spiro Mounds State Park is closed every Monday, and Tuesdays from November to April. Daytime hours are from 9 a.m. to 5 p.m., except for Sundays, when the hours are noon to 5 p.m. Other artifacts from the Spiro Mounds are on display at the University of Oklahoma in Norman, the Oklahoma Historical Museum in Oklahoma City, and the Philbrook Museum in Tulsa.

Return to US 271 and proceed to **Spiro**. Founded in 1895 when the Kansas City Southern Railroad was extended through the region, Spiro is primarily a service and trade center for the surrounding villages, farms, and ranches.

Continue on US 271 for 4 miles to **Panama**. Named for the Panama

Canal, which was under construction at the time, the town was established as a coal-shipping point when the Kansas City Southern Railway expanded south through the Ouachitas. Many of the homes date back to the turn-of-the-century coal-mining era when the town prospered. The view to the south reveals a prominent landmark, Cavanal Mountain, which marks the location of the town of Poteau. The road crosses Coal Creek just before the creek empties into Poteau River to the east.

After another 5 miles, US 271 enters **Poteau**, seat of Le Flore County. For details on Poteau and Cavanal Mountain, see Drive 29.

Leaving Poteau, continue on US 271 for 9 miles to **Wister**. This town began in 1890 when the Arkansas and Choctaw Railroad came westward into Oklahoma and formed a junction with the St. Louis and San Francisco Railroad's Texas branch. Today, due to its strategic location at the junction of US 270 and US 271, Wister is experiencing modest growth and serves as a center for hunters, fishermen, and tourists. Two miles south of Wister on US 270, Lake Wister and **Lake Wister State Park** provide camping, boating, fishing, and camping. Hiking is also available on the Lone Star Interpretive Trail. The area has a variety of habitats including oak and pine uplands and grassy glades. Waterfowl and bald eagles can be seen in fall and winter and a variety of songbirds and raptors are present the rest of the year. Otters are occasionally sighted in nearby streams.

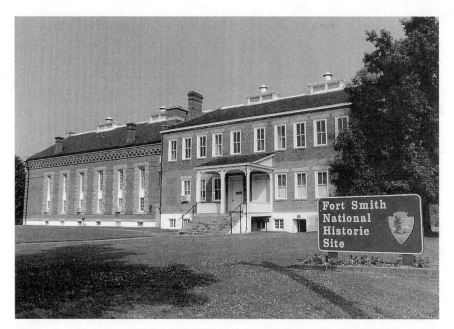

Once a federal courthouse, this building now houses a gift shop and exhibits depicting events surrounding the establishment of Fort Smith.

Passing through the nearly abandoned community of **Caston**, the road heads south towards the majestic Winding Stair Mountains, some of the highest and grandest in the region. In a couple of miles the road crosses Fourche Maline Creek, which in French designates that it is a sharply branching creek. The creek is dammed east of here to form Lake Wister, a 4,000-acre lake surrounded by 33,428 acres set aside as a wildlife management area. The road passes through this special area, which is called **Wister Wildlife Management Area**.

In a little over 3 miles, the road begins to climb the north slope of the **Winding Stair Mountains**. About a mile later, the boundary of the **Ouachita National Forest** begins. US 271 skirts the western edge of the national forest, which extends eastward to near Little Rock, Arkansas. The 1,276,973-acre national forest provides 33 developed recreation areas, 7 scenic areas, 7 wilderness areas, and 480 miles of trails. Information on activities can be obtained at the supervisor's office in Hot Springs or from any of the twelve district offices.

There are 7 miles of loops and switchbacks as the road climbs to the summit of the Winding Stair Mountains, 1,289 feet above sea level. US 271 then intersects with Oklahoma Highway 1, **Talimena Scenic Drive** (see Drive 28 for more details), and Talihena Visitor Information Center. Publications and information on activities in the area are available at the center.

About a mile beyond the visitor center, **Talimena State Park** provides camping and access to the **Ouachita Trail**. The trailhead initiates a 222.5-mile-long journey eastward to Pinnacle Mountain State Park, just west of Little Rock, Arkansas. The trail was constructed from 1971 to 1981 by Forest Service and state park personnel and groups of volunteers. Although the trail has had a bad reputation in the past for poor design and development, recent improvements and a stronger commitment by the Forest Service have greatly improved the trail. This stretch of the trail goes 23.7 miles to the Winding Stair Campground and is considered the most difficult section of the Ouachita Trail to hike.

US 271 descends the Winding Stair Mountains and in 7 miles enters **Talihina**. Settled in 1888, the town's name is derived from a Choctaw Indian word for "the great iron road," signifying the arrival of the St. Louis and San Francisco Railroad, which laid its tracks through the Winding Stair Mountains. The town, having grown up around the railroad, still remained fairly isolated until 1919 when a reliable road was built through the forest by convict labor. Nestled in the valley of the Kiamichi River, impressive views are offered of the Winding Stair range to the north and east, the towering Kiamichi Mountains to the south, and the knobby Potato Hills to the east.

31

Cherokee Nation

Sallisaw to Tahlequah, Oklahoma

General description: A 58-mile drive beginning at Sallisaw in the Arkansas River valley and traveling west and then north into the Ozarks to the heart of the Cherokee Nation at Tahlequah.

Special attractions: Sequoyah's Home Site, Sequoyah National Wildlife Refuge, Robert S. Kerr Lake, Lake Tenkiller, Cherokee Courthouse Historic Site, Murrell Home, Cherokee National Museum, and Cherokee Capitol Building; scenic views, hiking, camping, swimming, fishing (including trout), and hunting.

Location: Arkansas River valley and southwestern edge of the Ozarks. The drive is from Sallisaw to Tahlequah.

Drive route numbers: U.S. Highways 59 and 64 and Oklahoma Highways 82 and 100.

Camping: Tenkiller State Park has 40 native stone and timber cabins for rent plus 10 camping areas with a total of 221 campsites. These vary from primitive sites to modern ones with electricity, water, showers, and restrooms. Cherokee Landing State Park has 100 campsites with 59 electric hookups, water, showers, and restrooms. On Lake Tenkiller, the U.S. Army Corps of Engineers has 18 recreation areas, 15 of which have campsites. Restrooms, electrical hookups, showers, and water are provided depending on recreation area. On Robert S. Kerr Lake, the Corps offers 13 recreation areas, 8 of which have designated camping. Facilities vary according to camping area.

Services: All services at Sallisaw, Vian, Gore, and Tahlequah. Food and gas at Cookson and Keys. Gas at Flat Ridge.

Nearby attractions: Sallisaw State Park, Fort Smith, Spiro Mounds Scenic Drive, and the Illinois River.

 The drive

The drive begins in the Arkansas River valley in what is known as the Arkoma Basin, which separates the Ozarks from the Ouachita Mountains. Mountain remnants viewed to the south were isolated from the main Ouachitas by basin settling and the erosive action of rivers over millions of years. The Arkansas River valley was once primarily a mixture of prairie

Drive 31: Cherokee Nation
Sallisaw to Tahlequah, Oklahoma

SITES

1. Sequoyah's Home Site
2. Sallisaw Creek State Park
3. Sequoyah National Wildlife Refuge
4. Cherokee Courthouse Historic Site
5. Lake Tenkiller Overlook
6. Tenkiller State Park
7. Cherokee Landing State Park
8. Murrell Home
9. Cherokee National Museum

and bottomland hardwood forest, with some marshes and sloughs left behind by the meandering Arkansas River. Today, the deep, fertile soil produces crops and provides pastures for cattle. The northern part of the drive enters the Cookson Hills on the western edge of the Ozarks. The terrain is less mountainous, being characterized instead by large, rolling hills covered with upland hardwood forests of oak and hickory. In some parts of this region the forests were more like woodlands or savannas with scattered trees and an understory of prairie grasses and forbs (wildflowers). Elk and bison once roamed this land, as did the Caddo and then the Osage Indians, long before the time of European settlement and the displacement of eastern Indian nations to this part of Oklahoma.

Easy access to **Sallisaw** is provided off of I-40, but the rest of the drive will take advantage of two-lane roads that offer the opportunity to sightsee at a much slower pace. Sallisaw's name originated with French trappers who called the place *Salaisiau*, meaning "salt provision." Indians, early settlers, explorers, and trappers were familiar with the natural salt deposits found along many nearby streams. John Steinbeck, author of *The Grapes of Wrath*, used Sallisaw as the starting point for the novel's "Okies" fleeing to California to escape the dust bowl of the 1930s. Actually, it was in western Oklahoma that blowing winds created dust clouds from the dry, flat land that suffered from poor farming practices.

From Sallisaw, a side trip north on US 59 offers an opportunity to see **Sequoyah's home site**. Take US 59 3 miles north to OK 101 and go 6.7 miles east to the homesite. This wooded, ten-acre site features Sequoyah's log cabin housed in a Works Progress Administration (WPA) cover building. There are also walking paths, a visitors center and gift shop, and a daytime picnic area. Sequoyah was perhaps the best educated of the Cherokee statesmen and is credited with devising the written alphabet of the Cherokee language. He was born in the lower Appalachian region of Tennessee in about 1770. His mother was Cherokee; his non-Indian father left the family when Sequoyah was very young. As an adult, he became known as a skilled blacksmith and silversmith and for his drawings and paintings. In 1809, he began experimenting with a written alphabet for the Cherokee language. After years of experimenting, he found that developing an alphabet of letters would not work. Instead, he devised different symbols for each word of his language. Although the alphabet was not accepted at first, tribal members eventually were won over, and Sequoyah was recognized as a knowledgeable and respected man. He moved his family to Oklahoma and shortly after built a one-room log cabin. This 1829 structure was designated in 1966 as a national historic landmark by the Secretary of the Interior.

Sequoyah became famous worldwide as the inventor of a nation's written language. He was selected as one of Oklahoma's two greatest men in the National Statuary Hall of Washington D.C. Also, California's giant redwood

*A dramatic portrayal of Sequoyah, the father of the Cherokee alphabet,
can be seen at Sequoyah's home site.*

tree, the Sequoia, was named after him.

Returning to Sallisaw, another side trip is recommended, especially in the fall and winter. The **Robert S. Kerr Lake** is located 8 miles south of Sallisaw. A U.S. Army Corps of Engineers lake on the Arkansas River, the area below the dam offers outstanding opportunities to view bald eagles in fall and winter. Waterfowl, white pelicans, and shorebirds are also seen during migration in the fall and spring. A visitors center with observation decks overlooks the lock and dam. The 5.4-mile Short Mountain Hiking Trail is located near the lock and dam. With steep climbs at either end, the trail eventually reaches the top of Short Mountain for a commanding view. For those who want to take a swim, Kerr Beach is the largest sand beach in Oklahoma.

Return to Sallisaw, and proceed west on US 64. In 2.8 miles, **Sallisaw Creek State Park** offers picnicking and fishing on Brushy Creek Lake. Shortly after Sallisaw Creek, the road crosses the extreme lower edge of the Ozarks. The rest of the drive west and north will explore deeper into the Oklahoma Ozarks.

Continue to the town of **Vian**. In this small community, turn south onto OK 82, and follow the signs for 3.5 miles to the entrance of **Sequoyah National Wildlife Refuge**. Established in 1970 to provide habitat for waterfowl and other migratory birds, the refuge contains 20,800 acres, half of them in Kerr Lake. A visitors center is located at the refuge headquarters, and a 6-mile auto tour winds through woodlands, marshes, and along the lakeshore. Much of the rich bottomland is planted in winter wheat, soybeans, milo, and corn. This is cost-shared with local farmers who plant and harvest the crops, leaving a portion for wildlife. In the winter, the refuge hosts between 15,000 to 20,000 snow geese, making it home to the largest concentration of snow geese in the state. Bald eagles and white pelicans can also be seen during migration and in winter. The best viewing is from the 0.5-mile hiking trail that goes to an observation platform. Other wildlife, such as bobcats and river otters, can also be seen.

Returning to Vian, turn west and continue on US 64 for 6 miles to the **Cherokee Courthouse Historic Site**. The buildings here served as the original western capital of the Cherokee nation from 1829 to 1839, when a portion of the eastern nation migrated to the Oklahoma Territory after the Treaty of 1817. It was here that Chief John Jolly established a settlement and capital, called Tahlanteeskee, with a National Council House and Courthouse, near the Illinois River. When the eastern Cherokee nation was driven from its homeland on the "Trail of Tears" in 1838-1839, the two nations were reunited, and the capital was reestablished at Tahlequah. A visitors center and gift shop occupies one of the restored log cabins.

Leaving the historic site, US 64 crosses over the Illinois River. The river begins near Hogeye, Arkansas, and flows north and west through the

Ozark National Forest and south into Oklahoma to empty into the Arkansas River. The upper reaches, to the point where the river enters Tenkiller Lake, are very popular for canoeing. A section above Tahlequah has been designated an Oklahoma Scenic River.

After crossing the Illinois River, continue on to **Gore**. Originally named "Campbell" and then "Illinois" (after the nearby river), it was renamed "Gore" when statehood was achieved, in honor of Senator Thomas P. Gore. Located 7 miles south of Tenkiller Lake, the town serves as the gateway to the lake area for visitors arriving from the south and west. It is known as the "Trout Capital of Oklahoma," as it is located within a mile of the lower Illinois River, which offers year-round trout fishing. The water temperature, forty-eight degrees Fahrenheit, is caused by its being released from the bottom of the dam at Lake Tenkiller; this is the ideal temperature for trout.

In Gore, take OK 100 north 6 miles to the **Lake Tenkiller** dam overlook. Before the dam was built, there was a ferry crossing in this area operated by a Cherokee Indian family named Tenkiller. They sold the land to the U.S. Army Corps of Engineers for the lake's development. At the overlook, the Island View Nature Trail edges along the lake for 2 miles to Strayhorn Landing. The first 0.5 mile is developed, with bridges and a gravel base. The rest of the trail is more strenuous. From seventy to one hundred bald eagles can be seen in the fall and winter, as they fish along the surface of this exceptionally clear lake.

Stay on OK 100, crossing the dam with Tenkiller State Park on the left. This is a popular, sometimes overcrowded state park during the summer. It might be best to visit this state park during the off season, or else choose one of the Corps of Engineers' park areas during the busier times.

Continue on to the intersection with OK 82. This is the principal road leading to Tahlequah. The road turns north and crosses the Cookson Hills, offering a rugged, scenic drive over steep wooded hills, sandstone outcrops, and crystal clear streams. Because of its rugged and inaccessible landscape, Charles "Pretty Boy" Floyd and other notorious outlaws used the Cookson Hills as a hideout during the 1930s.

In 13 miles, OK 82 crosses over the upper end of Lake Tenkiller and passes **Cherokee Landing State Park**. After another 8.4 miles and just before the intersection of OK 62, OK 10, and OK 88, turn right on Murrell Road. Follow the road 1 mile to **Murrell Home**. Built by George Michael Murrell in 1843, the home was the center for many social and political activities among the Cherokee. The mansion is now operated by the Oklahoma State Historical Society and is open daily, except for Mondays and holidays, and except from November through April, when it is open Wednesday through Saturday.

Opposite the Murrell Home, follow the road north 0.7 mile to the **Cherokee Heritage Center**. Established in 1963 by the Cherokee National Historical Society, a private, nonprofit corporation, it was designed to preserve the history and culture of the Cherokee people. The center is on the site of the Park Hill Mission, established in 1836 by Presbyterians as a religious and educational center for the Cherokees. The mission included homes for missionaries and teachers, a boarding hall for students, a grist mill, shops, stables, and a printing office and book bindery. Thousands of schoolbooks and extracts from the Bible were published, many in the Cherokee alphabet developed by Sequoyah. In 1851, a Cherokee Female Seminary was built and dedicated to the perpetuation of the Cherokee heritage in the resources of its young women. Fire destroyed the structure in 1887; only three of its brick columns still stand today.

The **Cherokee National Museum** opened in 1975, and displays more than 4,300 artifacts related to Cherokee history and culture, as well as valuable art objects. The 24,000-square-foot building also houses the Cherokee National Archives and a library with more than 4,100 volumes related to Cherokee history and culture. A gift shop at the entrance of the museum displays handcrafted items designed by Native American craftspeople.

Be sure to take the guided tour of the Ancient Village at Tsa-La-Gi. Completed in 1967, the Ancient Village recreates the lifestyle of the Cherokees during the sixteenth century, prior to European contact. It has been

A young Cherokee woman provides a guided tour through the Ancient Village at Tsa-La-Gi.

rated as one of America's finest living museums. The tours are available from May through late August. From early June to late August, every night except Sunday, the amphitheater at Tsa-La-Gi provides the setting for the "Trail of Tears" drama. Beginning with the removal of the Cherokees from their ancestral homeland in 1838, when 4,000 of the 16,000 tribal members died in a forced march, through the statehood of Oklahoma in 1907, the historic drama captures the life of the Cherokee people and the struggles that they overcame after reaching Indian territory.

Leaving the Cherokee Heritage Center, turn right and then left onto Willis Road. Follow the road to the intersection of OK 10, OK 62, and OK 82, turn right and proceed 2 miles to **Tahlequah**. With a population of 10,400, it is the largest city in the Oklahoma Ozarks. Tahlequah became the permanent capital of the Cherokee nation on September 6, 1839, when the eastern and the western Cherokees met on the site of the present square to sign a new constitution. The Cherokee Capitol, completed in 1870, stands on that square today . It now houses the Tahlequah Area Chamber of Commerce and the Cherokee Gift Shop. Follow Muskogee Avenue to the downtown square to see the capitol. Today, Tahlequah is primarily a service center and college town, being the home of Northeastern State University. And, according to the chamber of commerce, for the past eight years the town has been ranked as the fourth best retirement location in America, based on a study of climate, health care, personal safety, housing, cost of living, and leisure activities.

Appendix
For More Information

*For more information on lands and events, please
contact the following agencies and organizations.*

Drive 1

Cape Girardeau Convention and
  Visitors Bureau
2121 Broadway
Cape Girardeau, MO 63701
(573) 335-1631
(800) 777-0068

Cape Girardeau Conservation Service
  Center
2302 County Park Drive
Cape Girardeau, MO 63701
(573) 290-5730

Cape River Heritage Museum
538 Independence
Cape Girardeau, MO 63703
(573) 334-0405

Historic Sites Division
Illinois Historic Preservation Agency
313 S. 6th St., 2nd Floor
Springfield, IL 62701
(217) 785-1584

Jonesboro Ranger District
521 North Main Street
Jonesboro, IL 62952
(618) 833-8576

Missouri Department of Conservation
P.O. Box 180
Jefferson City, MO 65102
(573) 751-4115

Illinois Department of Natural
  Resources
524 S. 2nd Street
Springfield, IL 62701-1787
(217) 782-7454

Missouri Department of Natural
  Resources
Division of Parks, Recreation, and
  Historic Preservation
P.O. Box 176
Jefferson City, MO 65102
(573) 751-2479
(800) 334-6946

Shawnee National Forest
Route 45 South
Harrisburg, IL 62946
(618) 253-7114

Trail of Tears State Forest
RR1, Box 1331
Jonesboro, IL 62952
(618) 833-4910

Trail of Tears State Park
429 Moccasin Springs
Jackson, MO 63755
(573) 334-1711

Drive 2

Fort de Chartres State Historic Site
1350 State Highway 155
Prairie du Rocher, IL 62277
(618) 284-7230

Great River Road Interpretive Center
66 South Main
Ste. Genevieve, MO 63670
(573) 883-7097

Hawn State Park
12096 Park Drive
Ste. Genevieve, MO 63670
(573)-883-3603

Historic Sites Division
Illinois Historic Preservation Agency
313 S. 6th St., 2nd Floor
Springfield, IL 62701
(217) 785-1584

Illinois Dept. of Natural Resources
524 S. 2nd Street
Springfield, IL 62706
(217) 782-7454

Maeystown Oktoberfest
c/o The Corner George Inn
  Bed and Breakfast
P.O. Box 103
1101 Main St.
Maeystown, IL 62256
(618) 458-6660
(The Corner George Inn acts as the
Chamber of Commerce for this small
town.)

Missouri Department of
  Conservation
P.O. Box 180
Jefferson City, MO 65102
(573) 751-4115

Missouri Department of Natural
  Resources
Division of Parks, Recreation, and
  Historic Preservation
P.O. Box 176
Jefferson City, MO 65102
(573) 751-2479
(800) 334-6946

Drive 3

Mark Twain National Forest
401 Fairgrounds Road
Rolla, MO 65401
(573) 364-4621

Missouri Department of
  Conservation
P.O. Box 180
Jefferson City, MO 65102
(573) 751-4115

Missouri Department of Natural
  Resources
Division of Parks, Recreation, and
  Historic Preservation
P.O. Box 176
Jefferson City, MO 65102
(573) 751-2479
(800) 334-6946

Drive 4

Mark Twain National Forest
401 Fairgrounds Road
Rolla, MO 65401
(573) 364-4621

Missouri Department of
  Conservation
P.O. Box 180
Jefferson City, MO 65102
(573) 751-4115

Missouri Department of Natural
  Resources
Division of Parks, Recreation, and
  Historic Preservation
P.O. Box 176
Jefferson City, MO 65102
(573) 751-2479
(800) 334-6946

Drive 5

Maramec Spring Park
The James Foundation
320 S. Bourbeuse
St. James, MO 65559
(573) 265-7124
(573) 265-7387 (reservations)

Mark Twain National Forest
401 Fairgrounds Road
Rolla, MO 65401
(573) 364-4621

Meramec Caverns
P.O. Box 948
Stanton, MO 63079
(573) 468-3166

Missouri Department of
Conservation
P.O. Box 180
Jefferson City, MO 65102
(573) 751-4115

Missouri Department of Natural
Resources
Division of Parks, Recreation, and
Historic Preservation
P.O. Box 176
Jefferson City, MO 65102
(573) 751-2479
(800) 334-694

Drive 6

August A. Busch Memorial
Conservation Area
2360 Highway D
St. Charles, MO 63304
(314) 441-4554
(314) 441-4669

Hermann Visitor Information Center
306 Market Street
Hermann, MO 65041
(573) 486-2744

Missouri Department of
Conservation
P.O. Box 180
Jefferson City, MO 65102
(573) 751-4115

Missouri Department of Natural
Resources
Division of Parks, Recreation, and
Historic Preservation
P.O. Box 176
Jefferson City, MO 65102
(573) 751-2479
(800) 334-6946

Drive 7

Arrow Rock State Historic Site
P.O. Box 1
Arrow Rock, MO 65320
(816) 837-3330

Cedar Creek Ranger District
4549 State Road H
Fulton, MO 65251
(573) 592-1400

City of Columbia Convention and
Visitors Bureau
300 South Providence Road
Columbia, MO 65205
(573) 875-1231

Finger Lakes State Park
Route 7
1505 East Peabody
Columbia, MO 65202
(573) 443-5315

The Friends of Arrow Rock [tours]
P.O. Box 124
Arrow Rock, MO 65320
(816) 837-3231

Mark Twain National Forest
401 Fairgrounds Road
Rolla, MO 65401
(573) 364-4621

Missouri Department of
    Conservation
P.O. Box 180
Jefferson City, MO 65102
(573) 751-4115

Missouri Department of Natural
    Resources
Division of Parks, Recreation, and
    Historic Preservation
P.O. Box 176
Jefferson City, MO 65102
(573) 751-2479
(800) 334-6946

Missouri Department of
    Conservation
P.O. Box 180
Jefferson City, MO 65102
(573) 751-4115

Missouri Department of Natural
    Resources
Division of Parks, Recreation, and
    Historic Preservation
P.O. Box 176
Jefferson City, MO 65102
(573) 751-2479
(800) 334-6946

Ozark Caverns
Lake of the Ozarks State Park
Route 1, Box 371
Linn Creek, MO 65052
(573) 346-2500

Drive 9

Mark Twain National Forest
401 Fairgrounds Road
Rolla, MO 65401
(573) 364-4621

Missouri Department of
    Conservation
P.O. Box 180
Jefferson City, MO 65102
(573) 751-4115

Missouri Department of Natural
    Resources
Division of Parks, Recreation, and
    Historic Preservation
P.O. Box 176
Jefferson City, MO 65102
(573) 751-2479
(800) 334-6946

Drive 8

Ha Ha Tonka State Park
Route 1, Box 658
Camdenton, MO 65020
(573) 346-2986

Lake of the Ozarks State Park
P.O. Box 170
Kaiser, MO 65047
(573) 348-2694

Ozark National Scenic Riverways
National Park Service
P.O. Box 490
Van Buren, MO 63965
(573) 323-4236

Van Buren Ranger District Office
US Forest Service
P.O. Box 69
Van Buren, MO 63965
(573) 323-4216

Drive 10

Big Spring Lodge
c/o The Landing
P.O. Box 697
Van Buren, MO 63965
(573) 323-4332
(They are the concessionaire for the
Big Spring restaurant and cabins.)

Big Spring Ranger District
c/o Ozark National Scenic Riverways
P.O. Box 490
Van Buren, MO 63965
(573) 323-4236

Eleven Point Ranger District
Route 1, Box 1908
Winona, MO 65588
(573) 325-4233

Mark Twain National Forest
401 Fairgrounds Road
Rolla, MO 65401
(573) 364-4621

Missouri Department of
  Conservation
P.O. Box 180
Jefferson City, MO 65102
(573) 751-4115

Ozark National Scenic Riverways
National Park Service
P.O. Box 490
Van Buren, MO 63965
(573) 323-4236

Drive 11

Arkansas Fish and Game
  Commission
#2 Natural Resources Dr
Little Rock, AR 72205
(501) 223-6300

Arkansas State Parks
One Capitol Mall
Little Rock, AR 72201
(501) 682-1191

Eleven Point Ranger District
Route 1, Box 1908
Winona, MO 65588
(573) 325-4233

Fred's Fish House
201 Main Street
Mammoth Springs, AR 72554
(501) 625-7551

Mammoth Spring National Fish
Hatchery
P.O. Box 160
Mammoth Spring, AR 72554
(501) 625-3912

Mammoth Spring State Park
P.O. Box 36
Mammoth Spring, AR 72554
(501) 625-7364

Mark Twain National Forest
401 Fairgrounds Road
Rolla, MO 65401
(573) 364-4621

Missouri Department of
  Conservation
P.O. Box 180
Jefferson City, MO 65102
(573) 751-4115

Missouri Department of Natural
Resources
Division of Parks, Recreation, and
Historic Preservation
P.O. Box 176
Jefferson City, MO 65102
(573) 751-2479
(800) 334-6946

Drive 12

Ava Area Chamber of Commerce
206 E. Washington St.
Ava, MO 65608
(417) 683-4594

Ava Ranger District
1103 South Jefferson
P.O. Box 188
Ava, MO 65608
(417) 683-4428

Mark Twain National Forest
401 Fairgrounds Road
Rolla, MO 65401
(573) 364-4621

Missouri Department of
  Conservation
P.O. Box 180
Jefferson City, MO 65102
(573) 751-4115

Mountain Home Resident Office
U.S. Army Corps of Engineers
P.O. Box 369
Mountain Home, AR 72653
(501) 425-2700

Theodosia Park is the specific Corps
campground
HC 5, Box 5030
Theodosia, MO 65761
(417) 273-4626

Drive 13

Branson Chamber of Commerce
P.O. Box 220
Branson, MO 65616
(417) 334-4136

Missouri Department of
  Conservation
P.O. Box 180
Jefferson City, MO 65102
(573) 751-4115

Missouri Department of Natural
  Resources
Division of Parks, Recreation, and
  Historic Preservation
P.O. Box 176
Jefferson City, MO 65102
(573) 751-2479
(800) 334-6946

Missouri Conservation Department
  Headquarters
2630 N. Mayfair
Springfield, MO 65803
(417) 895-6880

Springfield Conservation Nature
Center
4600 S. Chrisman
Springfield, MO 65804
(417) 888-4237

Table Rock Lake Project Office
U.S. Army Corps of Engineers
P.O. Box 1109
Branson, MO 65616
(417) 334-4101
(417) 271-3215 for Eagle Rock
Campsite reservations
(417) 271-3860 for Viney Creek
Campsite reservations

Table Rock State Park
5272 State Highway 165
Branson, MO 65616
(417) 334-4704

Drive 14

Kaelke Bed and Breakfast
Rt. 3, Box 49
Lockwood, MO 65682
(417) 232-4925

Missouri Department of
    Conservation
P.O. Box 180
Jefferson City, MO 65102
(573) 751-4115

Missouri Department of Natural
    Resources
Division of Parks, Recreation, and
    Historic Preservation
P.O. Box 176
Jefferson City, MO 65102
(573) 751-2479
(800) 334-6946
[1-9,11,13-15]

Missouri Prairie Foundation
P.O. Box 200
Columbia, MO 63144

The Nature Conservancy
Missouri Field Office
2800 South Brentwood Boulevard
St. Louis, MO 63144
(314) 968-1105

Prairie State Park
P.O. Box 97
Liberal, MO 64762
(417) 843-6711

Drive 15

Cassville Ranger District
Highway 248 East
P.O. Box 310
Cassville, MO 65625
(417) 847-2144

Mark Twain National Forest
401 Fairgrounds Road
Rolla, MO 65401
(573) 364-4621

Missouri Department of Natural
    Resources
Division of Parks, Recreation, and
    Historic Preservation
P.O. Box 176
Jefferson City, MO 65102
(573) 751-2479
(800) 334-6946

Roaring River State Park
Route 2, Box 2535
Cassville, MO 65265
(417) 847-2330

Table Rock Lake Project Office
U.S. Army Corps of Engineers
P.O. Box 1109
Branson, MO 65616
(417) 334-4101
(417) 271-3215 for Eagle Rock
Campsite reservations
(417) 271-3860 for Viney Creek
Campsite reservations

Drive 16

Missouri Department of
  Conservation
P.O. Box 180
Jefferson City, MO 65102
(573) 751-4115

Drive 17

Norfork Lake Office
U.S. Army Corps of Engineers
P.O. Box 369
Mountain Home, AR 72653
(501) 425-2700

Norfork National Fish Hatchery
Route 3, Box 349
Mountain Home, AR 72653
(501) 499-5255

Ozark Folk Center State Park
P.O. Box 500
Mountain View, AR 72560
(501) 269-3851 (information)
(800) 264-FOLK [3655] (lodging
and conference facilities)

Ozark National Forest
605 West Main
Russellville, AR 72801
(501) 968-2354

Sylamore Ranger District
P.O. Box 1279
Mountain View, AR 72560
(501) 757-2211

Drive 18

Bayou Ranger District
12000 State Road 27
Hector, AR 72843
(501) 284-3150

Buffalo National River
P.O. Box 1173
Harrison, AR 72602
(501) 741-5443

Buffalo Ranger District
Highway 7 North
P.O. Box 427
Jasper, AR 72641
(501) 446-5122

Jasper/Newton County Chamber of
  Commerce
P.O. Box 250
Jasper, AR 72641
(501) 446-2455

Newton Country Resource Council
P.O. Box 513
Jasper, AR 72641
(501) 446-5898

Ozark National Forest
605 West Main
Russellville, AR 72801
(501) 968-2354

Pruitt Ranger Station
HC 73, Box 222
Dogpatch, AR 72648-9729
(501) 446-5373

Drive 19

Arkansas Natural Heritage
  Commission
1500 Tower Building
323 Center Street
Little Rock, AR 72201
(501) 324-9619

Buffalo National River
P.O. Box 1173
Harrison, AR 72602
(501) 741-5443

Buffalo Ranger District
Highway 7 North
P.O. Box 427
Jasper, AR 72641
(501) 446-5122

Ozark National Forest
605 West Main
Russellville, AR 72801
(501) 968-2354

Pruitt Ranger Station
HC 73, Box 222
Dogpatch, AR 72648-9729
(501) 446-5373
Contact for river conditions and
emergencies only.

Buffalo Ranger District
Highway 7 North
P.O. Box 427
Jasper, AR 72641
(501) 446-5122

Eureka Springs Chamber of
  Commerce
P.O. Box 551
Eureka Springs, AR 72632
(501) 253-8737

Lake Dardanelle Project Office
U.S. Army Corps of Engineers
P.O. Box 1087
Russellville, AR 72811
(501) 968-5008

Ozark National Forest
605 West Main
Russellville, AR 72801
(501) 968-2354

Pleasant Hill Ranger District
Highway 21 North
P.O. Box 190
Clarksville, AR 72830
(501) 754-2864

Pruitt Ranger Station
HC 73, Box 222
Dogpatch, AR 72648-9729
(501) 446-5373

Drive 20

Buffalo National River
P.O. Box 1173
Harrison, AR 72602
(501) 741-5443

Drive 21

Boston Mountain Ranger District
Highway 23 North
P.O. Box 76
Ozark, AR 72949
(501) 667-2191

Ozark Lake Project Office
U.S. Army Corps of Engineers
Route 1, Box 267X
Ozark, AR 72949
(501) 667-2129
(501) 667-1100 for Aux Arc Campsite reservations

Ozark National Forest
605 West Main
Russellville, AR 72801
(501) 968-2354

White Rock Mountain
  Concessionaires
P.O. Box 291
Mulberry, AR 72947
(501) 369-4128

Winthrow Springs State Park
Route 3
Huntsville, AR 72740
(501) 559-2593

Drive 22

Holla Bend National Wildlife Refuge
Route 1, Box 59
Dardanelle, AR 72834
(501) 229-4300

Ouachita National Forest
Federal Building
P.O. Box 1270
Hot Springs, AR 71902
(501) 321-5202

Petit Jean State Park
1285 Petit Jean Mountain Rd.
Morrilton, AR 72110
(501) 727-5441

Lodge and Cabin Reservations:
Mather Lodge
1069 Petit Jean Mountain Rd.
(501) 727-5431

Pinnacle Mountain State Park
11901 Pinnacle Valley Road
Roland, AR 72135
(501) 868-5806

Winona Ranger District
1039 Highway 10 North
Perryville, AR 72126
(501) 889-5176

Drive 23

Arkansas Natural Heritage
  Commission
1500 Tower Building
323 Center Street
Little Rock, AR 72201
(501) 324-9619

Hot Springs National Park
P.O. Box 1860
Hot Springs, AR 71902-1860
(501) 624-3383
(501) 623-1433 (Fordyce Bathhouse
Visitor Center)

Jessieville Ranger District
P.O. Box 189
Jessieville, AR 71949
(501) 984-5313

Ozark National Forest
605 West Main
Russellville, AR 72801
(501) 968-2354

Ouachita National Forest
Federal Building
P.O. Box 1270
Hot Springs, AR 71902
(501) 321-5202

Winona Ranger District
1039 Highway 10 North
Perryville, AR 72126
(501) 889-5176

Lake Ouachita State Park
5451 Mountain Pine Road
Mountain Pine, AR 71956
(501) 767-9366

Ouachita National Forest
Federal Building
P.O. box 1270
Hot Springs, AR 71902
(501) 321-5202

Drive 24

Magazine Ranger District
P.O. Box 511
Paris, AR 72855
(501) 963-3076

Ozark National Forest
605 West Main
Russellville, AR 72801
(501) 968-2354

Drive 25

Hot Springs National Park
P.O. Box 1860
Hot Springs, AR 71902-1860
(501) 624-3383
(501) 623-1433 (Fordyce Bathhouse-
Visitor Center)

Lake Ouachita Project Office
U.S. Army Corps of Engineers
P.O. Box 4
Mountain Pine, AR 71956-0004
(501) 767-2101

Drive 26

Lake Ouachita Project Office
U.S. Army Corps of Engineers
P.O. Box 4
Mountain Pine, AR 71956-0004
(501) 767-2101

Lake Ouachita State Park
5451 Mountain Pine Road
Mountain Pine, AR 71956
(501) 767-9366

Mena Ranger District
1603 Hwy 71 N.
Mena, AR 71953
(501) 394-2382

Oden Ranger District
P.O. Box 332
Oden, AR 71961
(501) 326-4322

Ouachita National Forest
Federal Building
P.O. box 1270
Hot Springs, AR 71902
(501) 321-5202

Queen Wilhelmina State Park
3877 Hwy 88 W.
Mena, AR 71953
(501) 394-2863
(501) 394-2864
(800) 447-4178 (reservations only)

Womble Ranger District
P.O. Box 255
Mount Ida, AR 71957
(501) 867-2101

Drive 27

Caddo Ranger District
101 Smokey Bear Lane
Glenwood, AR 71943
(501) 356-4186

Lake Greeson Project Office
U.S. Army Corps of Engineers
Route 1
Murfreesboro, AR 71958
(501) 285-2151

Ouachita National Forest
Federal Building
P.O. Box 1270
Hot Springs, AR 71902
(501) 321-5202
[22,23,25-30]

Womble Ranger District
P.O. Box 255
Mount Ida, AR 71957
(501) 867-2101

Drive 28

Choctaw Ranger District
HC64, Box 3467
Heavener, OK 74937
(918) 653-2991

Mena Ranger District
Route 3, Box 220
Highway 71N
Mena, AR 71953
(501) 394-2382

Ouachita National Forest
Federal Building
P.O. Box 1270
Hot Springs, AR 71902
(501) 321-5202

Queen Wilhelmina State Park
HC-07, Box 53A
Mena, AR 71953
(501) 394-2863
(501) 394-2864
(800) 447-4178 (reservations only)

Talimena State Park
Box 318
Talihina, OK 74571
(918) 567-2052

Drive 29

Choctaw Ranger District
HC64, Box 3467
Heavener, OK 74937
(918) 653-2991

Heavener Runestone State Park
Route 1, Box 1510
Heavener, OK 74937
(918) 653-2241

Kiamichi Ranger District
P.O. Box 577
Talihina, OK 74571
(918) 567-2326

Lake Wister State Park
Route 2, Box 6B
Wister, OK 74966
(918) 655-7756

Oklahoma State Parks
500 Will Rogers Bldg.
Oklahoma City, OK 73105
1-800-654-8240

Ouachita National Forest
Federal Building
P.O. Box 1270
Hot Springs, AR 71902
(501) 321-5202

Talimena State Park
Box 318
Talihina, OK 74571
(918) 567-2052

Drive 30

Choctaw Ranger District
HC64, Box 3467
Heavener, OK 74937
(918) 653-2991

Fort Smith Convention and Visitors
  Bureau
2 North B Street
Fort Smith, AR 72901
(501) 783-8888
(800) 637-1477

Fort Smith National Historic Site
P.O. Box 1406
Fort Smith, AR 72902
(501) 783-3961

Kiamichi Ranger District
P.O. Box 577
Talihina, OK 74517
(918) 567-2326

Oklahoma State Parks
500 Will Rogers Bldg.
Oklahoma City, OK 73105
1-800-654-8240

Ouachita National Forest
Federal Building
P.O. Box 1270
Hot Springs, AR 71902
(501) 321-5202

Talimena State Park
Box 318
Talihina, OK 74571
(918) 567-2052

Drive 31

Cherokee Heritage Center
P.O. Box 515
Tahlequah, OK 74465
(918) 456-6007

Cherokee Landing State Park
HC-73, Box 510
Park Hill, OK 74451
(918) 457-5716

Oklahoma State Parks
500 Will Rogers Bldg.
Oklahoma City, OK 73105
1-800-654-8240

Robert S. Kerr Lake Project Office
U.S. Army Corps of Engineers
HC-61, Box 238
Sallisaw, OK 74955-9445
(918) 775-4475

Sequoyah National Wildlife Refuge
Route 1, Box 18A
Vian, OK 74962
(918) 773-5251

Tenkiller Lake Project Office
U.S. Army Corps of Engineers
Route 1, Box 259
Gore, OK 74435
(918) 487-5252

Tenkiller State Park
HCR 68, Box 1095
Vian, OK 74962
(918) 489-5643
(918) 489-5641 (cabins, RVs, and
campsites)
(800) 654-8240 (cabin reservations)

Suggested Reading

Cline, Andy. 1992. *The Floater's Guide to Missouri*. Helena, Mont.: Falcon Press, 1992.

Dufur, Brett. *The 1995 Katy Trail Guidebook*. Columbia: Pebble Publishing, 1995.

Earngey, Bill. *Missouri Roadsides: The Traveler's Companion*. Columbia: University of Missouri Press, 1995.

Ernst, Tim. *Arkansas Hiking Trails*. Fayetteville, Ark.: Ernst Wilderness, 1994.

————. *Buffalo River Hiking Trails*. 2nd Ed., Fayetteville, Ark.: Ernst Wilderness, 1994.

————. *Ouachita Trail Guide*. Fayetteville, Ark.: Ernst Wilderness, 1993.

————. *Ozark Highlands Trail Guide*. 3rd ed. Fayetteville, Ark.: Ernst Wilderness 1994.

Flader, Susan, ed. *Exploring Missouri's Legacy: State Parks and HIstoric Sites*. Columbia: University of Missouri Press, 1992.

Henry, Steve. *The Mountain Biker's Guide to the Ozarks*. Helena, Mont.: Falcon Press, 1993.

Kennon, Tom. *Ozark Whitewater: A Paddler's Guide to the Mountain Streams of Arkansas and Missouri*. Birmingham, Ala.: Menasha Ridge Press, 1989.

Rafferty, Milton D. *The Ozarks: Land and life*. Norman: University of Oklahoma Press, 1980.

Rafferty, *The Ozarks Outdoors: A Guide for Fisherman, Hunters, and Tourists*. Norman: University of Oklahoma Press, 1985.

Rafferty and John Catau. *The Ouachita Mountains: A Guide for Fisherman, Hunters, and Travelers*. Norman: University of Oklahoma Press, 1991.

Rossiter, Phyllis. *A Living History of the Ozarks*. Gretna, La.: Pelican Publishing, 1992.

Toney, Thomas E. *Public Prairies of Missouri*. Jefferson City: Missouri Department of Conservation, 1994.

Index

247

About the Author

Don Kurz has spent over twenty years working to inventory, acquire, protect, and manage natural areas, endangered species sites, and other special features. For the past fifteen years he has been employed by the Missouri Department of Conservation and is currently assistant chief of its Natural History Division.

Don is also a writer and nature photographer specializing in landscapes, wildlife, insects, and plants. His photos have appeared in calendars and magazines such as *Natural History* as well as numerous wildflower books including Falcon Press's *Tallgrass Prairie Wildflowers*.

His countless trips into the Ozarks and Ouachitas have originated from his home on ten wooded acres outside of Jefferson City, Missouri.

THE WATCHABLE WILDLIFE SERIES

Alaska Wildlife Viewing Guide
Arizona Wildlife Viewing Guide
California Wildlife Viewing Guide
Colorado Wildlife Viewing Guide
Florida Wildlife Viewing Guide
Idaho Wildlife Viewing Guide
Indiana Wildlife Viewing Guide
Iowa Wildlife Viewing Guide
Kentucky Wildlife Viewing Guide
Montana Wildlife Viewing Guide
Nevada Wildlife Viewing Guide
New Mexico Wildlife Viewing Guide
North Carolina Wildlife Viewing Guide
North Dakota Wildlife Viewing Guide
Oregon Wildlife Viewing Guide
Tennessee Wildlife Viewing Guide
Texas Wildlife Viewing Guide
Utah Wildlife Viewing Guide
Vermont Wildlife Viewing Guide
Virginia Wildlife Viewing Guide
Washington Wildlife Viewing Guide
Wisconsin Wildlife Viewing Guide

BIRDER'S GUIDES

Birding Arizona
Birding Minnesota
Birder's Guide to Montana

SCENIC DRIVING GUIDES

Scenic Byways
Scenic Byways II
Back Country Byways
Scenic Driving Arizona
Scenic Driving California
Scenic Driving Colorado
Scenic Driving Georgia
Scenic Driving Montana
Scenic Driving New Mexico
Scenic Driving Oregon
Scenic Driving Texas
Travel Guide to the Lewis & Clark Trail
Traveling the Oregon Trail
Traveler's Guide to the Pony Express Trail

ROCKHOUND'S GUIDES

Rockhounding Arizona
Rockhound's Guide to California
Rockhound's Guide to Colorado
Rockhounding Montana
Rockhound's Guide to New Mexico
Rockhounding Texas

FALCON
1-800-582-2665

P.O. BOX 1718
HELENA, MT 59624

To order any of these books, or to request an expanded list of available titles, including guides for viewing wildlife, birding, scenic driving, or rockhounding, please call 1-800-582-2665, or write to Falcon, PO Box 1718, Helena, MT 59624.